church follows c

Hippies — Jesus people.

Rock → Larry Norman

Yuppies → mega-churches.

post-modernists → ECM

Dynamic growth of Xianity, adapting
to social △

Future?
  — hard to see prolonged growth
  w/out organization, though that's
  not a goal.
  — transform existing orgs or
  spawn new ones.
  — 20 years from now.

The demand for this expression creates
its supply

# The Deconstructed Church

ALSO BY GERARDO MARTI

*A Mosaic of Believers:*
*Diversity and Innovation in a Multiethnic Church*

*Hollywood Faith:*
*Holiness, Prosperity, and Ambition in a Los Angeles Church*

*Worship across the Racial Divide:*
*Religious Music and the Multiracial Congregation*


ALSO BY GLADYS GANIEL

*Evangelicalism and Conflict in Northern Ireland*

*Evangelical Journeys:*
*Choice and Change in a Northern Irish Religious Subculture*
(with Claire Mitchell)

# The Deconstructed Church

*Understanding Emerging Christianity*

GERARDO MARTI
*and*
GLADYS GANIEL

OXFORD
UNIVERSITY PRESS

# OXFORD

UNIVERSITY PRESS

Oxford University Press is a department of the University of Oxford.
It furthers the University's objective of excellence in research, scholarship,
and education by publishing worldwide.

Oxford   New York
Auckland  Cape Town  Dar es Salaam  Hong Kong  Karachi
Kuala Lumpur  Madrid  Melbourne  Mexico City  Nairobi
New Delhi  Shanghai  Taipei  Toronto

With offices in
Argentina  Austria  Brazil  Chile  Czech Republic  France  Greece
Guatemala  Hungary  Italy  Japan  Poland  Portugal  Singapore
South Korea  Switzerland  Thailand  Turkey  Ukraine  Vietnam

Oxford is a registered trade mark of Oxford University Press
in the UK and certain other countries.

Published in the United States of America by
Oxford University Press
198 Madison Avenue, New York, NY 10016

Cataloging-in-Publication data is on file with the Library of Congress

9780199959884

1  3  5  7  9  8  6  4  2

Printed in the United States of America on acid-free paper

*From Gerardo:*
*For Laura and our children*
*Miranda, Zachary, Nathan, and Genevieve*

*From Gladys:*
*For Brian*

It is something beyond all these forms, a new form of Christianity, to be expected and prepared for, but not yet to be named. Elements of it can be described but not the new structure that must and will grow; for Christianity is final only in so far as it has the power of criticizing and transforming each of its historical manifestations.

—Paul Tillich, *The Protestant Era*

Believers of every conceivable background open up new religious freedoms for themselves. They recast pre-existing religious world-views and develop composite religious identities in the various stages of their personal spiritual journey. These subjective searchings and the composing of individual religious narratives represent conscious breaks with the ideal of purity to be found among the clerical guardians of the truths of institutionalized national churches. What is astounding is that people who feel free to take these liberties continue to call themselves "Christians."

—Ulrich Beck, *A God of One's Own*

# CONTENTS

# PREFACE

Driving through the countryside of Northern Ireland, Gerardo turned to Gladys and said, "We should write a book together." The conversation happened just a few days after the start of a small gathering of Emerging Christians, including Peter Rollins, Phyllis Tickle, and Dave Tomlinson, which was hosted by Gladys' institution, the Irish School of Ecumenics, Trinity College Dublin at Belfast. The days spent in the presence of passionate innovators were intense, and meetings swung from buzz-filled classrooms to the compressed streets of Belfast, the liveliest events occurring in McHugh's Bar and The Black Box. Gladys had published on the innovative workings of the Belfast-based collective Ikon, in addition to having good relationships with Emerging Christians across the United Kingdom and Ireland. Gerardo was gathering new data for a research project stemming from his acquaintance with the Emerging Church Movement (ECM) and several of its leaders in North America since the 1990s. The resonance of our cumulative findings suggested the time was right to bring together a transnational assessment of a developing religious phenomenon.

This book explores the persons, practices, and sociological significance of Emerging Christianity. The ECM is a creative, entrepreneurial religious movement that strives to achieve social legitimacy and spiritual vitality by actively disassociating from its roots in conservative, evangelical Christianity. In presenting our understanding of this movement, we focus on the religious orientation of Emerging Christians and the practices within their congregations (often called "gatherings," "collectives" or "communities" rather than "churches"). The ECM's resonance with the wider trends and values of our age lead us to conclude that the principles underlying Emerging Christianity will persist, perhaps even thrive. We see this book as a pioneering volume in the growing scholarly literature on the ECM, but more importantly as contributing to more general understandings of the ongoing relationship between modern religion and contemporary social change.

Thanks first and foremost to friends, new and old, who shared with us varied aspects of the movement. By opening their lives and their communities, participants in the ECM allow researchers like us privileged access to this dynamically evolving religious orientation. Any errors committed in our sincere attempt to accurately describe the multiple, layered aspects of Emerging Christianity are solely our own.

For gathering data and writing up the findings, Gerardo received grant support from the Changing Spirituality of Emerging Adults project, funded by the Lilly Endowment under the direction of Kathleen Garces-Foley, that allowed the collection of much of the ethnographic data for this research. The analysis was greatly deepened through his involvement as a member of the Congregational Studies Project Team also funded by the Lilly Endowment. Davidson College provided additional funding through the L. Richardson King professorship and a Faculty Study and Research Grant. Gladys' early research on Ikon was funded through a grant from the Royal Irish Academy for her wider doctoral project. A period of research leave in 2013 allowed her to devote time to finishing the manuscript. This was enriched by a period at the Southwest Institute on Religion and Civil Society at the University of New Mexico in Albuquerque, which was generously facilitated by Richard Wood.

During the writing of the book, Gerardo also benefited from productive scholarly interactions while directing a research seminar on "Congregations and Social Change" through the Seminars in Christian Scholarship program at Calvin College in 2010. Joel Carpenter and John Witvliet were wonderful hosts. Other fruitful dialogues occurred during a symposium in 2012 organized by Brian Steensland and Philip Goff on "The New Evangelicalism and Social Engagement" through the Center for the Study of Religion and American Culture at Indiana University. Helpful discussions occurred while presenting papers at the annual meetings of the Association for the Sociology of Religion (2010), the Society for the Scientific Study of Religion (2010, 2013), and the Postmodernism, Culture and Religion conference on "The Future of Continental Philosophy of Religion" at Syracuse University (2011). Gladys benefited from comments she received while presenting papers at the Southwest Institute on Religion and Civil Society at the University of New Mexico in Albuquerque (2013), and the meetings of the Sociology of Religion Research Network of the European Sociological Association (2012), the Irish Society for the Academic Study of Religions (2013), and the European Sociological Association (2013).

In shaping the manuscript, special thanks go to Steve Warner, Penny Edgell, Bill McKinney, Nancy Ammerman, Omar McRoberts, Jim Nieman, Larry Mamiya, Robert Schreiter, Joyce Mercer, and Jack Wertheimer for feedback and commentary as the book developed. Gratitude is extended especially to John Bartkowski who took time to share especially constructive comments at a critical point. Paul Goldman also offered feedback at just the right moment in the development of the project. Paul Olson collaborated on generating results from the quantitative survey data. James Bielo and Josh Packard graciously provided timely feedback on the near-final manuscript. Matthew Engelke allowed us to read an advance copy of *God's Agents*. Participants in the Ikon collective read portions of the manuscript, with Pádraig Ó Tuama providing especially detailed, helpful suggestions. Jon Hatch, while a doctoral candidate at the Irish School of Ecumenics, commented on portions of the manuscript and could always be counted on for insightful conversations over tea. Gladys also benefited from interaction with Siobhán Garrigan, Katharine Sarah Moody, and James Kapalo.

At Davidson College, very special thanks to Damian White and Joe McGinley for research assistance, Leigh Chandler for formatting assistance, and LuAnne Sledge for grant account management. Gerardo also thanks Michael Emerson, Samuel Sánchez y Sánchez, Kevin D. Dougherty, and Gayle Kaufman for their friendship and camaraderie. At Trinity College, Gladys received administrative support from Caroline Clarke, library assistance from Bríd O'Brien, and encouragement from Karen Nicholson, Vincent O'Sullivan, and David Tombs. Siona Masters and David Masters assisted with the transcription of interviews. Gladys was further encouraged by readers of her blog (www.gladysganiel.com) who commented on her posts on Emerging Christianity and others who pushed her to clarify her thoughts, including Kyle Alexander, Ed Cooke, Graham and Sarah Dean, Martin Magill, Graeme McKibbon, Dave Minion, Arlene Moore, Chris and Janet Morris, Steve Stockman, and Ethel White. Judy Anderson was a wonderful host in Albuquerque.

Cynthia Read, executive editor at Oxford University Press, was always efficient and gracious in working through all stages of the project, and Charlotte Steinhardt managed the complex processes largely invisible to authors yet essential for their published work.

# The Deconstructed Church

# Introduction

Christianity is the only mad religion; which is perhaps, the explanation for its survival—it deconstructs itself and survives by deconstructing itself.

—Jacques Derrida

In a downstairs room of a pub in Belfast, Northern Ireland, people are plotting "insurrection."[1] No, it is not the darkest days of the Troubles—it has been more than a decade since Northern Ireland's historic peace agreement. What's happening is a staged religious event, instigated by philosopher-theologian Peter Rollins and two friends from the Belfast-based Ikon collective. The event is designed to stimulate and provoke the gathering of about 150 people, many of whom are in the city for a conference organized by Rollins called "Re-Emergence."[2]

Rollins and Ikon, a group that he helped found in the year 2000, could be considered part of the Emerging Church Movement (ECM), a religious innovation that, while now several decades old, has only recently begun to attract the attention of social scientists.[3] Both Rollins and Ikon are located on the radical fringes of the ECM by both sympathizers[4] and critics.[5] Many who have been involved with Ikon locate themselves *outside* the ECM, although this reluctance to be labeled is common among other ECM groups. Nevertheless, Rollins's philosophy and Ikon's "theo-dramatic" performances illustrate and embody much of what makes the ECM sociologically and theologically distinct.[6]

The ECM is, among other things, experiential, so we invite you to join us in that lower room in Belfast where people are clustered around bar tables with flickering candles.[7] A long, open bar to the right is packed with people talking as they wait for the event to begin. As anticipation builds, a screen on a far wall features a black-and-white video loop of a church building engulfed in flames. Just after seven o'clock, Pádraig Ó Tuama, his long hair pulled into a ponytail, approaches the microphone, and says, "The Lord be with you." Some reply: "And also with you." He then initiates a "call to worship," saying:

In the name of the Father, of the Son, and of the Holy Spirit.
In the name of goodness and love and broken community.
In the name of meaning and feeling and I hope you don't screw me.
In the name of sadness, regret, and holy obsession, the holy name of
    anger, the spirit of aggression.
In the name of beauty and beaten and broken down daily.
In the name of seeing our creeds and believing in maybe, we gather
    here, a table of strangers, and speak of our hopeland and talk of our
    danger.
In the name of Mary and Jesus and the mostly silent Joseph.
In the name of speaking to ourselves, saying this is more than I can
    cope with.
In the name of goodness and kindness and intentionality.
In the name of harbor and shelter and family.[8]

By now, the room has hushed. To the right, Rollins sits at a table with a massive, antique book, a veritable tome of movie-like quality, and tells everyone it contains "the story of tonight." Opening the book, he pretends to read, talking out loud about the people sitting in the front row, the woman with the afro, the guy who looks like he's never set foot in a bar. People start smiling, getting into the joke. Rollins says the book contains many chapters, but he wants to start here: "Chapter One: To Believe is Human."

Rollins stands up, long hair swaying as he talks about a man stranded on a desert island with . . . the beautiful, Academy Award–winning actress Halle Berry! It takes time, but the man eventually succeeds in seducing her, and after a night of glorious passion, he is so excited that he asks her to put on a disguise. He gives her a hat and tells her to hold a branch under her nose like a moustache. He leaves. When he returns, he tells her, "You'll never believe who I just kissed." The point, says Rollins, is that humans need others to witness their stories. Believing is easy. In the desert, the thirsty invent mirages. Everyone laughs. Rollins says he used to try to convince people to believe, but then he found believers everywhere. He has come to see that leading people to the cross means leading people to doubt. Evangelism means offering people a desert in the midst of an oasis.

Ó Tuama returns with a guitar and sings a lament shaped by the Hebrew Bible's book of Jeremiah:

You are strength when I am weak
You are strength when I am weak
You are strength when I am weak
Maranatha

I've given up sometimes when I've been tired
I've given up sometimes when I've been tired
I've given up sometimes when I've been tired
Does it move you?
I've fucked it up so many times
I've fucked it up so many times
I've fucked it up so many times
Hallelujah
I've found my home in Babylon
I've found my home in Babylon
I've found my home in Babylon
Here in exile.

Rollins returns to the big book, flipping pages to another portion, and reads, "Chapter Two: To Doubt is Divine." Rollins says churches protect people from the trauma of doubt. Ministers shield people with their sermons of certainty. Worship leaders comfort them with songs that gush like puppy love. Rarely do Christians approach the cross in all its devastation because they look for shortcuts to the resurrection, ways to bypass the darkness of the cross. So many people discuss their doubts, but they never feel their force because pastors and worship leaders believe on their behalf. As a result, no one gets close enough to Christ, who believes God has abandoned him on the cross.

Those sitting at the tables and standing at the bar listen quietly. Coasters for setting drinks on show the clenched fist of a revolutionary with blood dripping from the wrist. It is a striking image, a gritty graphic cropped from a larger image of the crucified Christ. The fist is nailed to a cross, and dark blood obscures where the nails have been pounded. On that patch of blood, a small set of white letters reads "I Believe in the Insurrection." Rollins tells the group he is calling for an insurrection, a resurrection that starts with stripping oneself of religion and society and politics and identity, then replenishing life in all its forms. He says: "*Resurrection* is nothing if it is not *insurrection*, hurting the powers and structures of the world."

Rollins now carries a large mug of beer and continues to read through different chapters. More stories and metaphors fill the evening as he mixes the surreal alongside the mundane. He describes an "aha" moment about Hitler and the nature of evil he experienced while reading a vintage issue of *Homes and Gardens* magazine. He recounts a parable from a rabbi on the capacity to change the future. He offers observations on Facebook and the desire to protect our image. He reveals the confessions of doubt from the diaries of Mother Teresa, a modern saint.

Eventually, Rollins turns back to the massive book and glances at a final page. He says that the book tells him that nothing will change, that those gathered will return to their mediocrity. Worship leaders will keep singing about Jesus as their boyfriend, and people will keep telling themselves the lies that let them live as they do now. The church will remain the alcohol that keeps people from confronting their desperation. Instead of shock and annihilation, people will continue looking to the cross for comfort and sedation.

Setting aside his beer, Rollins closes his book. He says that while his gut tells him that people will go back upstairs and return to their lives without change, each listener has the power to alter their destiny.

Ó Tuama closes with a benediction:

> The task is ended.
> Go in pieces.
> Our faith has been rear-ended
> certainty amended
> and something might be mended
> that we didn't know was torn.
> And we are fire.
> Bright, burning fire,
> turning from the higher places
> from which we fell,
> emptying ourselves into the
> hell
> in which we'll find
> our loving, and beloved
> brother
> mother
> sister
> father
> friend.
> And so, friends, the task is ended.
> Go in pieces
> to see
> and feel your world.[9]

Throughout the performance, most people maintain an interested and thoughtful silence as they sip their pints. Some elements of the night, such as using the huge book as a prop, might prompt a wry smile or the rolling of eyes, but most accept or appreciate these elements as part of the staging of the event. In the informal conversations that follow—and Emerging Christians are keen to emphasize the importance of these conversations—people discuss the substance of what was said or relate how they reacted to certain images, such as the church building consumed with fire.

## Defining the Emerging Church Movement (ECM)

Experiencing the theo-poetic drama of Ikon's "Insurrection" event serves as a heuristic introduction to the larger dynamics addressed in this book. We do not claim that Ikon or Rollins are "typical" of the ECM, but this brief description provides contextual information about a form the ECM often takes (a "pub church" meeting), the type of "preaching" often featured (storytelling and poetry), the visuals often used (props and video loops), and the critique of existing church institutions for which the ECM is known. Both scholars and the general public do not yet know much about the ECM, and speculation—both positive and negative—drives the agenda and the critique of the movement to date. Although much is unknown, our research leads us to conclude that the ECM is one of the most important reframings of religion within Western Christianity in the last two decades. As social scientists, we do not attempt to provide an argument in support of or against the movement. Rather, we describe the workings of the movement and evaluate its significance most particularly in the American and British/Northern Irish landscapes, while also considering other Western contexts. To address the gap in our scholarly and public understanding, we analyze the origin, practice, and significance of the ECM.

In attempting a social scientific analysis, we acknowledge that we focus on a set of groups that resist definition. In some cases the resistance is passionate and obsessive. With so many voices, groups, and organizations participating in the ECM, few are willing to "define" it,[10] though authors have offered various definitions.[11] As John Drane notes, "It is a work in progress," and "the groups that claim this label are very diverse."[12] Participants at all levels prefer to call it a "conversation," albeit a lively one, that embraces irony and contradiction.[13] Those advocating more radical theological approaches are eager to see all semblance of connection to Christianity virtually eliminated. The lack of systematic coherence among Emerging Christians contributes to the frustration of their more conservative counterparts who work within theological structures furnished with tidy, holistic frames of critique that finely distinguish between the "correct" and "incorrect" varieties of modern Christianity.[14]

Because participants in the movement know there is resistance from conservative Christianity, avoiding labels is part of avoiding stigma. This avoidance of stigma is a core dynamic within the movement as a strategy to find breathing space in the creation of new frameworks in the face of more public and powerful definitions of Christianity, both conservative and liberal. Indeed, it is interesting to note that even when offered anonymity, one person we spoke with for this project eventually requested that we not quote or draw on the interview material, fearing any association with the ECM could taint their reputation and threaten prospects for future employment. Our observation shows that the avoidance of labels functions to allow variety and fluidity within the movement itself. It also makes gatherings associated with the ECM hard to pinpoint without qualitative immersion in ECM networks and access to insider knowledge. Cory E. Labanow cautions researchers that the ECM is "a diverse and heterogeneous network which no single church can fully represent."[15] Moreover, manifestations of the ECM—including Ikon—are fleeting and impermanent. As John D. Caputo writes, "Ikon is hardly an institution at all, a more literally and visibly deconstructive quasi-institution. It is relatively new and no one knows how long it will be around."[16] Our consequent labeling and isolating of the ECM in this book is not intended to ignore the varied and evanescent strands of the movement, particularly when the movement values autonomy, diversity, and dissent, but to find analytic ways to examine the ECM as an intriguing instance of religious institutional innovation.

Our use of the label "Emerging Church Movement" could be considered problematic. Many insiders who initially embraced the label now see it as marred, inaccurate, and misappropriated. Yet we still find it useful. In our choice of the term "Emerging Church Movement" we agree with Tony Jones, who compares networks of emerging congregations to new social movements.[17] Like Jones, we have observed how the activities of Emerging Christians resemble those of social activists in other social movements. We also think the term "movement" captures the fluidity and dynamism of emerging congregations. At the same time, we recognize that the term "movement" may sound too grand a word to describe what these congregations are doing, especially since most people we consider Emerging Christians do not identify with the ECM by name.

Nevertheless, we argue that Emerging Christians are a discernable, transnational group who share a *religious orientation* built on a continual practice of deconstruction. We deliberately choose the term "religious orientation" rather than "religious identity." A number of distinct religious identities already exist *within the ECM*, ranging from those who explicitly identify with labels such as "emerging," "emergent," and "emergence," to those who discard (or are not aware of) these labels. Other observers have invested more significance in the distinctions between these identities. Mary Gray-Reeves and Michael Perham claim that "*emergence* was a word used to communicate the movement as a whole . . . *Emergent* currently tends to reflect churches inclusive in character of all sorts of conditions of people; *emerging* is more representative of churches that are evangelical and conservative in nature."[18] Phyllis Tickle also has noted these distinctions, identifying them first in *The Great Emergence* and then claiming that the boundaries between the factions have grown more solid in her follow up book *Emergence Christianity*.[19] In fact, Tickle argues that there was a crisis within Emergence Christianity (the term she uses for the ECM as a whole) in 2009 and 2010, which crystallized when Andrew Jones asked "if 2009 was to be the end of the Emergent ethos?"[20] Jones's comments stirred debate within the movement and ultimately revealed plenty of life.

By the end of 2010, the US-based network Emergent Village had been included in the American *Handbook of Denominations*, a sure sign of recognition in the American religious landscape.[21] Tickle also says that 2010 was the year of Emergence Christianity's "Marburg," referring to a meeting in Germany in 1529 among leaders within the Protestant Reformation, where they could not reconcile their theological differences. Tickle's latter-day Marburg was catalyzed by the publication of Brian McLaren's *A New Kind of Christianity*, the subtitle of which is *Ten Questions That Are Transforming the Faith*. It was McLaren's answers to those questions that confirmed a split:

> The howl of protest over his proposed answers was as loud almost as were the opposing cries of affirmation. Skilled theologians like Scot McKnight, who had always proclaimed himself as emerging/emergent, now went on record as Emerging, no longer Emergent. Pastors like Mark Driscoll of Mars Hill Church in Seattle, who had claimed and operated originally under the two labels as interchangeable, now reemphasized his place as Emerging and not Emergent in any way, shape, or form. Emerging Christianity and Emergent Christianity would forever be distinguishable one from the other, both between themselves and before the world at large.[22]

Tickle prefers the term "Emergence Christianity" because it chimes with the moniker she says has been applied to our present era: "The Great Emergence."[23] She explains how scholarly understandings of our period of history have drawn on emergence theory and systems theory to come to be called the Great Emergence. But in our fieldwork experience, the term "The Great Emergence" has not entered the everyday lexicon, being even more unfamiliar to our informants than the terms "emerging" or "emergent." We agree with Tickle that divergence and disagreement within the movement is very real, but we are less sure that people have coalesced around the labels "emerging" and "emergent" as definitively as she claims. Finally, as it relates to terminology, we also recognize that not all groups in the ECM would call themselves "congregations" or "churches"—some, like Ikon, characterize themselves as "collectives" or use terms like "community" or "group."

We are also aware that while many we consider Emerging Christians resist definition, our acknowledgement of that may seem inadequate when we then proceed to offer our own definitions. It may appear we are trying to put people in boxes that they would resist going in. As Ó Tuama wrote in an e-mail:

> I know that you highlight that many folks resist such identification— but in a way, you have set up a bind within that. I either read definitions that simply feel inadequate to me, or else I voice clarification/objection and then I wonder if it'll be said "Oh, that's such an emergent thing to do, this resisting definition." For me, being part of the Ikon Collective is one part of many parts—being Catholic, Irish, Nationalist, gay, in- volved in peace, a poet.... Certainly reading the distinctions between "Emerging" and "Emergent" left me bewildered—and left me think- ing that my participation in Ikon has absolutely nothing to do with such syntactical semantics.[24]

Such nuances are vital for understanding the ECM. Still, when considered from an international perspective, "emerging" seems to be the most com- monly used label within the movement as a whole, thus our adoption in this book of the terms Emerging Church Movement (ECM), Emerging Christians, and emerging congregations. Throughout the book, we will often use the term "congregation" in recognition of its sociological significance,[25] albeit recogniz- ing that it is not a term everyone within the ECM uses.

Further, for us the term *orientation* rather than identity better captures the package of beliefs, practices, and identities shared by people within the ECM. *Orientation* allows us to convey that there is a wide spectrum of beliefs and practices within the ECM. While people may disagree, they can still be con- sidered part of the *movement*. It also allows us to recognize that people within the ECM hold multiple identities simultaneously and that identification as "emerging" may be only occasionally important in their everyday lives (if ever). This leads us to characterize the ECM as an *institutionalizing structure,* made up of a package of beliefs, practices, and identities which are continually de- constructed and reframed by the *religious institutional entrepreneurs* who drive the movement. But Emerging Christians are somewhat unique institutional entrepreneurs, in that one of their primary purposes is to resist the institution- alization of their faith rather than to reform or create new institutions.[26] This desire to resist institutionalization explains our adoption of the term "institu- tionalizing structure" to describe the swirl of activity generated as Emerging Christians intentionally reframe Christian belief and practice.

Even though we see the ECM as a significant development in Western Christianity, we'll be blunt—in comparison with other religious orientations within global Christianity, the ECM is not numerically large. "Renewalist" expressions of Christianity, which include Pentecostal and charismatic churches as well as charismatics within traditional denominations, are the fastest growing forms of Christianity. About one in four Christians worldwide is now Renewalist—impressive growth, indeed. If one dates the beginnings of modern Pentecostalism to the Azusa Street revivals in Los Angeles (ca. 1906–1915), this growth has occurred over a period of about a century.[27] No such explosion of growth is evident in the ECM as yet. However, observers may be looking for the expansion of the ECM in the wrong way.

Estimates of emerging communities range widely depending on the sources and the definition one uses. In *Emerging Churches*, Eddie Gibbs and Ryan K. Bolger used an Internet search of Western countries combining googling for key words and contacting leaders of emerging congregations directly, who then provided further information on congregations in their networks. Gibbs and Bolger identified about 200 communities that fit their criteria, mostly in the United States and the United Kingdom. These numbers are not large, but Gibbs and Bolger's definitional criteria were strict and failed to include emerging-type groups within traditional congregations or take account of how the ideas behind Emerging Christianity are being explored and incorporated in established denominations.[28] Denominational connections occur more often than is commonly supposed, but they are veiled and often illicit operations concocting religious mixtures that may be unacceptable to established authorities. Knowing this, one emerging congregation in Florida funded by the United Methodist Church jokingly calls itself "The Meth Lab."

The existence of underground, emerging congregations within established denominational structures especially obscures the number of emerging groups in the United Kingdom. For example, a few months after the publication of Dave Tomlinson's 1995 book *The Post-Evangelical*, the British evangelical magazine *Third Way* published a survey in which 25% of its readers identified themselves as "post-evangelical." As Tomlinson reflected in a 2003 interview with Gordon Lynch, "This was really pretty remarkable given that the idea had only just been launched."[29] Similarly, Michael Moynagh's figures for the prevalence of "Fresh Expressions" congregations in the United Kingdom are surprisingly large. He reports that, "In 2010, the Methodist Church counted 941 fresh expressions, associated with 723 churches out of a total of 5,162—14%. In 2011, the Church of England identified at least 1,000 parishes—6% of the total—with a fresh expression of church."[30] Although Josh Packard argues that the Fresh Expressions figures should be independently verified, he does not dispute that Fresh Expressions is a significant development within British Christianity.[31]

Further, Matthew Engelke's study of the British and Foreign Bible Society affirms that Emerging Christianity is prominent within this historically important and strategically placed organization. Key staff members have been influenced by the ECM, reflected in choices made about activism and in its popular Theos think tank and website.[32]

Another figure is found in anthropologist James S. Bielo's book *Emerging Evangelicals*, which includes an estimate of over 700 communities just in the United States. In another book, Packard's "indicators" for "the reach of the movement" are the Emergent Village cohorts, sponsored in more than "60 cities in the U.S. and around the world in Japan, Ghana, and South Africa." He also notes the Ginkworld database of "self-identified Emerging Church congregations," which "lists 300 in 39 U.S. states and Washington, D.C., 6 Canadian provinces, and 10 European countries along with New Zealand and Australia."[33]

Going beyond these numbers, we suggest that the aggressive advocacy of emerging congregational forms through conferences organized by entities including Emergent Village, TransFORM, and Big Tent Christianity as well as promotion of the ECM through practical seminars on "establishing missional communities" given by leaders (both in person and through online "webinars") indicate broader, international confluence than is apparent when individual emerging congregations are considered in isolation.[34] The leaders, regular members, and occasional visitors to these conferences and workshops are stimulating a broad current of people reading books, hosting dialogues, seeking consultations, and launching new communities both within the confines of established congregations as well as alternative and religiously inconspicuous sites. Their presence is felt across the Christian landscape. As Packard admits, "In my years of studying religion as a sociologist . . . I have yet to come across anyone involved with a mainstream congregation who was not aware of the Emerging Church in at least a very general way. In other words, the Emerging Church certainly has penetrated the common consciousness within religious circles even if their overall numbers do nothing to threaten the viability of more established congregations and denominations."[35] In short, the awareness of ECM groups has disseminated widely alongside indistinct notions of the principles believed to be inherent to the religiosity of Emerging Christians.

Bielo has argued that being an Emerging Christian "is a viable form of identity on the American religious landscape and is present in nearly every region of the United States."[36] While we prefer the term "orientation" rather than "identity," we agree that the ECM is creating social spaces for newly invigorated religious *identities* to emerge and coalesce. Accordingly, we think that the influence of the ECM is greater than the sheer numbers of explicitly allied gatherings. The ECM's significance does not come from its attendance size but from the way it is contributing to the development of an intriguing, distinctively modern religious orientation.[37] That this orientation can be found transnationally is also significant. Although each emerging congregation is unique and embedded in its local context, emerging congregations localize similarly across national contexts. Many Emerging Christians are aware of the wider movement, with some participating in transnational networks (primarily online) and utilizing resources from other emerging congregations to enhance their own local practices.

## Introducing the ECM as a Religious Orientation

In our previous research, both of us have employed ethnographic methods. We share a commitment to the "thick description" of social practices and events, and to privileging the experiences and voices of participants. We also think that direct observation from sites chosen based on insider knowledge is best suited to provide the information that is needed to understand the ECM. Based on our fieldwork, and to further introduce the movement, we provide four descriptive "snapshots" of various manifestations of the ECM: pub churches, Emerging Christian conferences, web-based networks, and neo-monastic communities. All of these manifestations can be found transnationally. We then outline the history of the ECM, emphasizing its evangelical roots yet locating it within wider religious trends such as ecumenism. We suggest that the seeming "successes" of evangelical Christianity, especially in the United States, inadvertently stimulated a broadening critique of conservative Protestantism that resulted in the ECM. We then start to build our argument about the sociological significance of the ECM, describing it as an "institutionalizing structure." This institutionalizing structure provides a framework through which some Christians are strategically renegotiating their religious orientations to the extent that from a sociological perspective Emerging Christian should be considered a viable religious orientation—as distinct and identifiable (although as equally contested) as the evangelicalism from which so many of these Christians "emerged."

## Snapshot: Pub Churches

Pub churches are a distinct and widespread phenomenon that encapsulates many principles embedded within the ECM. The vignette with which we opened this book provides a glimpse of what the "pub churches" of the ECM are like. Rollins's "Insurrection" tour, which traveled from Northern Ireland to North America with stops in several major cities, served as a portable model of the pub gatherings developed by Ikon in the (now closed) Menagerie Bar in Belfast. But not all pub churches are as theatrical as Ikon gatherings. The "Holy Joe's" pub gathering associated with Dave Tomlinson in the United Kingdom in the early 1990s was heavier on conversation and lighter on performance than most Ikon gatherings.

Indeed, conversation seems to be the key to pub churches, as Gerardo found on his first visit to one in Charlotte, North Carolina. Gerardo had arranged to meet the host in the lounge of a popular restaurant. Gerardo takes over the narrative from here:

The email said to look for a guy with glasses and a beard at a table in the back. "I'll be looking for you," he wrote. With a few business people and small clusters of friends talking quietly on this Tuesday night, it wasn't crowded so I didn't have trouble finding my contact. Lawrence was wearing a black "RAMONES" T-shirt and sitting with two other men at a small table.

"Hey, man," he said and stood up to shake hands. With a bright smile, he asked, "Is it *Hur-ar-doe*?"

"Actually, it's *Jer-rahr-doe*, thanks. Nice meeting you."

After being introduced to the others, I took a seat as a waitress set down three beers. She asked if I wanted a drink, and I said I'd start with a water for now. The guys continued their conversation, talking about their jobs, pressures with classes, travel plans, girlfriends, and family issues—they seemed to have known each other for a while. Soon, two more people came, a man and a woman, greeted warmly, and then another woman who was a "guest" like me. Lawrence eventually looked at his watch.

"Well, I guess we should get started." Lawrence brought out a book from his messenger bag. One of Lawrence's friends seated at the table was an author I didn't recognize. They met in seminary. He had written a new book and was traveling through town, so Lawrence had him come to meet the group. "This is us," he said, and for the next hour we launched into a broad ranging discussion on personal relationships, the church, world history, a few Bible references, and a smattering of other topics in a haphazard, round-robin fashion.

Everyone contributed. Stories were told, and personal experiences shared. Even the new woman, Sarah, got to talking about how she was "in transition" with her faith. She had moved to the area six months ago, bounced from church to church, and was trying to find people to connect with. She said she appreciated the conversation several times.

At some point, Lawrence looked at his watch and simply said, "I need to get home." We gathered our things, shook hands, shared big smiles all around, and moved out the door. When I got close to my car, I heard Lawrence yell, "Nice meeting you!" I turned to wave and saw him writing on a piece of paper to give to Sarah as she nodded enthusiastically.

This was Gerardo's first experience of a pub church. Since then, we both have seen many gatherings that meet in pubs, bars, cafes, or restaurants and feature conversation, sharing poetry, parables, or other deliberately provocative readings over a pint.[38]

Pub churches are "doing church" in ways that are distinctly non-church-like. Some pub church gatherings are an extension of an existing church ministry.[39] One of the first recorded pub churches was sanctioned in 1955 by the rector of Saint Anne's Church in the Soho area of London.[40] But often pub churches are nonsponsored assemblies organized as underground meet-ups largely untracked by survey researchers or denominational consultants. They are not obviously churchy or even Christian because there are no hymns or conventional liturgy. There is no push for tithing, giving, volunteering, or even responding. Instead, beer loosens the tongue in an effort to promote conversation about matters of life and faith.

Organizers of pub churches intend to shake mainstream Christianity out of what they see as its so-ordinary, so-familiar, and oh-so-relevant orientation to create a fresh and distinctly unformulaic response to the Spirit. As Nadia Bolz-Weber, Lutheran pastor at House for All Sinners and Saints (HFASS) in Denver, puts it: "There's nothing we love more than being Church in bars."[41] Describing the feedback she received from people who had attended a HFASS event in a bar: "They mentioned how amazing it felt to pray in the basement of a bar, how the space felt sacred, and how they realized that there was nowhere else in their lives where their deepest longings could be voiced and held. To which I responded, 'That's why you need a *church*. When your mom dies, your yoga teacher isn't bringing you a casserole.'"[42] In writing about their events in a bar, Bolz-Weber simply says, "It's fun and quirky, and we love it."[43]

Those who participate in pub churches see them as an escape from churchy atmospherics and a refuge for open discussion centered on an unpretentious, egalitarian, and spiritually neutral space. Sharing his experience, Timothy Snyder reports, "What we discovered at Jesus at a Pub was that many of our friends, as well as friends of friends, needed a safe space to ask questions that have no good answers, to deconstruct their past experiences of church, and to voice the fragility of whatever faith they did have."[44] Snyder adds, "The point was never to do anything other than provide a safe space for these conversations to take place. It was not about conversion or getting anybody to worship or anything else."[45] The leader is a facilitator, and everyone has the opportunity to share without the obligation to do so. Spontaneity is valued; not the spontaneity of Spirit manifestations in prophecies or supernatural ecstatic actions but rather an unforced, free response of individuals toward each other, toward God, and toward one's self. What pub church organizers most reject is an authoritarian, dictatorial stance toward leadership. Pub church leaders seek to minimize exploitation, maximize authentic relationships, and achieve humane fulfillment of religious values without violence or victimization.

Although the long-term sustainability of pub churches is uncertain, the variety of such gatherings creates an experimental, entrepreneurial dynamic. They have no overhead, they require no official ordination for leadership, and can be initiated by almost anyone. Pastors, like Bryan Berghoef, are actively promoting pub churches by providing inspiring stories and accessible resources.[46] There is even an initiative in the United Kingdom (http://www.pubchurch. co.uk/) that offers training and support in pub church practices.[47] For them and others, the pub church embodies the flattening of clerical hierarchy and the reimagining of liturgy that are so important in the ECM. Although critics have argued that pub churches are just another gimmick for gaining religious converts, we see the pub church format as the underlying liturgical model for the ECM. Its format (e.g., flat leadership, open conversation, and leisurely setting) is found in many ECM-influenced congregations as part of their regular services. Some are "established" churches meeting in refurbished sanctuaries, while others are new and experimental communities meeting in homes and rented facilities. Others are much more occasional—even haphazard. Yet all promote what Ben Edson describes as "an environment within which people feel comfortable talking about their faith, their lack of faith, and other related issues."[48]

## Snapshot: Emerging Christian Conferences

Pub churches are not isolated entities. We found that leaders of these gatherings are connected to broader networks of Emerging Christians who see themselves as actively renegotiating the beliefs and practices of mainstream Christianity. In November 2010, Gerardo attended the annual Emergent Village conference along with more than 300 pastors, parachurch leaders, seminarians, and dedicated lay people from across America. The conference included a mix of the curious and the committed, those who operated both inside and outside of ECM networks and were motivated to come because they wanted to hear the now-famous Brian McLaren speak or to reconnect with old friends from previous conferences or to simply explore alternative approaches to Christianity.

From the moment of approaching the church building housing the conference, Gerardo saw attendees gathered in clumps talking, and a buzz of earnest conversation and warm embraces were evident throughout the conference. It was a diverse group in terms of denominational background and social class, yet attendees were mostly men, mostly white, and mostly late twenty- to early thirty-year-olds. More importantly, they included people with various affiliations, including those involved with LGBTQ issues and advocacy, practitioners within neo-monastic communities, and members of the "Outlaw Preachers"—a group inspired by the "rebel-preacher" Jay Bakker (son of televangelists Jim and Tammy Faye Bakker).[49] What drew them together is a shared sentiment that the pretentiousness of Christianity as they have known it must change.

Judging from the excited talk from morning to evening, everyone seemed to have strong opinions on modern Christianity. At times comforting and at other times confrontational, the conference created a meeting ground for issues regarding the practice of Christian community by mixing both inspiration and practicality. The intensity at times was overwhelming; nevertheless, there was also a notable casualness in the air that suggested the ambiance of a church social hour. About a dozen "breakout" sessions expanded on "hot" issues, including details involved in setting up intentional communities, conceptual issues to solve for constructing a new hermeneutic of atonement, experiments with liturgy (including pub churches), a charged session discussing homosexuality in the church, and more. In one session—a classroom packed so tightly that people sat on the floor—a megachurch pastor described his "coming out" as gay during his Sunday sermon. A young woman sitting in the front began to cry; and as she was invited to share her experience, she talked about how she had struggled for years to serve God in youth ministry while hiding her sexual orientation. She spoke through her tears, and a sense of camaraderie imbued others around her. It was her first emerging conference, and these new relationships showed her a way to embrace both her spirituality and her sexuality. In these and other engaging, often emotional, sessions, the tone was less philosophical than relational as the meeting continually emphasized tolerance, sensitivity to trauma and brokenness, and a willingness to support any participant dubbed to be "sincere" toward God and themselves.

We observed similar dynamics at the Re-Emergence conference in Belfast, where we met for the first time. There, speakers like Phyllis Tickle inspired listeners with the idea that the movement with which they were involved—by virtue of being at the conference, it seemed—was leading a re-formation of Christianity that would have historic implications on par with the Reformation. Her talk galvanized the group, and the collective zeal was palpable. It created a sense among people that they were engaged in something of deep significance for the future of the Christian church as a whole, and that they should therefore take what they had learned back to their various faith communities in the United Kingdom, Northern Ireland, Ireland, Europe, and the United States. Like other conferences, it also provided an opportunity for making new friends and meeting new collaborators, stimulating relationships that would be sustained electronically over time and through geographical space.

Large Christian festivals with thousands of attendees, like the Greenbelt Festival in the United Kingdom and the Wild Goose Festival in the United States, similarly provide strategic meeting points for Emerging Christians. Such festivals include panel discussions by prominent figures in the ECM, as well as music and artistic activities. In a pastorally orientated book titled *Losing My Religion? Moving on from Evangelical Faith*, Gordon Lynch recommends that former or postevangelicals who are transitioning and cannot find support in their local areas attend "annual festivals like Greenbelt," as these can be "an important way of meeting with other people who are sharing a similar spiritual journey."[50] Equally important are smaller, more intimate meetings with far fewer participants like the invitation-only Pyrotheology in Praxis gathering at Peter Rollins's home in Greenwich, Connecticut, that brought strangers together in tight quarters for daylong discussions, weaving heady discussions of philosophy alongside deeply emotional exchanges of intimate religious experiences, spiritual disillusionments, and life aspirations.

These are only samples of the many conferences—local, national, and international—that serve as vehicles for sustaining networks of relationships and modeling alternative practices among Emerging Christians. Conferences are important for people in the ECM because insiders to the movement do not define themselves by conventional means like their denominational affiliation or a shared church membership. Their connections do not come from what they are *joining* but rather from a shared sense of what they are jointly *leaving*. Emerging Christians have a contested relationship with the established structures of mainstream Christianity and willingly take on a badge of being "misfits" and "outsiders." Yet, despite their orientation of being marginalized, all share a deep sense of mission at these conferences regarding the future of Christianity. Together, they seek to revitalize Christianity and extend new values and practices in their own religious communities, whether their local gatherings are sanctioned as official "church ministries" or not.

As a scattered, loose-knit network, ECM insiders from different emerging congregations do not often see each other face to face. Gerardo was told several times by participants at these conferences, "It's not about the meetings. It's about getting together *after* the meetings." Old friends continued to catch up as new friends were brought into the conversation. Any comfortable setting with food and drink stimulates opportunities to build new connections and to refresh old ones. Conferences therefore allow Emerging Christians surprisingly frequent opportunities to meet with their religious colleagues while simultaneously incorporating new people into the movement. In finding like-minded folks and emotional catharsis at conferences, Emerging Christians are not unique. But in the absence of traditional avenues of communication through denominational structures like seminaries, general assemblies, and the like, these conferences provide a key function for the ECM.

## Snapshot: Online Networks

From the beginnings of the ECM, the Internet and social media have occupied important places in lending coherence to it as a dispersed network of believers.[51] The digital network of relationships was initially forged in smaller conferences and persisted through websites and e-mail, and now larger networks are fostering more expansive social connections through Twitter, Facebook, and other social media.

One of the most significant and longest-lasting manifestations has been the web-based community Emergent Village (www.emergentvillage.com) created in 2001. Even as its centrality begins to fade, it has served for many years as a clearinghouse for ideas, announcements, gatherings, resources, and conferences.[52] During the writing of this book, Emergent Village and the TransFORM Network managed a near-constant stream of tweets from various Twitter accounts.[53] In November 2011, the ECM gained its own section on the patheos.com blog, called "Emergent Village Voice," which it bills as a forum where fifty leading voices in the ECM comment on various matters. In effect, this moved the emergentvillage.com conversation to patheos, a catch-all religion site with eleven "Faith Channels": Atheist, Buddhist, Catholic, Evangelical, Hindu, Jewish, Mormon, Muslim, Pagan, Progressive Christian, and Spirituality. Emergent Village Voice falls under the Progressive Christian channel. Doug Pagitt describes it on the site like this:

> This blog is an experiment.
> We are seeking to include as many voices as are willing to join together and tell stories, create ideas, and generate friendships that will compel us to the future. There are more than 50 people who will be

adding their voices to this conversation. Some will write, some will post audio, some will post video.

You will hear from Christians and Jews; denominationalists and free-range spiritualists; conservatives and liberals; the faith-filled and the faith-hesitant.

We are a collective of people who are not only concerned about the "right and left" but now and the future. Emergent Village is a community that wants to make something together.

We invite you to join us.[54]

Pagitt's welcome post demonstrates the value placed on inclusivity, ecumenism, and conversation in the ECM—as well as the priority put on using social media.

Pagitt's explicit mention of "now and the future" underscores Emerging Christians' eagerness to employ new methods for communication and spiritual development (like the World Wide Web), and their willingness to change and adapt. A forward-looking temporality is key to the ECM, and it is electronically embodied online. The World Wide Web allows for the creation of multiple forums through which the ECM practices an ongoing self-criticism (which is revealed mostly through blog posts) and supplements informal conversations and occasionally formalized presentations at conferences (e.g., Emergent Village annual conversations). Further, the Internet is an important platform for the charismatic stars of the ECM—Brian McLaren, Rob Bell, Tony Jones, Peter Rollins, Nadia Bolz-Weber, Rachel Held Evans, and others—who use Twitter, Facebook, YouTube, Vimeo, and personal blogs to promote their ideas, lectures, and initiatives. Such figures also commonly post on blogs with wider general readership, such as patheos or the Huffington Post. Other examples include Rollins setting up a "Dis-Courses" Facebook page to facilitate discussion among groups who are embarking on projects similar to those developed by Ikon, namely, the Last Supper, the Evangelism Project, Atheism for Lent, and the Omega Course.[55] This Facebook page later developed into a more elaborate "Pyrotheology" website, which provides more information about these practices and includes videos featuring Rollins and testimonials from people involved with Ikon.[56] The CANA Initiative, launched in 2013, is yet another attempt to mobilize networks of committed insiders and catalyze further connections that uses social media as a means to promote new projects. For participants in the ECM, social media provides a viable, legitimate, and personal means for promoting events, keeping in touch, supporting each other, sharing ideas, and building virtual, networked communities of like-minded people.

# Snapshot: Neo-Monasticism

In 2013, Gladys visited East Central Ministries in Albuquerque, New Mexico.[57] East Central Ministries is located in the rough International District, a multicultural, multiethnic community that is home to a number of "undocumented" migrants. Director John Bulten explained that the group was inspired by John Perkins's Christian development approach, which entails living and working *alongside* (not *for*) the poor.[58] Many of those involved with East Central Ministries live near each other in a housing cooperative in the community, thus embodying the practices recommended by Perkins and also by other, city-based neo-monastic communities. East Central Ministries has an array of programs, including Growing Awareness Urban Farm, Community Food Co-op, Casa Shalom Housing Co-op, One Hope Centro de Vida Health Center, English as a second language and computer classes, Creation Park, After School Club, Juntos Youth Program, Kids' Club, Youth Internships, Escuela Luz del Mundo School, and one-off events.

East Central Ministries is made up of several buildings, including a homely welcoming area patrolled by a cat, as well as a shop, a large warehouse for a food co-op, work and storage areas, a doctor's office, and greenhouses. Gladys and her husband were led around the site, and East Central workers explained how the varied projects they had started responded to needs in the local area. As they discussed the problems faced by individuals living near East Central, they often stopped to greet people who dropped in. Gladys was struck by the cheerful buzz as people came and went about their business, smiling and chatting. Women were cleaning up after the co-op after having distributed food. Men were bringing lumber they had salvaged for building items for the store. A small group, including a Catholic priest, prayed together. John described the work as fulfilling but was frank in admitting that it was sometimes stressful and tiring. He said that the community's shared meals, prayers, and fellowship were essential in sustaining their activism.

With its housing co-op, shared spiritual practices, and commitment to urban community development, East Central Ministries is an example of a neo-monastic community. Neo-monastics are "intentional communities" of Christians who either live together in a large house or close to each other in a specific geographical area.[59] They commit to compassionate service to each other and the local community, and attempt to live self-sustaining lifestyles often combining craftsmanship, environmentalism, and charitable work.[60] In contrast to the casual connections of pub churches or the occasional gatherings at conferences, neo-monastic communities are characterized by intense and holistic commitment. Neo-monasticism does not emphasize celibacy and is not committed to poverty but rather uses historical elements of community living (found in documents like *The Rule of St. Benedict*) to cultivate a deeper level of Christian fellowship that is reminiscent of the first church community described in the Book of Acts Chapter 2 where "all the believers were together and had everything in common," meeting together daily for worship, sharing food and faith, "with gladness and simplicity of heart." While neo-monastic communities can vary widely, Bielo provides a list of common practices that characterize them.[61] He describes them as including communities organized around the sharing of resources (food, money, housing, clothing, and transportation); individuals and communities prioritizing becoming debt free; groups eating communally on a daily basis; members encouraging each other to not live on 100% of their income; decreasing reliance on "the system"; communities eliminating ownership of a church building, thus freeing time and resources to devote to other expressions of faith; individuals working together to eliminate various addictions, from alcohol to shopping; and individuals and small groups regularly attending weekend or weeklong silent prayer retreats.

Perhaps more than the previous expressions of the ECM that we have featured in these snapshots, neo-monastic communities seem to appeal to people from both Protestant and Catholic backgrounds, rather than being traceable to developments within evangelical Protestantism. Some see the impetus for the recent expansion of neo-monasticism in the inspiration from earlier efforts such as the Catholic Worker movement, the ecumenical Iona Community in Scotland, or the Taizé community in France. In Northern Ireland, the context from which Ikon emerged, now defunct neo-monastic groups, such as the ecumenical Columbanus Community (1983–2003) and the Cornerstone Community (1982–2012), emphasized the importance of Catholics and Protestants living intentionally together *as fellow Christians* in a religiously divided society.[62] The descriptions of Fr. Michael Hurley, a Jesuit priest and founder of the Columbanus community, of the daily structure of communal prayer and fellowship of the group, are typical of contemporary neo-monastic communities.[63] For example, in Ireland, the Magis organization for young adults, a collaboration between lay Catholics and Jesuit priests, supports young people living in intentional communities in Dublin. This includes assisting in the development of communal practices such as shared meals and the "Examen" method of prayer developed by Jesuits.[64]

Neo-monastic communities do not become congregations. Instead, they encourage members to commit to local congregations as an extension of their commitment to the local community. In this way, these groups are not intended to be insular but missionally expansive and engaged. Two of the most prominent contemporary examples are the Simple Way in Philadelphia and Moot in London. The focus of these and other groups on microcommunity and sustainable living, along with a decentering of doctrinal correctness and social conservatism, resonates with the ECM as a whole. Emerging Christians appear committed to a radical reconsideration of what they see as a consumerist, apathetic, privileged, and violent status quo. For them, the goals they have been told to strive for as young adults are soured as inauthentic ideals that merely support a heartless and destructive world system. In sum, neo-monasticism represents a movement of Christians to live in committed community, to foreground life-structuring ideals, and to reconsider their taken-for-granted stance toward their relationships to the capitalist system, different faith traditions, and the environment.

## The ECM in Historical Perspective

Many observers date the origins of the ECM to the early 1990s when the movement became most visible in North America. In their popular writings, pioneers of the ECM in the United States such as Doug Pagitt and Tony Jones have described the events of that decade, emphasizing the evangelical roots and youth-orientation of the ECM.[65] On the other hand, Doug Gay, writing from a UK context, argues that the origins of the ECM are located further back and linked to wider trends within global Christianity, such as reforming impulses in what he calls Low Church Protestantism (LCM), the ecumenical movement, and the loosening of denominational boundaries after Vatican II.[66] Unlike in the United States, the ECM in the United Kingdom can be more readily linked to developments within established denominations, such as the joint Anglican-Methodist "Fresh Expressions" project, the Church of England's 2004 *Mission Shaped Church* report, and the Church of Scotland's "Church Without Walls" initiative.[67] The logic behind these initiatives is that traditional forms of church are failing to reach people in largely secularized Britain—hence the emphasis on mission. For example, mission is a major theme of *Church for Every Context: An Introduction to Theology and Practice*, published in 2012 by Michael Moynagh, a Church of England minister and member of the national Fresh Expressions team. This book, running to nearly 500 pages, offers a theological rationale for Fresh Expressions and other "new contextual churches," as well as chapters full of practical advice about how to start and sustain such congregations. Moynagh writes that "the secularization thesis is wrong" and "church demise" is not "inevitable." Rather, "the problem has been the church's failure to adapt; new contextual churches are the Spirit's means of reversing decline."[68]

In the more highly "churched" United States, the ECM now seems to place less emphasis on mission and more on critique of the existing churches, although the UK context has not been without its critics, either. Tomlinson's popular book *The Post-Evangelical* served as a sort of critical manifesto for UK Christians, and Ganiel considers Ikon, in its Northern Irish context, as an embodied critique of traditional Northern Irish evangelicalism.[69] That said, in the United States, one of the major initial stimuli for the ECM was an evangelical-led, mission-style project aimed at youth—not unlike *The Mission Shaped Church*.

## Growing Up and Moving Out of Evangelicalism

In the United States, the ECM began as a youth-oriented movement rooted in a concern for the religious experience of young adults.[70] Much of the leadership and the focus on outreach during the 1990s was based on reformulating strategies to minister to twenty-somethings. There was a strong belief that the rise of postmodernism presented a combination of threat and opportunity, so meetings were set to deal with perceived challenges presented by contemporary young adults. Organizationally, the beginnings of the ECM took shape through an initiative of the Leadership Network, a private parachurch evangelical organization that stimulates innovation and dialogue among church leaders. The Leadership Network established the Young Leaders Network in the late 1990s with an enterprising group of pastors and youth ministers under forty to confront what they defined as the greatest problem of the contemporary church—namely, its lack of being "contemporary." Concerns ranged from theology to aesthetics. These leaders believed churches were losing the next generation due to their failure to keep up with the culture and concerns of younger cohorts.

In the concern for youth, the movement owed its origins to conservative evangelical Christianity. But some have come to regret their initial experimentation. Fueled by images of heresy in their religious imagination, many conservative Christians very much fear the ECM because of a perception that its adherence to "sound doctrine" is softening (like the virgin birth) or because of its rejection of "orthodox" Christian rituals (like "closed" communion/Eucharist). As the movement developed, it came to integrate people who had already rejected forms of Christianity—especially evangelical fundamentalism—and sought new ways to express their lingering faith. When Gerardo talked with a pastor in his late fifties attending an ECM conference and asked if the movement was the answer to reaching young adults, he said, "It's one answer." He was quick to say that "the church" should welcome this experimentation and "let young people do things and dig in the past for the gold of our tradition." This pastor was no fan of the constraining structures of his denomination. "They [young people] want elbow room and understand how constraining it is."

Shortly after the formation of the Young Leaders Network, a string of conferences (like the New Edge Conference and the Terra Nova Project) and Internet sites raised issues on interpreting the Bible, approaching "nonbelievers," considering connections between "ancient" and present-day liturgy, and evaluating spiritual practices, all with a view toward reinventing contemporary evangelism.[71] In these beginnings, the conversation within the ECM took conservative evangelicalism as its base of critique,[72] and much of its conversation still consists of stories of "de-conversion" from fundamentalist-tinged orientations.[73] Such discussions consistently frame modern Christianity as a problematic institution. Given these reactionary roots, the ECM is sometimes considered to be merely a reinvented evangelicalism. But this minimizes the resonance that the overall message of the movement has had once the orientation spread outside its original clusters to mainline, other Christian, and non-Christian believers.[74] For example, while we cannot claim the surveys we draw on in this book are representative of the ECM as a whole, we found that 29% of our respondents from eight ECM congregations indicated they come from an evangelical background, and a higher percentage (31%) indicated their background as Mainline Protestant. In addition, Roman Catholics (13%) and those from nonreligious, agnostic, or atheist (9%) backgrounds participate in these ECM congregations.[75]

Our observation suggests that the ECM does not appeal most to younger, college-age adults but rather to older, more educated, and still-single young adults who have gained their independence and seek to uncover outlets for a more flexible Christianity. Our survey data supports this, revealing that nearly 32% of ECM respondents were 18–25, but a larger percentage—37%—were 26–35 years old. In terms of education, 95% have at least some college education, with 23% having earned a graduate degree. Slightly more than half (50.3%) of them were single, and even if married (43%), more than two-thirds (68%) of our respondents had no children.[76] Participating in events and dialogues inspired by the movement, Emerging Christians find places that allow for independence of thought, expression of religious questions and opinions, and an uncertain commitment to institutions. Young adults in their older twenties and early thirties committed to the movement may be active careerists in secular jobs or they may be in seminary. Traveling to conferences and events can be expensive, so participants tend to have both the income and the flexibility to attend. Some are married couples who do not yet have the time-consuming demands of childrearing; indeed, the primary reason given for the ending of the Without Walls Emergent Village cohort in Newtownards, Northern Ireland was "kids." As they wrote on their website: "[Kids are] all incredible blessings and an answer to prayers but it was also the beginning of the end for Cohort. We were no longer free to meet up so regularly. Baby-sitters were needed, free-time was gobbled up, tiredness and extra parental responsibilities simply meant that Cohort could no longer be what it once was."[77] Packard speculates that emerging congregations may become "stops" on people's religious journeys between the institutionalized churches of their childhoods and the institutionalized family-friendly churches of their adulthood.[78]

What characterizes these younger Emerging Christians is their aptitude for articulating an "expertise" on what "the church" is and how it has failed. Moreover, the few young adults who come from *nonreligious* backgrounds are glad to find a place that tolerates their skepticism about "church" and their uncertainties about the doctrines and practices of Christianity. ECM events are places defined by an active renegotiation of orthodoxy, so both sets of young adults (those who view themselves as experts on the "failure" of the church and those uncertain of any faith) find a workable middle ground. Older adults who have passed beyond their thirties round out the movement (32% of our survey respondents are over thirty-five), sometimes as attendees, other times as even more aggressive questioners of the faith and promoters of a new future.[79]

By 2004, blogs, conferences, articles, and books coalesced around a new set of imperatives representing the movement. Most especially, Brian McLaren's *A Generous Orthodoxy* attempted to isolate a religious identity that was as definitive as it was ambiguous.[80] A combined statement and manifesto, the subtitle of the book seeks to capture its message: *Why I am a missional, evangelical, post/protestant, liberal/conservative, mystical/poetic, biblical, charismatic/contemplative, fundamentalist/Calvinist, Anabaptist/Anglican, Methodist, catholic, green, incarnational, depressed- yet hopeful, emergent, unfinished Christian.* Tickle considers McLaren's book to be the "analog of Martin Luther's Ninety-Five Theses on the door of Wittenberg Church."[81] Certainly many people were introduced to the ECM through this bestselling book.[82]

## Growing in New Ecumenical Spaces

In the United Kingdom, Doug Gay dates the immediate origins of what he prefers to call the "Church: Emerging" to the "alternative worship" movement of the late 1980s.[83] He locates this within "post charismatic" and "post-'reformed'/post-evangelical" currents. Again, the ECM's British origins have much in common with the ECM's American (evangelical) origins. Yet Gay also argues that the alternative worship movement was "heavily precedented by more isolated and marginal experiments in practice within a range of traditions from at least the 1960s onwards,"[84] and that such experiments were possible in part because of "three contextual shifts":[85] the broadly diffused influence of the ecumenical movement, the new climate produced by the Second Vatican Council, and the influence on Low Church Protestants of a new wave of missiological thinking, forged in the post–Second World War experience of decolonization.

We agree with Gay that it is important to be mindful of these broader shifts, not least because they helped create contexts—on both sides of the Atlantic—in which it became easier and less threatening for people to critique their own Christian traditions and to be open to the insights and gifts that they might gain from engaging with other Christian traditions. On the other hand, Gay admits that participants in the ECM do not often recognize the influence of the ecumenical movement on their own movement, and that most scholars and ECM practitioners have failed to make connections between ecumenism and the ECM.

Gay makes ecumenism central to the closest he "venture(s)" to a definition of the ECM:

> The Emerging Church can perhaps best be understood (and defended) as an irreverent new wave of grassroots ecumenism, propelled from within low church Protestantism by a mix of longing, curiosity, and discontent. It is what we in the UK might call DIY ecumenism, constructed by means of a series of unauthorized remixing and emboldened by an (evangelical) ecclesial culture of innovation and experimentation. It is a variant of ecumenism which for the most part is ignorant of the history and protocols of institutional ecumenism, but which "frankly might not give a damn" for them in any case, since it still carries a genetic confidence about remaking the Church and its mission in response to the Spirit's prompting.[86]

Gay's ecumenically centered definition resonates with many of the ideas and practices of the ECM explored in this book, including the appropriation of ideas, rituals, and liturgical practices from a variety of Christian traditions. Influenced by Gay's work, we think that if evangelicalism is the seed from which the ECM has sprouted, the diffuse influence of the ecumenical movement has, almost unnoticed, provided the fertile soil in which it has grown.

## The Deconstructed Church

We title this book *The Deconstructed Church* and define Emerging Christians in terms of sharing a *religious orientation* built on a continual practice of deconstruction. We characterize the ECM as an *institutionalizing structure,* made up of a package of beliefs, practices, and identities that are continually deconstructed and reframed by the *religious institutional entrepreneurs* who drive the movement and seek to resist its institutionalization. As such, the ECM is best seen as a mix of both reactive and proactive elements, vying for the passion and attention of Christians and nonbelievers. Emerging Christians *react* primarily against conservative/evangelical/fundamentalist Protestantism but also against other forms of traditional Christianity that they have experienced as stifling or inauthentic. At the same time, they *proactively* appropriate practices from a range of Christian traditions (Gay's "DIY" ecumenism) to nourish their individual spirituality and to enhance their life together as communities.[87]

Among Emerging Christians, the term "deconstruction" is not consistently used and therefore not a term actively discussed except occasionally and among self-consciously philosophical members.[88] But in examining the ways in which Emerging Christians renegotiate religious beliefs and practices, we note with sociologists Stephan Fuchs and Steven Ward that *the practice of "deconstruction" is a form of micropolitics in which actors establish competitive arenas in response to pressures for conformity.*[89] The focus of such work is on the personal religiosity of members. Emerging Christians create ongoing opportunities to push off religious pressures to comply with standard narratives. Labanow writes that Emerging Christians are "aware of the extreme complexities of their world and their faith" and "will never be satisfied with final interpretations." Moreover, "Since deconstruction and reconstruction are such fundamental characteristics of the emerging church, its practitioners are encouraged to give ample attention to these challenges."[90]

Deconstruction, then, represents an opportunity for actors to "irritate, if not overthrow" an overarching regime "by pointing to its contingent and arbitrary status."[91] In this way, we understand that members of the ECM actively deconstruct congregational life by placing into question the beliefs and practices that have held sway among conventional Christians. For Emerging Christians, the Christian institutions they experienced had little "wiggle-room" for belief and practice. Their entire religious orientation as an Emerging Christian necessarily resides in relation to conventional Christianity. Yet Emerging Christians strive for a renegotiation of Christianity precisely because they want to stay within the broader tradition while creating more room to navigate within it. Emerging Christians want to create Christian communities that allow for a sustainable religious autonomy, ones where a broad scope of freedom in individual belief and religious conviction reign.

But an autonomous religious self necessarily entails friction with the conflicting goal of institutions to urge conformity and avoid disruption.[92] Emerging Christians actively challenge multiple forms of religious conformity they encountered in their past and heartily welcome all critiques of institutionalized Christianity based on the push for conformity. Therefore, as Emerging Christians try to change the mainstream institutions of modern Christianity, we observe a sometimes subtle yet often overt political wrangling of meanings and practices. As one ECM leader said, "I want to subvert my church—which I love. But she needs to change."

The work of sociologist Erving Goffman implies that such institutional "micropolitics" are a natural consequence of institutionalized religious life, especially to the degree that an institution is perceived to be demanding and confining. Individuals require social structures for their "selves" to exist; nevertheless, Goffman states that an individual "takes up a position somewhere between identification with an organization and opposition to it."[93] The importance of Goffman's insight is his recognition that various institutionalized arenas of society threaten to swallow individuals whole within their normative and comprehensive definitions of what committed "selves" should be. And individuals find ways to push back.

So, where does a religious self reside? Does a properly religious self exist merely through socialization into expected norms of behavior? No, according to Goffman, "Our sense of selfhood can arise through the little ways in which we resist the pull." Goffman concludes, "It is thus against something that the self can emerge." Indeed, Goffman uses a provocative phrase by writing, "Our sense of personal identity often resides *in the cracks*." It is therefore possible to define one's religious self as resting between absorption and opposition to an institution. Goffman states that such ongoing oppositions comprise "the underlife" of institutions.[94]

Following Goffman's insights, the ECM corresponds to "the underlife" of mainstream Christian institutions. Acts of deconstruction are happening both at the elite level of highly mobilized current and ex-pastors (including current and ex-seminarians) who are reconstructing religious communities and among grassroots Christians (including "seekers," "the unchurched," "the dechurched," and generally "spiritual people") who are negotiating the mundane practice of their private Christian faith. In general, five aspects of the ECM's deconstruction stand out as particularly notable:

First, *Emerging Christians consistently characterize themselves as anti-institutional*. A bold spokesperson for the ECM, Tickle simply states, "Emergence Christianity is, first and foremost, deinstitutionalized."[95] Using empirical data, both Bielo and Packard have argued that the ECM's anti-institutional stance is central to its identity and to its appeal.[96] Anti-institutional—implying an active posture against institutions—is a stronger term than deinstitutionalized, which Tickle seems to use in a descriptive way. For us, anti-institutional is a more appropriate term. For Bielo, Emerging Christians' anti-institutional sentiment is consistent across ECM groups and persistent across time. For Packard, the ECM continues to thrive, albeit on what he characterizes as the "margins" of American Christianity, because it employs strategies to resist what is often considered the sociologically inevitable process of institutional-ization. Such strategies include deliberately limiting the power and influence of professional clergy; expecting laypeople to take initiative within congrega-tions; limiting flows of information between professional clergy and laypeople to a need-to-know basis (since laypeople are not expected to "report back" on all their activities); allowing congregational activities to end before they become institutionalized; deliberately disrupting normally taken-for-granted religious ideas, routines, and rituals; emphasizing inclusivity rather than reli-gious boundaries; and stressing the independence of local religious commu-nities. Within the ECM there is considerable openness among leaders (and potential leaders) for creating small, informal, and nonhierarchical assemblies that are not connected to sanctioned theological seminaries or staffed denom-inational structures. Although the long-term sustainability of such groups is uncertain, the variety of gatherings rapidly being formed stimulates an experi-mental, entrepreneurial dynamic that propels leaders to connect with other leaders through both face-to-face and online conferences and networks. These larger gatherings consistently demonstrate an emphasis on relationships over programmatic structures, a sentiment reflected in a tweet from Tony Jones quoting the Russian theologian Alexis Khomiakov, "The Church is not a doc-trine, not a system, and not an institution. The Church is a living organism, an organism of truth and love, or more precisely: *truth and love as an organism.*"[97] The importance of network alliances is highlighted while overly close connec-tions to larger, more established structures of religious training and dialogue are desperately avoided.

 Second, *Emerging Christians' approach to issues ranging from salvation, sanctification, and eschatology—especially alongside a great concern for social justice—encourages a form of ecumenism that transcends many theological and ecclesial boundaries.* Mainline and evangelical Christians who formerly found themselves divided over issues like LGBTQ rights and aggressive evangelistic tactics now meet together in a common critique of "right-wing evangelicals." Moreover, Emerging Christians draw freely from strands of Christian tradi-tions in a shared desire to create tradition-rich, yet culturally relevant, local church experiences. Groups from various Christian orientations partner on social initiatives (providing vocal and legislative support for gay marriage) and share ideas on re-creating liturgical formats that mix different types of musical instrumentation and new media technology.[98] This transcending of boundar-ies reinforces the ECM's goal of "inclusivity," as Emerging Christians strive to welcome a range of theological and ethical viewpoints to the "conversation" that they see as central to their movement. The emphasis on conversation also reinforces the encouraged processes of deconstructing modern Christianity and deconstructing individuals' personal religious beliefs and identities. Using a term employed by Emerging Christians, Packard and George Sanders emphasize the "messiness" of the ECM. For them, "Messiness can be understood as the opposite of over-coded and striated spaces and interactions that delimit and divide experiences and people."[99] Packard claims—and we agree—that the ECM would not be able to maintain its emphasis on deconstruction if it became more "institutionalized," because the very process of institutionalization would by definition mean that more rigid boundaries must be drawn.[100]

Third, *Emerging Christians actively seek to avoid entrenched power structures by bringing young adults into leadership and decision-making in their local church context*. Young adult leadership is widely assumed within the movement, and for many outside the movement *Emerging = Under 30*, an equation that further legitimizes giving greater programmatic control to young adults. Inside the movement, participants have a much broader range of ages, and it is not unusual to meet people in gatherings and at conferences who are in their fifties and sixties. But age hierarchies are openly challenged, and young adults are expected to take leadership responsibility, such that sympathy with the ECM coincides with encouraging young adults to lead worship, speak in public assemblies, direct project teams, and create new programs as a way to encourage participation and "shift" the culture of the church toward the next generation.

Fourth, *experimentation and creativity are core dispositions among Emerging Christians*. Creativity is evident both from the popular leaders of the movement—public figures whose books and blogs offer "new" theological justifications for the ECM—and from participants, who are expected to be involved in shaping and choosing congregational practices. The sheer variety of practices within emerging congregations illustrates how Emerging Christians are eager to innovate based on older religious forms. Many Emerging Christians lament that their previous, usually evangelical, traditions neglected artistic expression. They now endeavor to use the arts to facilitate individual spiritual development. Activities foster games and nonformal interaction. Playfulness and participation are highly esteemed. And creative approaches to liturgical processes are welcomed.

Fifth and finally, *Emerging Christians negotiate potential religious polarization by striving to create a new type of "neutral religious space" that is church-ish without being church-y*. The ECM is dependent on established institutions at the same time it attempts to win independence from them. Emerging Christians believe they are living in a changed religious landscape in which foundational Christian doctrines are no longer assumed and some traditional church practices are viewed as irrelevant. Furthermore, Emerging Christians see themselves as rescuing core aspects of Christianity from the entanglement of modernity, bureaucracy, and right-wing politics. Emerging Christians are also rescuing their own selves from the shallowness, hypocrisy, and rigidity of their religious past. And while some Emerging Christians are open and explicit in their commitment to the movement, we know from our fieldwork that there are other "secret" adherents with leadership and internship positions in established denominations who keep their sympathies and affiliations quiet so as not to create a disturbance.

So when approaching the ECM, rather than noting its "anti-institutional" orientation and succumbing to a hopeless lack of definition, we view it as a form of institutional innovation, that is, *an institutionalizing structure* that relies less on formal organizations than informal networks. We argue that the ECM is driven by *religious institutional entrepreneurs* who share a particular *religious orientation* based on deconstruction. We conceive of the ECM as a relatively stable package of beliefs, practices, and identities that exist via a series of relationships, affiliations, and affinities, which is sustained both *formally* through partnerships and collaborative efforts and *informally* through friendships and shared ideals. The ECM is therefore *relatively coherent* yet *haphazardly organized. It is* deliberately *messy.* [101] This somewhat amorphous quality makes it at once easy to pinpoint figureheads of the movement while dismissing the more substantive social structures and everyday participants that perpetuate it. Emerging Christians are themselves caught in a distinctively sociological dilemma: how to revitalize the Christian "church" while simultaneously avoiding what they see as the "trappings" of church institutions. The apparent chaos observed in the ECM stems from the way its practices serve to exaggerate the inherent heterogeneity of Christianity itself. The ECM accepts and encourages *multiple approaches* to spirituality. Indeed, the apparent nebulousness of the movement has prompted some scholars in their casual observations to dismiss the relative substance of the larger undertaking. Yet gauged by the continued activity within the movement itself—as well as the aggressive polemic against the movement from outside critics—the ECM is a stable and significant aspect of US and UK religion.[102]

Emerging Christians may or may not explicitly identify with the ECM through its figureheads or its conferences or its websites, but they do identify with the aspects of the ECM's deconstruction that we describe throughout this book. Most especially, Emerging Christians should be considered to have a distinctive and viable religious orientation based on a fierce notion of individuality.[103] Through immersive communities that afford diverse practices, Emerging Christians enact a *strategic religiosity* that reveals itself in multiple ways. Recognizing this orientation helps us move beyond previous scholarly and popular speculation that participants in the ECM are "innovation consumers" who relish novelty and actively seek out opportunities to experience the spectacle of whatever is new or are simply Christian "hipsters" who, in effect, seek style over substance.[104] What we describe is also more than a vaguely defined, fluid, postchurch religiosity. Their "switching" is not a casual happenstance but an intimate and intentional part of their religious lives. They are not disaffected religious "nones." Participants in the ECM define their various congregations as a type of "haven" that supports a valued aspect of their personal identity.[105] Their participation is often associated with personal and emotional strain rather than exuberance in a recreational pursuit. Yet all believe they have found a place that allows them to be "themselves." In the end, through their congregations and their involvements Emerging Christians work to accomplish a strategically enacted *religious individualization*. Religious individualization enables them to fulfill their religious imperatives however ambiguously they may be defined.

## The Structure of This Book    *What they do.*

In the rest of this book, we describe what it is like to be an Emerging Christian and analyze Emerging Christians' activities and their significance in the wider Western religious landscape. We privilege the lived experience of Emerging Christians, utilizing a unique data set drawn from congregations, parachurch organizations, and informal ECM-type communities. Our conclusions are based on more than a decade of research within the ECM, primarily in the United States and Northern Ireland.[106] The majority of our data were collected from ECM participants, communities, and conferences from 2010 through 2013 using participant observation, focus groups, and in-depth interviews with leaders and participants; observation and interaction using social media; and examination of available textual sources. Numerous intense conversations at ECM gatherings are also part of this data. Public figures were not considered representative of the movement as a whole, although their writings helped clarify and crystallize some of the key aspects of Emerging Christians' religious orientation. Our material was supplemented with data collected by Tony Jones for his doctoral dissertation in practical theology at Princeton Theological Seminary. Using his "insider's" knowledge of emerging congregations, Jones visited eight representative congregations across the United States in 2005 and 2006, groups that are examples and models within the movement and whose leaders are well networked; and he conducted interviews, focus groups, and congregational surveys. Although Jones's primary interest was in helping emerging congregations develop their theology, he gathered data in a manner relevant to social science researchers like us. We are impressed with the quality of the data, and he kindly granted us access.

Chapter 2, *Pluralist Congregations,* characterizes the congregations of the ECM as *pluralist congregations,* seeing them as rare examples of religious institutions that—rather than failing to recognize or trying to suppress diversity—instead try to facilitate it. The ECM is a congregational faith, one that relies on patterned relationships, regular gatherings, and ongoing involvement. The pluralist congregations of the ECM are distinct in that they promote individualism while at the same time providing a basis for community around shared experiences and relationships. Pluralist congregations exemplify what sociologist Ulrich Beck has called "cooperative egoism," as they strive to form the basis for a religious orientation that straddles the tension between individualism and collective identity.

Chapter 3, *Being an Emerging Christian,* shares the stories of Emerging Christians, highlighting their individual experiences of deconstruction, often characterized as "deconversion" stories. We emphasize the common experiences of Emerging Christians, such as disillusionment with evangelicalism, megachurches, or rigid mainline denominations; and the liberating effects reported from reading Brian McLaren books. This chapter introduces the concept of *strategic religiosity* and shows that what appears on the surface to be a freewheeling heterodoxy reacting to the established institutions of contemporary Christianity is, on more investigation, a strategically framed religious self that is nurtured, legitimated, and sustained through congregational involvement.

Chapter 4, *Faith as Conversation,* emphasizes the value placed on dialogue and discussion within the ECM. Understanding how institutional entrepreneurs use discourses helps explain the effectiveness of the "faith as conversation" approach of the ECM. Drawing on the literature on institutional entrepreneurship, we argue that Emerging Christians are *religious institutional entrepreneurs.* The "conversation" of the ECM is an almost paradigmatic example of the type of "meaning work" that has been so central to studies of institutional entrepreneurship. Moreover, the common and expected participation in dialogue reveals the ECM as a form of *collective institutional entrepreneurship.* We analyze the content of the ECM conversations, focusing on the importance placed on asking questions and on the distinct ideas about the nature of truth, embracing doubt, and the nature of God, exploring how these ideas shape Emerging Christians' religious orientations.

Chapter 5 *Deconstructing Congregational Practices,* analyzes Emerging Christians' renegotiation of congregational practices. We argue that the ECM has two dominant conversational partners in its reshaping of congregational practice: the "Seeker Megachurch" and the "Solemn Mainline" experience. For us, Emerging Christians' renegotiations of congregational practices embody their critiques of the "mega" and the "mainline," especially their approaches to preaching, leadership, public worship, and the physical locations of church. Further, emerging congregations' practices are deliberately open, inclusive, and drawn from a variety of traditions—all in an effort to make people feel comfortable and to allow them *multiple paths* to choose which religious practices work best for them.

Chapter 6, *Following Jesus in the Real World,* explores how Emerging Christians live—or strive to live—in the "real world." While many emerging congregations got their start as "church plants" or "missional" communities, Emerging Christians disagree about the extent that they should be living their lives to try and "convert" others. Some Emerging Christians choose lifestyles that they see as inherently political, believing that this is the best way for them to live out their Christianity. For them, Jesus's mission was a *political* one on behalf of the poor and marginalized, so they seek to emulate Jesus by identifying with disadvantaged communities, or working for peace and reconciliation, through conventional political engagement, forming neo-monastic communities, creating Temporary Autonomous Zones (TAZs), and choosing careers that enable them to work for social justice. Overall, immersive relationships with people outside their congregations and involvements with loftier ethical and political concerns provide Emerging Christians multiple, necessary opportunities for experimenting and implementing a newly individuated religious self.

Chapter 7, *Understanding Emerging Christianity,* not only synthesizes the broader argument of the book but also places it in contrast to common interpretations of the ECM, such as that it is merely evangelicalism in disguise, liberal Protestantism in another guise, religious consumerism, or a movement that has already run its course. We argue that the structure and practices of Emerging Christianity represent a distinctive approach to *religious individualization.* We describe the religious orientation or "self" of the Emerging Christian as "legitimate," "sacralized," and "pluralist," which is supported by congregations that facilitate a *cooperative egoism.* While labels may change, we argue that the ECM developed and will continue to persist well into the future because it is a striking manifestation of increasingly ubiquitous elements characteristic not only of the wider Christian landscape but, more significantly, of all modern religiosity.

# 2

# Pluralist Congregations

I had not put it into words, but when I saw it, I said, "Yes, that's what
I envision a church should be: a lot of people doing things that feel
right to them—but doing it together."
— Sydney, *on what attracted her to her church*

There is so much variety among emerging congregations that it is difficult to
generalize about their structure or form. But what holds almost all these congregations together is their openness and commitment to tolerating radically
diverse viewpoints, which translates into their willingness to incorporate a
wide range of devotional and liturgical practices. As a starting point for understanding, we characterize the congregations of the ECM as *pluralist congregations*, seeing them as rare examples of religious institutions that try to facilitate
rather than fail to recognize or try to suppress diversity. *We define pluralist congregations as social spaces that permit, and even foster, direct interaction between
people with religiously contradictory perspectives and value systems.* In defining
"pluralist congregation," we agree with Beck's approach in defining "pluralization" as "the coexistence of different and frequently contradictory world perspectives and value systems in a space where they directly interact."[1] Pluralist
congregations promote individualism while at the same time providing a basis
for community around shared experiences and relationships.

As we describe in chapter 3, the experiences of deconstruction and deconversion are central to Emerging Christians' identities. Through the practice of
deconstruction, all Emerging Christians craft a type of religious self, yet *any
religious self, even a critically oriented religious self, cannot thrive without a community of others.* At first glance, the focus on one's self through relationships may
seem like a kind of therapeutic, self-help type of religion in which others are
seen as means to an individual end—a dismal "me-first" attitude that defeats
the notion of community as the egoistic self participates in religious gatherings in order to have their own needs fulfilled. But what our research consistently reveals is bonded groups of individuals who share a religious orientation.

Emerging Christians experience a warm and accepting atmosphere in their congregations and find that their individual religious journeys are bound up with the journeys of others.

Emerging congregations therefore strike an apparently contradictory balance as they create religious communities in which the autonomy of the individual is held as a core value in the very midst of an often-stated emphasis on relationship and community. Emerging Christians do not strive for the instrumentalized or therapeutic religious identities that are often (rather stereotypically) associated with evangelicalism. Instead, Emerging Christians maintain a modern (or postmodern) religious orientation by participating in highly open relational spaces that welcome self-asserting, critically reflective attitudes toward "religion" while striving for a holistic sense of self that is consistent with their everyday lives. The self is viewed as fully human and fully integrated only in the context of relationships—with others and with God.

In short, even within the most loosely organized emerging "churches," *the ECM is a congregational faith*, one that relies on relationships, regular gatherings, and involvement. Emerging Christians' pluralist congregations exemplify what Ulrich Beck has called "cooperative egoism," a concept we examine more fully in chapter 7. Cooperative egoism helps form the basis for a religious orientation that straddles the tension between individualism and collective identity. In the rest of this chapter, we explore what it is like for Emerging Christians to participate in pluralist congregations. We describe how Emerging Christians' practice of pluralism extends all the way from public worship (see chapter 5) to allowing, even encouraging, people to hold a plurality of beliefs around faith and morals in their private convictions (see chapter 3).

## Introducing the Pluralist Congregations of the ECM

To illustrate the various pluralist congregations of the ECM, we share descriptions of the public gatherings of three emerging congregations, highlighting their pluralist practices.

### Church of the Apostles, Seattle

Church of the Apostles in Seattle meets in a self-consciously cool-looking, street corner coffee shop, which was formerly a homeless shelter. The congregation deliberately chose this location as a hub from which to revitalize the community through the church's presence. The space is small, with a capacity of around thirty-five people. The room was packed, with the only available seats up front. Being such a small space, it was impossible for a visitor to blend in. Yet those present made the few visitors there feel welcomed and even appreciated.

All available space was carefully crafted to create ambiance. An iconic crucifix was propped on top of a speaker, and incense filled the room. A white sheet was draped over the ceiling lights to subdue the lighting. Professional-standard artwork lined the walls, not on canvas but on plain white paper. Another sheet was stretched artistically across the front wall, and a cartoon of Jesus's life played on a video screen. Yet another large screen flashed announcements, worship lyrics, images, and scripture texts (no verse references noted so people would not necessarily know that they came from the Bible). A table covered in a royal, majestic tapestry held the communion elements, and a plastic, opaque bowl was illuminated by a light from underneath. Candles sat on the table, and a Celtic cross was laid before the elements. People were shaking gourds and musical instruments, getting ready for worship. The band—bass, piano, percussion, xylophone—played a repetitive jazz riff in a minor key.

It was a late Sunday afternoon, and just after five o'clock people were invited to stand and sing (if they were able). The worship music was led by an amplified guitar, a female vocalist, and three violins, and most songs were unfamiliar with the exception of "Amazing Grace" (although this was done with an unexpected rhythm). A short time of singing led into what was called "Translation Time." An unreferenced scripture text was flashed on the screen, and those gathered were told to break up into groups of five or six to consider and discuss their own translations. In groups, people mostly reflected on the use of metaphor, images, and symbolism and how they enhanced our understanding and internalization of the text. The dialogue was active, with people feeding off each other's ideas. After a period, each group was encouraged to share the important aspects of their conversation. Then there was a short prayer, during which the speaker described the Holy Spirit as "she." A person serving as lead pastor for the service then stood to give an exposition of the scripture and how it applied to his life. It seemed like more of a poetic and artistic reading than a sermon *per se*. He talked about exposing sin and how Jesus brings all things into the light of truth. He then invited those gathered to partake in personal confession and expose one's sins before God. People were encouraged to come forward to the "altar"; write confessions with black markers on clear plastic Saran Wrap; and place them in the lighted clear plastic bowl, which was symbolic of offering prayers to God. Only a few people participated.

The gathering then sang the words, "Our darkness is never darkness in your sight. The deepest night is clear as the daylight," over and over again in Taizé fashion. During what they called "The Drum Beat," someone in the crowd read Psalm 23. People were invited to pick a percussion instrument and use their hands, sing, or make some kind of noise with cymbals to the beat of the psalm.

Next a scripture reading occurred that was spoken more like a narrated story than a reading of sacred text. Different people read the scripted parts. It was the story of Jesus healing a blind man. A video image of Jesus was shown on the overhead screen, first blurry and then slowly coming into focus—like what one would imagine the blind man saw as he gained sight. After the reading, the group said in unison, "Praise be to you, Lord Jesus Christ."

Following this was a time called "Open Space." Open Space is a regular feature where everyone can do whatever they feel like they need to do—whatever they want to do—to reflect on what they heard. In practice, this consists of seven to eight minutes for quiet reflection, prayer, contemplation of the icon, lighting a candle, talking with a friend, having a cup of coffee, drawing, or journaling. A sort of Middle Eastern rendition of "Amazing Grace" was played in the background. Open Space ended with a time of prayer for two people from the community who were preparing for their baptism on Easter Sunday. Everyone gathered around and laid hands on them.

Communion, or the Lord's Supper, which came next was very casual. Attendees came forward and took the elements from appointed lay leaders of the church. The pastor asked every person their name and spoke personally to each one as he offered the bread and the wine. It seemed that he wanted to know who each person was and to ensure every person was welcome in the community for however long they stayed. After the taking of the elements, the closing aspect of worship was called "Family Time," where people could make announcements relevant to the group. There was a brief discussion about a community house that was forming, an open invitation to a graduation party, and finally an invitation to become part of their community of faith. A lone pug dog wandered throughout the room during the worship service, fell asleep on the floor, and added to the noise with his loud snoring. No one seemed bothered by this.

## Journey Church, Dallas

The room was dark, shrouded in black cloth, and lit with candles. The band was small, using a track in lieu of drums. Several television sets projected the words to songs. The furniture was a mixture of pews, lounge chairs, and small tables with Bibles and some other literature on them. There was art on the walls, and a bar in the back with soda available to drink. The stage and two sections of seating formed a triangle, with a lectern in the middle. People wandered in, and all were dressed casually.

The service opened with a comedy monologue, fully irreverent, and a young man wearing jeans, a collared shirt, and a blazer (it was "Bad Blazer Night"), welcomed everyone. He led a collect on the screens, and the congregation sang four songs recognizable from the contemporary Christian music scene. A woman led the singing and took center stage, with men playing guitars and bass. As the songs went on, some remained standing while others sat down.

The first reading, from the book of Ezra, was done by a young woman as trance music played in the background. She read in a dramatic and engaging way, with a handheld mic behind a small lectern. Abstract art was projected on the screens. Then another woman, this time the leader of the congregation, got up to speak. She reflected on being "people of the Book" in her church as she was growing up. She referenced pop culture, a novelist, and some smart academic texts by contemporary theologians. She then asked people to share memories of stories they heard while growing up. A man talked about his dad reading *Where the Wild Things Are* while bouncing him on his knee. Another man remembered reading *The Catcher in the Rye* in high school and then said how much he hates that book now—it reminds him of how stupid he was. A woman shared watching the movies *Schindler's List* and *Dances with Wolves* and being confronted with others' pain for the first time. Another woman shared about reading *Sadako and a Thousand Paper Cranes*. She was deeply moved by the story and went on to fold 1,000 paper cranes in response. A half-dozen more people shared before the pastor asked them to share memories of experiences in their own church. A man shared about the pranks of the "Man Group" that led to lots of people piping in about their funny memories of that group.

The discussion got somewhat boisterous before the pastor shifted people to talk about their favorite stories from the Bible. A woman said that she liked the Mosaic plagues as a kid, and a man talked about Mephibosheth—the "gimpy kid" in the Hebrew Bible. Another man talked about the Tower of Babel. The pastor shared her favorites and then talked about the overall story of the text—concluding that it's telling us to "remember, remember, remember." She said:

> We want scripture to be central to our life of faith because the story is formative for us ... In our community we center our lives on the grand narrative of scripture, and I love that we put "grand" in front of it. We don't want to be the type of community who lets the Bible do the remembering for us. We want to do the remembering. We don't want to slip into amnesia, to forget where we come from.

She led a prayer, which transitioned to the offering time, introduced by a young woman who also gave announcements in a friendly, lighthearted way. There was a book club and an opportunity to lead worship at a community for mentally challenged persons. She also invited everyone to dinner after the service. Everyone recited a benediction in unison, and the feeling after worship was noisy and happy, even a bit raucous. There was no communion at this particular meeting.

## House of Mercy, St. Paul

House of Mercy in St. Paul meets on Sunday evenings in the sanctuary of First Baptist Church of St. Paul. The sanctuary is a large, high-ceilinged room with an imposing organ framed by dark stained wood. The formal architecture contrasts with the informal ambiance. Dress is very casual, including jeans and hooded sweatshirts. While some time was given to congregational music, more was given to the sermon from a guest, a professor in a local evangelical college. After his message, three pastoral leaders ascended the platform to lead communion.

The structure of communion was unexpected given the seemingly "Baptistic" orientation of the liturgy. On the communion table were three pottery cups, a matching pitcher, and a basket of bread. A candle burned on the table. Other votive candles were visible to the side. The lead pastor began with an open invitation and words traditionally used to instigate the Eucharistic ritual. The pastors served each other first, and then people came forward by pew. Communion was taken by intinction, the Eucharistic practice of dipping the consecrated bread into the consecrated wine before ingesting. Some people lit votive candles on the way back to their seats. As people took communion, an a cappella sextet sang an ancient-sounding chant in Latin recently composed by someone in the congregation. The tempo shifted for a final song. In a tip of the hat to the fundamentalist past, the closing hymn was "The Old Gospel Ship," a 1939 copyright gospel tune played in a bluegrass style: "O I'm 'gonna' take a trip in the good Old Gospel Ship, I'm going far beyond the sky; O I'm 'gonna' shout and sing until the heavens ring, when I'm bidding this world goodbye."

To evangelicals, the mix of liturgical approaches creates for them an unexpected emotional twinge. To them, the overall ambiance of the communion portion of the service feels nostalgic and "Roman Catholic." But for everything else, from the opening band to the sermon and closing "benediction," the presentation is simply casual and distinctly "low church." One member said, "What kept me here was that I really enjoyed the aesthetic of the service. It was really beautiful and weird. The service was quirky." Another member summarized, saying, "We're quirky. We do quirky things."

# Practicing Pluralism

Emerging congregations draw on a variety of religious practices in their public events. While this may look initially like religious consumerism or syncretism, Emerging Christians see their practices as honoring the depth and breadth of a variety of Christian traditions, while at the same time appealing to people who are coming from a plurality of Christian backgrounds. By incorporating a variety of practices from a range of denominational traditions, emerging congregations cultivate communities where people from different Christian denominational backgrounds are provided the opportunity to recognize a familiar ritual. So even when socioeconomic and ethnic diversity are lacking, people within emerging congregations say they incorporate many forms of diversity in their gatherings. Packard links the ECM's ability to accommodate this kind of diversity to its congregations being anti-institutional, "resistant organizations," which allow people with diverse viewpoints, identities, and liturgical practices to feel at home without having to change or compromise their already-existing religious familiarities.[2] Emerging Christians' encounters with at least some form of religious diversity encourage them to maintain an orientation that is intellectually open and focused on relationships rather than concentrated on pinning down a correct set of specific beliefs and practices. Even more, participation in these pluralist congregations is vital to maintaining Emerging Christians' distinct and individualized religious orientation.

## Diversity—"There's this way of being Christian and that way of being Christian."

Emerging Christians come from multiple Christian backgrounds.[3] Participants in the emerging congregations we studied included former pastors and youth pastors, seminary students and graduates, worship leaders, seminary professors and professors in evangelical colleges, a Christian camp director, missionaries working in foreign countries, children of missionaries, staff members in campus ministries and parachurch organizations like the Navigators and Campus Crusade for Christ (what one person called, "a good old-fashioned evangelical collegiate ministry"), others working in nonprofit foundations focused on poverty, an employee of a Christian media company selling services to megachurches, descendants of the "Jesus Movement," children and grandchildren of pastors, youth workers, and dedicated lay leaders who had served in churches large and small. Our congregational surveys and interviews revealed that very few people in emerging congregations come from atheistic or agnostic backgrounds. Instead, emerging congregations are a haven for the "dechurched," those who had a religious upbringing or background but had grown disillusioned with conventional religious institutions.[4] One man said, "A lot people who are coming here are disillusioned with the church. They have a church background. They feel like they were talked down to in the regular church and not getting enough [spiritually]."

Moreover, many had been immersed in several religious traditions through their life experiences. As one man said, "I was raised Catholic, and then Baptist, and then Presbyterian. Seems like three different lives." Or as a husband and wife said, "We've been Presbyterian, we've been Lutheran, Episcopalian." Many, like Felicia, called themselves a "lifer in the church" and "a lifelong church attender," or stated, "I've been to church all of my life." One woman was so "churched" she said, "I have had three baptisms": a catechistic baptism, a believer's baptism, and a baptism in a small group. It signified for her the various ways she experienced Christianity: a formal commitment, a conviction-based public declaration, and then a highly relational one in the pool of a church friend performed by her current pastor. Another man came from a conservative evangelical church, then went to a Catholic university where he got involved in mass. He said: "That was a really great experience for me. Different worship. A lot more liturgy and tradition involved, a stress on different parts of the faith." One man described his "journey" to his emerging congregation as moving from being a "total Wiccan Neo-Pagan guy" to "evangelical Christian" to claiming "now I'm a Catholic." Conner recounted his affiliations before coming to his emerging congregation, saying, "I became a Christian at a late age, became an evangelical for a really short period of time, then jumped ship and became a Roman Catholic of a pretty conservative persuasion. And that worked for me for all of my undergrad years, and it stopped working. I started searching a lot after that, and it's pretty much how I came here."

While Emerging Christians appreciate different liturgical forms and rites, they tend to choose from denominational traditions "what works for me." In the case of married couples from different Christian traditions, many emerging congregations combine elements of those traditions in a way that allows both to feel at home. One man said, "I grew up in the Catholic Church, and I liked coming to a church that was not Catholic but still had the liturgy." His wife was Baptist, so finding an emerging congregation that mixed the liturgy was ideal. As Claire said in talking about Protestant and Catholic churches, "I have a great respect for both approaches." And Emerging Christians from evangelical backgrounds often say, "I always liked the liturgical aspect of Catholic [or Episcopal] services." At the same time, the distance achieved from prior orientations leaves Emerging Christians less insistent that liturgy must be practiced in a specific way. For example, Taylor described his previous religious experience as being a "culturized form of Christianity," the practices of which reflected "modern" culture. As such, it should not be equated as the one, "true" expression of faith—as he had been led to believe. He said, "We came from being raised in this very modern Christianity and going through our own journey of letting that go ... What we grew up with was a 'culturized' form of Christianity and we wanted to break out of that."

Many Emerging Christians carry the experiences of diverse religious backgrounds within themselves. Their varied Christian experiences are disjointed in that they are not seen as readily harmonizing with each other; however, people always acknowledged them as valid pieces of themselves. One man said, "All these pieces have something to say about who I am, where I am now. It's hard to dig in and pull out one thing 'cause it's all those things blended together." As Hailey said, "I'm like a religious mutt." Another man said:

> I always held onto pieces of those earlier bits. Some people wonder why. "Why do you always do your Bible reading every morning? Why make that such a big deal?" I'm like, "This is something I learned from the evangelicals that has been really helpful to me, and I see nothing in my current church that tells me I ought to give it up."

He concluded, "There's this way of being Christian and that way of being Christian."

While on the surface this may appear to be simply a laissez-faire attitude, Emerging Christians see being open to multiple expressions of Christianity as vital to their personal spiritual growth. Conner explained that he attended his emerging congregation in part "to explore other ways of being Christian." Blake grew up in a Southern Baptist family and explained how in his Baptist college, "I started being pushed out of my tradition in a healthy way. I started desiring more paths of spirituality—finding that Christianity had more than what I had experienced." Another man had been a worship pastor but began "asking questions" and was removed from his position by his denomination. He began visiting other churches and participated in several congregations "trying to figure things out. [Our church] seemed to be a fit, something that made sense." As such, Emerging Christians express a willingness to explore, accept, and even legitimize experiences different from their own. Emerging Christians view themselves as honoring the depth and breadth of a variety of Christian traditions, both in the respect they declare for them and in their willingness to incorporate a range of practices into their gatherings.

The diverse denominational backgrounds of those active in the ECM reflect, in part, its primary origins in evangelicalism, which historically has been a transdenominational movement.[5] A significant portion of Emerging Christians in our survey say they come from evangelical backgrounds (28.5%) and continue to label themselves as evangelical (21.2%). However, we were surprised to find the *largest* percentage of respondents marked mainline Protestant as their religious background (30.7%), with some (8.1%) still retaining this self-definition. Just under 10% report coming from nonreligious, agnostic, or atheistic backgrounds. We cannot claim that our survey is representative of or can be generalized to the ECM as a whole. But future research might probe more deeply the extent to which Emerging Christians (and not just their high-profile leaders, who are almost unanimously evangelicals or former evangelicals) come from evangelical backgrounds.

## Religious Freedom—"You don't have to be right."

Emerging congregations not only do not demand that people conform to the beliefs and practices of a particular Christian tradition, they also resist "officially" identifying which Christian beliefs and practices should be central to their own communities. One woman said, "There's no pretence of having to be orthodox here. You don't have to be right." Another man said, "I'm really into talking about doctrine in the Bible. But I'm not going to push it on anyone, and I'm not going to say you're going to hell if you don't believe the way I do." This affirms Matthew Guest and Steve Taylor's description of ECM groups as making "a virtue of rejecting clear-cut theologies and accepting newcomers as they are, without any call for doctrinal conformity."[6]

Emerging Christians highly value the exercise of religious freedom—*within their own congregations*. People are encouraged to critique the beliefs and practices that have wounded them and to not insist on what beliefs and practices they maintain or adopt. As one man said, "The last thing we want to do is reject, because many of us probably feel alienated in the larger Christian [world]." Emerging Christians say they appreciated that their emerging congregations not only welcomed people from diverse denominational backgrounds but also allowed for a diversity of inward beliefs and outward appearances. One man said, "I grew up with an evangelical background. I believe in very different things than that. Some things are the same. I believe Jesus is God. But maybe how 'sin' is defined is very different." Openness to receive a diversity of viewpoints and religious perspectives is common. A woman said, "Acceptance for people whatever level they are, whatever place they are, whatever belief system they have, whatever they've grown up in, just a place to gather together and to grow together, and to reach out to people and accept people for who and what they are and still maintain your own position." As Katharine Sarah Moody also observes, "The emphasis is thus placed not upon *what* beliefs are believed, but *how* such beliefs are believed; 'holding beliefs lightly' is discursively promoted to keep the individual and community open."[7] This ability to "hold beliefs lightly" is vital to Emerging Christians' distinct religious orientation and is another way in which they see themselves as honoring the depth and breadth of a variety of Christian traditions.

Other Emerging Christians spoke about the link between respect for diversity and individual acceptance, with Max characterizing this as "our church's strength—we strive so hard to find diversity and to find acceptance." Another mentioned "affirmation and admiration of who that person is." This means that individuals do not feel pressure to become a particular type of person. Isaac said about his emerging congregation, "I like having room to be ourselves." Another man simply said, "No pressure to conform." Emerging Christians rejected what they saw as a false, enforced orthodoxy within their previous congregations, including an excessive focus on how people dressed or even styled their hair. One woman said that she "had purple hair growing up" and that this would not have been acceptable in her previous churches. Valerie also brought up in conversation the hair color of a person in her congregation: "One of the people who often leads communion has pink hair. [Lots of laughter] That says a lot about our church. [Lots of laughter] It says that it's OK if you're different. You can have pink hair and still be there." Individuals are encouraged to "come as they are" in terms of what they believe and how they dress.

The diversity of these congregations extends to incorporating people of different religious faiths—even those who do not believe in God at all. Ulrich Beck describes this as "the maxim that *freedom of religion is the freedom of other people's religion.*"[8] As one woman said, "I've always grown up with certain tenets of the faith about the Bible, but I've met people here who haven't and who still don't even believe that now. But still they're accepted here and even put in places where they can serve communion. We're all on this faith process." One man insisted that ECM congregations create "a safe environment for doubt." One woman estimated that "ten percent" of the church would not call themselves Christian or really struggle with belief in the most basic aspects of the Christian faith. A leader of a pub church said, "When these gatherings occur, there's as likely to be an atheist or two as a traditional believer, there may well be someone who is somewhere between faith and agnosticism, and on a good night, there'll be a Jewish person, perhaps a Muslim, and maybe even a Baha'i or Wiccan to keep the peace. You may also find a Methodist or Nazarene sneaking a pint."[9] As Beck notes, "The religion of others is not merely 'tolerated' [but] held rather to be an *enrichment* of one's own religious experience."[10]

Although Emerging Christians tend to come from churched backgrounds, their self-understanding emphasizes they have moved away from maintaining strict, orthodox sect memberships in their congregational relationships. Beck insightfully labels this as *religious cosmopolitanism*.[11] Religious cosmopolitanism "emphasizes the dignity and the burden of difference."[12] Encountering differences is unavoidable. As Beck writes, "The territorial exclusivity of religious *imagined communities* is coming to an end, and even where it still exists, the voices of the different religions collide with one another in a global society where communication knows no bounds."[13] Consistent with the reports from

Emerging Christians, "The alien faith, the faith of the stranger, is not felt to be threatening, destructive, or fragmenting. Rather, it is felt to be enriching."[14]

Consequently, Emerging Christians reject homogenization and encourage individualization. One woman said, "I just love that we're allowed to come together and have different opinions and to express how we see scripture, and we don't all have to agree." There's not "a certain uniform," said another member. Emerging Christians assert that their congregations constitute a pluralistic space. One member even said, "They're OK with pluralism." Max said, "We've learned how to relate to each other even though we are so different." Tony Jones also once conversationally described emerging congregations as characterized by "this nonjudgmentalness, this openness to diversity of opinions, this diversity of theological backgrounds, openness to many different beliefs."

In short, a desire to accommodate individuals in their diverse viewpoints and lifestyles is central to the religious orientation Emerging Christians are cultivating through their congregations. Max called such freedom "therapeutic," saying:

> [Our church] was therapeutic at the time that I needed it most. It was a safe space for me to rest—let, you know, whatever I had in me wash out—clean yourself out by the simple fact of being here and not having pressures on me about what's expected of me, how I should view religion, how I should view my life, how I should behave, how I should do all these things—but really just rest and let those things go away.

Further, Emerging Christians see their congregations as places that affirm their own identities. One woman said, "I feel like I can be completely myself." Another woman said, "It's not that certain parts of me go in and come out and certain parts of me don't go in. I bring my whole self to church, and I take church in its whole with me back."

In affirming others who are religiously different, Emerging Christians simultaneously affirm themselves. As Beck writes, "What is involved is an egoism of cosmopolitan religiosity: those who integrate the religious perspectives and traditions of others into their own religious experience learn more about themselves *and* about others."[15] A continuum between "belief" and "nonbelief" is both accepted and expected. In short, "religious cosmopolitanism distinguishes among non-believers, the broad spectrum of believers in other faiths. It regards them, however, not as a threat to its own religious monopoly on truth, but as an enrichment in a quite personal sense, and ultimately even as part of the normal state of affairs."[16]

## Moral Freedom—"There's no judging."

The freedom people experience means they frequently describe their congregations as "not judging" and "not legalistic." One person said, "There's no judging," and another member quipped, "Or at least the bar is a lot higher." [Laughter] People also said their fitness for taking responsibility in the ministry of their congregation was not judged by their social behavior.

Examples of personal freedom abound in the interviews, some of them shocking. When Wyatt was asked by his church, "Do you want to be on leadership?," he responded, "Well, yeah, but I don't want to be a moral pillar or whatever. I'm still trying to figure this stuff out. Like, next week my friend is turning twenty-one, and we're going to take him out and get him drunk and go to a strip club." According to Wyatt, his plans did not disqualify him for leadership. "They're like, 'Yeah, we still want you to be on the leadership,' and I said, 'That's great. I would love to be on the leadership.'" He said his involvement in his church's leadership "was a really therapeutic thing for me."

The experience of moral openness contrasted with Emerging Christians' inherited expectations of a conservative social morality. One remark that drew a lot of laughs was a woman describing her experience of "the freedom or the openness—in a biblical way." She had graduated from a Baptist college and coming to her church, she was dumbfounded: "Whoa, you have a *beer* after *church*? With your *pastor*?!" She characterized this as her church's "lack of legalism and judgment." She said, "There are certain freedoms that I had been led to believe didn't exist. [In my previous church] there were all these black-and-white issues, and those things, like cussing or drinking, don't matter in a healthy context." One man said, "You can be drinking a beer with somebody who's not a Christian, and if somebody from [our church] walks in and sees you doing that, you don't feel like you have to explain yourself [Laughter]." Remaining in the everyday world, "there among the community being Christian and among them," is highly valued. One young woman said, "We go hang out at a local restaurant. People drink. They don't pretend they don't drink." She said, "It just seems so real."

Stella similarly said her current church is "very different from the experience where we were at. I was feeling strangled. I would leave church feeling, 'Phew, got that out of the way.'" Emerging congregations do not feature moral restrictions, strict biblicism, or obedience to spiritual authority as didactic priorities.[17] One man said, "If the appropriate word was 'damn,' then 'damn' was the word that was said." Brooke said, "They don't have a sermon on why you shouldn't have sex before you're married. In other churches they're like, 'Let's have a sermon on why we shouldn't smoke,' and 'Let's have another sermon on why we shouldn't drink.' They don't have sermons like that here."

She said, "The first time I came here I was by myself, my family didn't come, it was just me, and I felt like the Holy Spirit was welcome here. The Holy Spirit's not welcome everywhere, because when you welcome the Holy Spirit you have to let go of control. And we had come from an experience where control was the driving force, and it was strangling." Stella said, "I just felt a release, I felt like it was real, the workings of the Holy Spirit in this place."

In other churches, Emerging Christians say they felt like they were forced to adopt a false identity, one that indicated a correct religious persona. Claire said, "I always thought at other churches that I always had to be a good Christian but knew that I wasn't, and at [this church] I don't feel as if I have to be a 'good' Christian. I'm just a Christian." An older woman said, "You don't have to feel like you need to put up this big front like you're this 'Super Christian Person'—because nobody else is." One man said, "It's a place where I can be comfortable being imperfect." Liam said, "There are lyrics to songs in our church that are like, 'I'm weak, Lord'—but I was used to singing in charismatic churches, 'I'm a conqueror'—[Robust laughter]—I felt like singing, 'I'm a hypocrite.' I can't sing this stuff!" One young woman summarized, saying, "I found a community of people who were flawed and not trying to cover up their flaws."

Another woman explained, "I was brought up Southern Baptist—very strict—and this is the total opposite of conservative Baptist background. I needed to be in an environment where it's okay to not be strict." Churches from her background were places "where you have to do these things, and you have to believe a certain way, you have to live a certain way to be a Christian." Now she says that if someone fails to live up to these expectations, "God still loves you and that's okay." She said, "I was a pretty uptight person, and I've relaxed a lot because I don't care about guilt as much. I can go to bed, and if I didn't read my Bible before I go to bed, I'm okay with that. I can sleep all night, and I'm okay." She concluded, "I'm okay with my own faith."

## Getting Involved—"How can you be who God has made you to be in this place?"

Emerging congregations' use of practices from diverse Christian traditions and their rather loose attitudes toward doctrinal beliefs and moral standards may look like attempts to appeal to as many people as possible. But this is not the aim of most emerging congregations. Rather, they demand a high level of involvement from those who attend. Based on our survey of ECM participants, 24% attended weekly, and an *additional* 33% said they attended more than once per week. This level of involvement considerably blunts emerging congregations' individualistic tendencies.

The importance placed on "being involved" is significant given how much individual freedom and discretion is valued. All the Emerging Christians interviewed for this research indicated their immersion within the relational networks of their congregations, and they often recounted the many ways their ECM communities create informal opportunities for people to meet and greet in order to find their affinities. One woman explained her church has a small group of leaders come before public meetings, and they "talk about the group a little bit. So you can kind of go, 'Huh, they seem cool. I might like to join that group.'" As a result of multiple, open invitations, even though unintended, small groups end up oriented around social affinities. Consistent with Labanow's study of an emerging congregation in the United Kingdom, although members are not assigned to groups, "they tend to cluster in groups of similar age, geography, and (to a lesser degree) marital status."[18]

Emerging congregations also urge individuals to get involved in activities that are consistent with their own values and concerns. This takes their congregational involvement beyond Sunday gatherings and after-church meals. Even more, such ministry involvements come to concretely define what "church" means for them. For example, Alyssa said, "The minute I came here, it was like, OK, now you're doing children's ministry . . . and now you're doing this, and that is what church is to me." Packard's study similarly details how emerging congregations facilitate a variety of subgroups in which people can build relationships and/or pursue interests that they are passionate about, such as urban regeneration or working with the homeless.[19]

Within these congregations, the barriers to deep involvement are relatively few, as people generally do not have to demonstrate their doctrinal orthodoxy or a long tenure of membership to be trusted to serve in the congregation, as may be the case in other churches. One man said that in his congregation: "By your third or fourth time here, you're asked to read the scripture . . . At that point, usually somebody knows something about what you have to offer and says, 'Hey, how can we use this thing that you have to offer. Can you contribute that into our service?'" Another woman said that in her previous church, there was a list of jobs and the leadership expected people to try squeeze into one of those job descriptions. By way of contrast, she sees her emerging congregation as a place where people's talents are recognized, and the "jobs" are tailored to fit around their gifts. She described what this looks like in her congregation:

> A couple of people who showed up were running our hospitality station, and I just kept glancing over and watching their energy level get higher and higher and higher . . . I finally had to walk over them. I said, "You are doing what you are gifted to do. Doesn't it feel good?" They were just glowing. That's what's unique about [our church]. Rather

than saying, "Okay, here little Christian. Let's quickly plug you in," it's, "Let's get to know you. How are you wired? How can you be who God has made you to be in this place?"

The expectation that people will be heavily involved in their congregations is part of cultivating a religious life where people are not passive consumers of religious products. One woman was dismayed that their evening service seemed like a consumer experience for some local youth, who are "not necessarily really committing to the community." While this woman was troubled about this trend in her particular congregation, Packard argues that this problem is less common in emerging congregations than in other religious institutions. The expectation of involvement greatly alleviates the "free rider" problem. Free riders are people who consume the "goods" of religious organizations without investing much in return. Our research finds comments regarding free riders to be rare. As Packard concludes, "To use language more appropriate to the sociology of religion, it is difficult, if not impossible, to be a free rider when you are sitting on a couch in someone's living room, as many congregations do."[20] As Elaine affirmed, "You just don't sit there, you're involved." Another woman agreed: "I've invested into this church, you know. Not just time, emotionally."

As much as congregational involvement is emphasized among Emerging Christians, they strive not to pressure people to connect to the community. One leader said, "We want people to feel like they can be absolutely anonymous." That means that visitors can be ignored even in the midst of what is considered a highly welcoming community. Noah said, "The pastors are constantly getting calls for people wanting something to get to know other people in the church." The interviews consistently indicate that while community was available, it was up to the individual to break into their congregation's social networks. Alyssa is one of several who appreciated being free from pressure to participate in church activities. She said:

> You can do what you feel like doing. You can just sit there. There have been services where I just sat in the back and cried. And no one was going to call me out on it. But as I grow, there are things for me to do. If I want to get more involved, I can. If I want to be in more Bible studies, I can. It's kind of growing with me as I grow. And I like that.

Alyssa later said, "If you choose to be involved, you can easily do that, it's not like there are set people at that top that are running the show, and you're just in the audience." Isaac stressed that his congregation is characterized by "more personal ownership—where you bring to it what you want to."

The openness to connect with their congregation's ministries as they are ready is nearly always contrasted with the strictness of their previous churches. One woman said, "The whole reason we left the church is because people were telling us what to do." She added, "This has been something that has kept me here: the freedom from that and enjoying being in community."

## Cultivating Relationships—"Feel the love"

Relationships were a strong and consistent theme in our conversations with Emerging Christians. Wyatt said, "I love the community." "What's kept me here," said one man, "is the relational aspect... there's a relational aspect that's full of the heart of God." He was accepted by others "even though they didn't know me from Adam." One woman said, "What keeps me coming here that touched me is the community thing." Joel said, "Relationships trump every other consideration." The importance of community comes up frequently, especially in congregations that focus on building smaller communities that meet in homes or in the neo-monastic movement where so much of spirituality is channeled in and through one another's homes. Valerie said, "Not everything at our church is about Jesus. It's community, it's like, let's share our lives, whatever it is, in our art and whatever. We don't have to be saying, 'Jesus loves you' every other sentence."

Max is one of many who said, "Community is one thing that [our church] knows how to do well." Deep relational connections with other people in their emerging congregations contrasted with their previous church experiences. A woman said, "Relationships have always been important to me, and I've never found a place where I can really be OK with that and have that be my thing instead of quiet times every day, or whatever." Felicia said, "At my other church, I had gone to it from kindergarten through college, and I didn't really know those people. I knew them, and it was like, 'Hey Bob, how ya doin'?' But it wasn't like seeing people. I see everyone here, and it's like I want to give them the biggest hug ever." Felicia states, "It's totally the people, and it's so emphasized here that we are the church. The building is not the church. It's so different." Another woman said, "We have true community here in a way that I have never experienced in any other church." Jackie said, "The number one thing is the sense of community I've never experienced anywhere else. There's this deep wanting to really know and be known and find out about you and why you're here. You want to hear about why I'm here, too. It's a very authentic sense of connection." One highly educated man, who previously taught classes at a wealthy megachurch, said that after attending two years he still did not have any friends. He found his emerging congregation around the corner from his house after being encouraged by another member. "Night and day difference when it comes to how quickly I was able to connect." Another woman said when she first came, "There was something more authentic, more relational."

The focus on relationships is connected with a stance against "institutions." One man contrasted institutions with his emerging congregation, saying, "I don't even like to say [the name of our church], referring to it as if it is another one of these institutions created by some sort of system, because it's not." For him "institutions" (exemplified by "a corporation or educational institution, or even these megachurches") are rational systems that create distance between people, "which creates these big churches, these big corporations, these big 'institutions'" in which relationships are sacrificed for the sake of the system. He said, "We're just people, and we like each other. I don't think we really have a structure that lives on without us. I think that it is just the people, and, to me, that's unique."

Communal relational schemas not only orient toward expressing personal commitment to relationships but also mediate the inherent difficulty of working in a new and unfamiliar religious environment.[21] Past research reveals that strong relationships are difficult to achieve in the context of novelty, meaning less familiarity with mutual expectations and greater uncertainty in coping with challenges.[22] But Ruth Blatt argues that the most important mechanism for challenging novelty—the difficulty of accepting something simply because it is "new"—is by adopting communal relational schemas which involve a deep caring about group member needs.[23] The communal schemas found among Emerging Christians encourage them to self-disclose and express themselves emotionally, which fosters respecting one another as unique individuals and then identifying more strongly with the team.[24] One man said, "We're not just a church that meets once a week. We have community, and we have church with each other in smaller groups or bigger groups in a variety of settings, doing a variety of different things." As one leader explained, "We're not deliberate about anything we do. I mean we're deliberate, but we don't have strategies. Theologically, we're all about the same thing. We trust each other immensely." Caring for mutual needs and making expectations explicit are key strategies for maintaining an entrepreneurial team.[25] Inherent to such coordination of action is trust. The affective bonds become very strong, and they allow people to overlook others' imperfections, ambiguities of structures, and uncertainties of congregational processes. One man summed up by saying that critics of the ECM needed to visit his congregation and "feel the love."

## The Challenges of Pluralist Congregations

While it is clear that Emerging Christians value their participation in pluralist congregations, they also talk about how the experience of pluralism in their congregations is challenging. People struggle with a lack of boundaries (particularly around issues of religious and moral freedom), find it difficult to break into close-knit congregations, feel their congregations are too disorganized, and become frustrated with vague or hidden leadership structures.

## Lack of Boundaries—"It was too unconditional."

The moral openness of emerging congregations is not always received as positive. One man said, "A lot of people that I know left because . . . it was too unconditional. It just didn't make sense to them. They just couldn't even grasp it." He said people found it "unsettling" and "even nauseating." Social freedom may be valued, but standards are still expected, especially since such freedom still lies within the broad institutional framework of Christianity.

Critical questions arise: How should Emerging Christians enforce moral boundaries? And which ones should be enforced? Wyatt made a point of saying his church had "virtually no church discipline." Similarly, Mason said, "We know how the fundamentalists deal with this. We know how we've always been taught to deal with this. We've got this whole new paradigm. How do we deal with this? Where do we draw the line ethically and morally?" Another member said, "It's a challenge." Another asserted, "It's a *huge* challenge." One volunteer leader stated, "My fear for [our church] is that we are going to become so open that we don't have any boundaries, that we don't have any stance, and we would be so afraid to insult someone or to say something wrong that we don't say anything at all."

While some people welcomed these social freedoms and found the ethos resonated with their experiences in other areas of their lives, others said they were deeply changed by this accepting attitude. One man said:

> In my past history of ministry with Campus Crusade I would run into people who were living lifestyles that I found totally disgusting and abhorrent. I could get away with shying away or not pursuing them. When I came here and saw the love shown toward these "marginalized people" or whatever, I asked God to help me love them, these marginalized people who had disgusted me. God worked in me to love those people. I'm still working on it, but I would rather be someone who loves than someone who's right on theology or doctrine. That's what I see as being a Christian. Being around these different people that I wouldn't have had anything to do with has motivated me and helped God to work in me to broaden my love base.

Stories like this are a different type of "mistake story," that is, a testimonial that reinforces a profound sense of personal failure and yet describes how spiritual growth has occurred from such failure.[26] Mistake stories provide models for how to live one's faith.

A gay man expressed similar surprise regarding his reactions to the sexual lifestyles of others in his congregation. He talked about people he had met who were in "a polyamorous relationship" that sidestepped notions of monogamy. He said, "it blows my mind, and it's so fascinating to talk to them and go, 'How does that work for you? You call yourself a Christian, and you're obviously engaged with this learning relationship with Christ. But how?' I mean, it's just mind-boggling to me." He said, "I was brought up to believe that God intends people to be monogamous—but at the same time I scratch my head, other people scratch their head at me going, 'You're gay, so how can you be a Christian?'—so it's a challenge to figure it out. We're all in this crazy mess together and still going back to the authority of scripture." He tried using the Bible to sort out his reaction to polyamorous relationships by saying, "It's interesting to read about these traditional Bible heroes that we make action figures out of and sell in Christian bookstores who have just as messy lives as we have—like, David and Solomon who had more than a polyamorous relationship going on with their concubines and their adulterous affairs and all this other stuff—and somehow God still worked in them. That's really a challenge for me." Despite his discomfort, he refuses to condemn this lifestyle. "I don't know if I can say, 'I don't think you should be in that relationship'—those hard words. That's really hard for all of us." He explained, "I'm constantly affirmed and constantly growing and constantly being challenged to rethink things and think outside the box. Always there's grace underneath all of that. It's really changing me in my understanding of God's grace and what grace really is about."

## Exclusive Relationships—"It's almost too much community."

Even though they value relationships, some members are frustrated with the consequences of stressing community. Members describe themselves as welcoming, but the value on highly involved relationships can hinder newcomers from easily fitting in. As strangers become friends, the formation of bonds through self-disclosure and shared experiences leads to cliques that are unintentionally closed to newcomers.

For example, Mason appreciated the community he found in his church, but he said, "I was kind of frustrated that I wasn't getting assimilated." Mason said it took a while for him "to break into the group because community is valued so much. We really develop a tight-knit community, like a family. So, it's almost like when you're bringing somebody into your family. You've got all these traditions, these inside jokes." Mason said, "It takes a little while to observe and feel the rhythm of it and feel the energy between people." He added, "Of course, you have to have someone who reaches out to that person. I'm not sure we're really good at that here." Again, Mason said, "I'm not sure how well we care about inviting others in."

A leader had a similar observation about the unintended consequences of focusing on building strong relational ties: "When visitors come, we're such a tight group that it's completely overwhelming." The leader also said, "It can work both ways, and it does scare me. It's almost too much community."

## Lack of Organization—"It's very chaotic."

Another consequence of the focus on informal relationships is the lack of a clear organizational structure. A common refrain is that their congregations are "not organized." One man said his congregation was "weird" in their "aversions of church" like "the aversion to bylaws, the aversion to voting." He said, "A couple of years ago, somebody was like, 'Should we take a vote?' And everybody was like, 'No, no, no, we don't want to vote,' and I'm like, seriously?" He added, "Our aversion to whatever smacks of the old ways is something that causes us to throw out the baby with the bathwater."

There is no "membership," said participants in several emerging congregations, and clearly "membership" is a word that grates on Emerging Christians. Alyssa said, "Since there isn't membership and there aren't meetings," communicating to people who are "on the periphery" is difficult. When there are issues, it is not clear whom to talk with in these congregations if you are not an insider. They ask: Who's responsible for what? For example, Mary said, "You don't know who the elders of the church are, who's not, so you don't really know who to take issues to or passions. You don't know who to go to."

The tolerance for an ambiguous structure may be a reaction to past congregational experiences. One leader said (as stated earlier), "We're not deliberate about anything we do. I mean we're deliberate, but we don't have strategies." Mary said, "When you've grown up in a church that has been so structured, so conservative, and that's all you've had, it's nice for a while to just have it kind of merge together." One woman said, "I'm the kind of person who would fall back on what I know of typical church organization and be like, 'We should have committees, we should have standing committees, we should write up by laws,' blah, blah, blah, and [our pastor] said, for one thing, they're not good at managing systems like that. But he also believes that's what kills churches." Another woman observed, "It's like hunting wild horses." Yet another woman asserted, "It's very chaotic."

# The ECM as a Congregational Movement

Nancy Ammerman encourages sociologists of religion to see a religious organization as "a shifting collection of persons, engaged in a complex set of actions and rhetorics, actions that are supported by and indeed define the collectivity they inhabit."[27] Our descriptions of the pluralist congregations of the ECM provide an intriguing case study of how a religious organization is shaped in a context where people hold a highly individualistic religious orientation, yet simultaneously identify strongly with "relationships" and "community." The data in this chapter demonstrate that it would be wrong to assume that the ECM appeals to participants because it feeds an individualized narcissism, that it merely facilitates a type of religious consumerism where people are concerned only with having their needs met and their identities affirmed. Rather, Emerging Christians locate the autonomy granted to individuals firmly within a communal framework.

John Drane characterizes the ECM as "consisting of Christians who have become angry and disillusioned with their previous experience of church . . . *who have established their own faith communities* that—far from being accountable to any larger tradition—are fiercely independent."[28] (Emphasis added.) Even when the ECM is characterized as consisting of "post-church groups," our observations and the observations of others affirm that *their congregations matter*.[29] A particularly interesting case is No Name near Fort Worth, Texas. No Name is a group of "post-evangelical-Christians" that has met together in a home for eight years. Part of what they do is share contribute funds amongst one another to assist individuals in the group with various projects, for example by contributing medicine and supplies for one of its members who is a nurse to take to a very poor area in Ethiopia. They also financially support another member in her work at a local crisis pregnancy center. To avoid any form of branding, monolithic structure, or other distant organizational form, they wanted to avoid naming their group altogether. Thus: "No Name." No Name is intended to be based on informal, affective relationships ("We're a lot of individuals") rather than on a formalized, bureaucratic charter. As Alan Jamieson writes, "Post-church groups are formed by people who have left 'established' forms of church and yet want to support and sustain each other in their spiritual journeys."[30] Repeatedly, we find that these Emerging Christians care about their congregation. One woman said, "I'm so vulnerable here, and I can't imagine losing this, it almost makes me want to cry right now. I hold it so dear."

We stated in chapter 1 that the ECM is an "institutionalizing structure," which indicates it is a set of religious ideas and practices that are being formed, in process, and not yet concretized. There is an incompleteness to the entire "movement" that is frustrating to both observers and participants. However, the unsettled nature of the ECM provides an opportunity for analysis of its relative coherence. As Bielo writes, "Ultimately, Emerging Christianity is about the creation of a new Christian identity . . . one whose precise contours and boundaries has yet to be finalized, and whose appeal has yet to be measured."[31] If we do more than merely note this incompleteness and strive to understand the circumstances and character of it, we find that the unfinished nature of the ECM points to a more substantive understanding of how religious innovation happens.

Emerging Christians are rooted in the Christian traditions that have come before them, both critiquing them and drawing on them to construct their own congregational practices. In their openness to a range of historic Christian traditions, we can see how they cultivate a religious orientation that promotes pluralism by striving to respect the validity of a variety of Christian traditions. As seen in the next chapter, pluralist congregations enable the enactment of the strategic religiosity of Emerging Christians. As such, the ECM involves an earnest attempt to fundamentally redefine the contemporary practice of Christianity, and this is being done *in and through congregations*.

# 3

## Being an Emerging Christian

*When people ask me, "Are you a Christian?," I say, "Yeah—
[pause]—but probably not the way you mean."*
*—Jake, shared during an evening gathering*

Late one night, a link came through Gerardo's Twitter feed to a blog post by Christian Piatt titled, "You Might Be an Emergent Christian If . . ." The post provided a handy list of supposed markers of an "emergent" Christian, a set of bullet points that included identifying as a denominational hybrid ("with a '-mergent' thrown on the end for good measure"); proud identification with atheists; mentioning Žižek and quoting Derrida in conversation; drinking "fair-trade soy latte"; owning a MacBook; self-conscious irony in identifying as a Christian; correctly identifying key insiders to the movement by name; men having bald heads, facial hair, and "hipster glasses"; using nontraditional words like "faith community" and "gathering" instead of "congregation" or "worship"; using gender-neutral language in describing God; routinely using words like "authentic," "context," "ecclesial," and "metaphoric"; queasiness at the notion of "substitutionary atonement"; strong reaction against evangelical pastors Mark Driscoll and John Piper; answering questions with "deep, reflective sighs"; propensity to boycott; and, finally, "You find you always use your fingers to make little air quotes when you use words like 'salvation' or 'sin.'" The post is clear that "you don't have to identify with all of these to be an emergent," then adds a final warning: "But whatever you do . . . don't actually call yourself an emergent. No self-respecting emergent would ever do such a thing."

Gerardo read and immediately retweeted the link with a simple question, "Accurate . . .?" Within moments came a public reply from Tony Jones, author, speaker, and first coordinator of the Emergent Village. His one word response: "No." And we agree. Simplistic caricatures abound when talking about Emerging Christians, and insiders to the movement do not help the confusion when they poke fun at themselves.

The most prominent caricature of Emerging Christians revolves around the idea that they are "reactionary," constantly deconstructing the church yet failing to reconstruct anything of value. Indeed, deconstructing and "deconverting" are central to how Emerging Christians describe their own religious journeys. For example, pastor, author, and popular speaker Kathy Escobar wrote a series of blog posts profiling individuals she labeled "deconstructors," those who can be considered Emerging Christians due to their experiences with Christianity.[1] These are "people who have gone, are going through . . . a gut-wrenching, excruciatingly painful and lonely season in their faith called 'deconstruction.'" She wrote:

> Some of us enter deconstruction willingly. We sat through too many church services that made us queasy with songs-with-words-we-stopped-feeling-good-about-singing, predictable messages, certainty, and focus on belief instead of practice. Something stirred within us, and we started asking the questions swirling around in our head. Others of us were pushed into deconstruction by wounding church experiences. We saw one too many inconsistencies, abuses of power, or crazy-stuff-that-only-insiders-sometimes-see that pushed us over the edge and called everything into question.

Her blog post continues to describe the disorientation of faith among sincere believers that results in *doubt, emptiness, loneliness, sadness, fear, anger,* and *confusion*. As Escobar laments, "One thing that makes me the most sad about 'church' is how few places we have for deconstruction." She continues, "On this process, we cannot follow the crowds or people-please or do-what-we-think-good-Christians-are-supposed-to-do. All of that will get us into more trouble." Rather than follow an institutionalized, conventionally defined faith, she encourages deconstructors to rebuild their faith in a personal way. "Rebuilding requires bravely finding our own unique path with God, and there are many ways to build something new."

Emerging Christians publicly discuss this process of destroying and rebuilding their religious lives; people like Lee, a young woman who shared at an ECM gathering how she went through what she called "the demolition experience." She said, "My entire life came crashing down. I lost everything I ever thought I knew." She had spent the last two years deconstructing and reconstructing a new set of convictions for her life. Gordon Lynch details how difficult and painful "deconstruction" can be, as people, like Lee, face losses of certainty, friendships, partners, and a sense of community. Lynch likens this to a process of grieving and wrote a pastoral book intended to guide people through this process.[2]

For Emerging Christians, deconstructing their previous, personal faith is central to their religious orientation. "Coming out of Christianity" stories are continual manifestations of deconstruction and regular, expected features of ECM gatherings. Deconstruction is often described as a process of "deconversion," which inverts the conventional (evangelical) emphasis on conversion.[3] Deconversion means journeying through an almost-always painful experience of dismantling their previous religious ideas and practices, and losing relationships with people in their former churches. It also means learning to articulate critiques of existing church structures, especially "showy" megachurches, "dead" mainline churches, or "hateful" politically conservative evangelical churches. Furthermore, deconversion includes an anxiety to avoid the stigma associated with conservative Christians—often caricatured as "right wing fundamentalists"—in the contemporary West. Emerging Christians want others to see different ways of being a Christian, and their identities are bound up in modeling those different ways. Of course, many Emerging Christians eschew the "emerging" label altogether or remain blissfully unaware of it.

As we argued in chapter 2, the *pluralist congregations* of the ECM provide an *institutionalizing structure* that facilitates people's ability to balance the individual and communal aspects of their religion. Pluralist congregations are structured with the intent to allow a maximum degree of individuality and openness to divergent viewpoints and maximize individuals' opportunities to self-direct their spiritual selves. At the same time, pluralist congregations provide a basis for community with others and draw deliberately on selected resources (rituals, theologies, and practices) already established by the Christianities they are deconstructing.

In this chapter, we focus on the stories of Emerging Christians, honing in on their personal and highly individualized experiences of deconversion and deconstruction. They manifest a distinct approach to *religious individualization*. But we want to be clear that our focus on the formation of *individual* religious orientations cannot be done without reference to people's experiences in the *relational* congregations of the ECM. While we agree with Ulrich Beck that "individuals use their religious experiences to construct their individual religious shelter," we also stress that such shelters are not closed, isolated, or sequestered spirituality.[4] Indeed, Beck writes, "Religious individualization and committed churchgoing are not mutually exclusive but may well reinforce each other." We agree. Their congregations are not only important as places to find caring relationships; they are sites affording the performance of their religiosity.

Because being an Emerging Christian is a form of personal religiosity that is expected to be intentionally (rather than customarily) enacted, this type of religious self cannot avoid being strategic in its activities, which are selected and enacted according to individual choice. We describe their actions as the enactment of a *strategic religiosity*. Conceptualizing their actions as a form of strategic religiosity helps to resist seeing a person's religious identity as essentialist—an unchanging, static, and highly bounded aspect of the self—and instead asserts that religious identity is contingent, circumstantial, and highly responsive to the surrounding social environment. *Strategic religiosity conceives religious identity as dominated by assessments of appropriateness, relationality, and self-image. In the process, certain forms of religiosity and religious identity are sought out and legitimated while other forms are regulated to being less desirable, ineffectual, or merely mundane.* Overall, Emerging Christians participate (often unknowingly) in a socially enabled, collective entrepreneurial process in which a distinct, though slippery, religious orientation is being formed. In doing so, they enact a strategic religiosity in the shaping of a legitimated religious self.

## Emerging Christian Stories

Mason and Judy have both deconstructed their previous faith and are now finding their religious selves shaped in relation to their involvement in the ECM. Our data reveal that stories of personal deconstruction like theirs are so frequent as to become an expected repertoire of the stories recounted by people who associate with emerging congregations. Therefore, focusing on Mason's and Judy's stories give us insight into the orientations of Emerging Christians, especially in highlighting that the ECM is not a solely individualistic religious project but rather a collective project nurtured by participation in pluralist congregations.

### Mason: "I was going to be a Baptist preacher."

Mason called his emerging congregation a "haven of deconstruction," especially for "recovering conservatives." Mason said, "For so many people, [this place] was their last chance—their last stab at church." For Mason, the beginning of his spiritual journey began in a jail cell as a teenager. Raised Southern Baptist, he threw himself into the Christianity of his youth after he left jail and "went hardcore fundamentalist right off the bat." He said, "Fundamentalism was so attractive because it provided all the answers." He became fully immersed in a fundamentalist world. "I learned all the apologetics of why the King James is the only correct version of the Bible and then proceeded to preach to all my friends at school." He dedicated himself to an evangelistic ministry. For his high school graduation present, he said he "asked for a black suit. I was going to be a Baptist preacher, so I had to have a black suit."

Mason got his black suit, and fortified by it, he spurned formal theological education (he thought the Bible alone was good enough for him) and went "straight into ministry." Building on a prior short-term missionary trip overseas, he traveled to the United Kingdom. But his hopes of saving souls were soon dashed. His grand scheme for a thriving youth ministry melted when he discovered that the lead pastor of his new church was not interested in evangelism. He only wanted to use Mason as a babysitter for members' children. "I came home totally defeated. I had gone over with all these goals. I felt this is what God had called me to do."

Mason returned from the United Kingdom "angry with God," only to be further disillusioned when he found that his home pastor had an affair with a woman he had been counseling at the church. "All these foundations I built my faith on are no longer valid." Nevertheless, he still deeply believed two things: one, "Christ cares about me and loves me," and two, "Christ wants to do something in this world." These twin convictions lay at the core of what he called "my deconstruction."

His religious journey of deconstruction continued when he eventually enrolled in a Bible college and volunteered in a campus ministry. The study of the New Testament encouraged a more expansive understanding of scripture. "I began to ask really critical questions." But his newfound analytical attitude was not welcome at the college. "I would ask questions and be told, 'Don't ask these questions' or told that I didn't have a mature faith." While he continued to serve in ministry, his reading expanded. He began to pursue new conversations with new friends. "We talked about postmodernism and got into that." He found new books using a Google search, discovering contemporary authors like Tony Jones, Leonard Sweet, and Brian McLaren. Especially important was McLaren's award-winning book *A New Kind of Christian*.

Mason eventually found his current emerging congregation through an Internet search. Mason said his church "has been this haven of deconstruction from whatever brand of fundamentalism we grew up in—whether it was charismatic Pentecostalism, or Baptist churches, or evangelical churches, or whatever." Members of his church "grew up in those circles, and they started asking questions like I did, and thank God they found [this church]. They found a safe place to ask those questions and didn't just fall off." It was an open space for exploration with no pressure. "The people at this church weren't trying to ram any kind of dogma down my throat, and they weren't trying to create some sort of new fundamentalism that has candles. It was, 'Hey, come here, there's space for you. This is sort of what we think. If you're into this, come get on board.'"

Mason summarized his Christian experience, saying, "I was involved in church my whole life. When that framework fails—when some morning you wake up and say, 'I really think my framework is flawed, what I think is true and what I've always taken for granted and has guided me is not right'—then everything falls apart." He said, "That happened me. So when you come to a place and you see that they allow you to have those doubts, for that system to not be there, and for people to say, 'It's OK. You don't need to freak out. We can work it out, and you'll be fine.' That is comforting. That is what this church offers."

## Judy: "I was jaded and just done with it."

A high school convert to Pentecostalism, Judy has been involved in her emerging congregation over fifteen years. Her religious experiences before arriving at her church were often fraught, bound up with what she felt was her own calling to serve God as a missionary, and yet tempered by disappointment with the way she was treated as a woman.

Judy was intensely religious as a young adult. After going on a teen mission to the Caribbean, she quit college and committed to becoming a career missionary. She eventually returned to college in her later twenties but began to question her church leadership about what she had been taught about Christianity. "Some things happened at my church at the time, which really disillusioned me." Part of the dismay was a lack of theological depth. She recalls a "spirituality" class she described as "just ridiculous, just hokum. 'Let the Spirit move you!' Ridiculous." Her dissatisfaction with the church's theology combined with a profound disgust toward the chauvinism of its male leaders. She vividly recalled several incidents, especially once during a class when an older leader said to her, "Come sit on my lap." For her, "Some of it was borderline, but some of it was definitely abusive. Just weird. Ridiculous." Judy attended an evangelical college but was disappointed by the lack of "any real spiritual life there." She soon avoided church and neglected chapel services. "I still felt like I was a believer, but I just couldn't handle the different ways that I was told to have a relationship with God. I was jaded and just done with it."

After graduating from college, she found a good job with an accounting firm but still hoped to work overseas as a missionary in long-term economic development work. With that goal in mind, she connected with several short-term mission trips. Her extensive missions background and experience justified appointing her to a leadership position, but she found that as a woman she was always expected to co-lead teams with men who failed to accept her as a legitimate leader. "They would pair me with a single man who was typically very conservative and had very specific ideas about gender roles and was very threatened by me. It became really hard." In addition to her other experiences, "That contributed to my whole disillusion thing."

Judy left her conservative church and began attending an Episcopal congregation, "which is ironic because I'd been told that 'ritual is bad,' 'tradition is bad,' and 'it needs to be expressive.'" Judy eventually married an atheist and had a woman officiate their wedding—aspects of her life that would have resulted in ostracism from her previous religious community. While she enjoyed the Episcopal liturgy, she felt she never made any lasting friendships. At the same time, many of her evangelical friends had also left their conservative evangelical churches and began attending an emerging congregation.

She initially resisted joining her ECM church. It seemed to be "a fad," and she did not want to "jump on the bandwagon" along with other disillusioned evangelicals. Her friends called themselves "survivors," people who had escaped various abuses of their Christian past. Ultimately, Judy "gave in" and found she particularly appreciated the pastor. "I couldn't really call them sermons, but just going to hear his thoughts or stories or whatever. I always came out of there with something to chew on, even if the whole time I'm listening and going, 'What the hell? Where does he get this? This doesn't make any sense.' It's thoughtful and gives me something to think about." Although she has had some difficulties in settling into a group of core friends within her emerging congregation, Judy said that what was most important is that she is accepted for who she is.

Judy's atheist husband is also a welcome member of her congregation. "I love it that he's been embraced as a member of the community. Accepted as who he is. It's like, 'We're going to embrace this man, and it's up to God what he decides to do with him.' Everyone seems to be OK with that. It's so important to me." Her husband plays in a musical group every week associated with the church. "He says he's an atheist." She said, "No one has ever attempted to talk with him about the state of his soul." Communion is open, and he participates. She disagreed with the conservative stance of other churches: "'If you're not saved, don't come.' Nonsense! Christ died for everyone."

She believes the ECM involves "the embracing of the secular, not the shunning of it. That's a big issue for me. I'm sick to death of people denying the world and spending their time praying, 'Lord Jesus, take us away.' What an insult to God, from my perspective." She also appreciates that many aspects of theology at her church are left ambiguous. "I've never pressed [my leaders], 'What do you really believe about this?' I love it that they're comfortable leaving some grey area, saying, 'It's a bit of a muddle. I'm just trying my best. But here's what seems right to me. Here's what makes sense.' It seems so right to me, the honoring of common sense and the mind that God gave you." It allows individuals discretion in their beliefs. "It lets people at different levels grapple with things at their own pace."

## Being an Emerging Christian

Mason's and Judy's stories provide exemplary highlights of what it is like to be Emerging Christians: people who have come or are coming through an often painful process of deconstructing their personal faith. They continually critique yet at the same time draw on existing expressions of Christianity as they live out their faith, and they do so as they participate with others in pluralist congregations.

### "A church for recovering Christians."

Emerging Christians are not offhand religious "shoppers" sampling spiritual wares; they are highly engaged and sincere people who in various ways came to the conclusion that they needed to leave the church they were at before their involvement in their emerging community. This process is often traumatic and means that their new emerging congregations serve as a refuge where they are supported by people who have had similar experiences. Becca said the people who come to her emerging congregation are "taking a break" from church, are "licking their wounds," and have "things that they're struggling with." Another woman said, "Many of us went through this [pain] alone, and we don't want others to go through it alone." One man said, "Many of us are refugees from the previous experience." Another man said, "We have nowhere else to go. This is our refuge." Yet another member said their church "is like a church for recovering Christians . . . It's one of the jokes we say all the time."

Many spoke of their disillusionment with evangelicalism or fundamentalism. As Trent explained, "My wife and I both grew up in a really evangelical, traditional kind of church background . . . 'traditional' is probably not the right word, 'fundamentalist' is probably a better word." Another person in the room said, "That's what I'm fleeing." Emerging Christians often contrast their evangelical experiences to their new congregation. Joel said, "The church I was in before was a typical evangelical church, and this didn't have the feeling of that." Sharon said, "I came to [this church] after a long, long journey at a very, very conservative Baptist church." Camden said, "I had grown up in a really fundamentalist, conservative Baptist church and had just gotten tired of it and left . . . just quit going to church." Nicole said, "I went to a really fundamentalist church." Another man, describing the ECM, said,

"It is a movement *from* something, and it seems to me that the movement was definitely away from the evangelical church, which was the scapegoat of its preaching. And when I first came here, I'm like, 'Hell yeah, that is exactly what I want to hear.'"

Others left their previous congregations due to emotionally heavy breakdowns in relationships, and their discussions are often characterized by memories of vicious behavior. Jeremiah said, "I came here because my dad was a pastor, and his church imploded and turned on him. And at that point it's like, 'I'm not going to that church anymore.'" One woman described the pressure she experienced from her previous church after leaving her husband. She said she had

> really valid reasons, and I told the church what was going on, but they refused to accept it. I had people calling me every day saying, "We'll work with your husband to get him to stop doing these things to you. You just need to stay married to him," and I'm like, "He's crazy. None of that's going to happen." Just these horrible phone calls every day—for hours—"Just come meet with us. Just be here"—really intimidating, threatening stuff.

She left the church because they insisted on her remaining in an abusive marriage. "It freaked me out so much that I never wanted to go to church again." Having gone to a Christian college and "built a life" with friends and family, she said, "I lost the entire life I had built." Another woman said, "I left the church I was going to because they had huge problems, and I got to the point where I went from being this good Christian girl to being the lowest of the low." Max said, "I was hardcore Pentecostal and, just before coming here, had gone through a huge fallout with my church. So, I was looking for a place to go, and I was angry." Another woman stated, "We had left our church under horrible circumstances . . . My husband was the chairperson at our last church . . . Coming out of a bad situation, it was refreshing."

Our research uncovered more "recovering Catholics" than we expected, given the evidence that the ECM is in large part a product of Protestantism. The survey data revealed 12.6% with Roman Catholic religious backgrounds, and they were well represented in the focus group interviews. A member in one church said, "There's definitely a post-Catholic group that comes here. I struggle going to mainline, evangelical churches. It's still not what I'm used to in the way the service is conducted. The communion thing [rarely done in this church] is a big difference." One man was an altar boy and became a liturgical minister and Eucharistic minister. "As things moved along I realized that the Catholic Church as a whole got caught up in trappings and not living the life we claimed to live." His wife is a devout Catholic and went to a Catholic college. Despite their lifelong commitment, he described a "breaking point" when they made a large cash donation toward a Catholic school that was never built. He said, "I paid 50 grand for a church I'll never go into, and I've never been back since." He said he started thinking, "Where would I go? Who's going to be any better? The Lutherans are claiming they're better than the Catholics, who claim to be better than the Presbyterians, who claim to be better than the Episcopalians. Everybody's got their claim, but who's actually doing it? Who's being real?"

### "I would never go back."

Emerging Christians contrast negative experiences in their old congregations with positive experiences in their new congregations. Many say they're "never going back" to their past churches. Elaine said she and her husband had no interest in "going back to the old way of doing church." Becca said, "I've been to those other places, and I'm not interested. I don't miss that. I would never return. To me, that would be so many steps backward in how I view community that I just would not, in my own heart, be able to go back." One man said, "I grew up at an evangelical church, and it's a great church. I don't want to talk bad about it but like—I hated it . . . I hated it." Another man explained, "My concern is that we would become, in some fashion, evangelical, and I don't want any part of that. I came up through a real evangelical situation and that just doesn't fly with me." He had even stopped attending his emerging congregation for a while because he believed it was headed in that direction. One woman said, "I grew up in this Baptist kind of thinking about things. This is different, and I love it."

Emerging Christians do not want to go back to what they assess to be the narrowness and shallowness of their prior churches. One woman said, "The sermons here are different and incredible because they actually use scripture. So much of what I grew up on took an idea and then tried to fit scripture into that idea and then did 'The Three P's of Progress' or 'The S's of Success.' [Laughter] Every point they made they tried to find a scripture that fit. And [our church] doesn't do that." Another man had been a very dedicated evangelical Christian. "When I was younger in college leading worship, I wanted to be real with it, which caused me to ask a lot of honest questions to the people I led worship with—even the senior pastor: 'If this is what you preach and believe, then let's do it.' When I started saying that, it was threatening. It started to unravel. It just seemed so fake and ridiculous to me." Another man stated, "In the evangelical churches, they were always trying to chase culture. Always mimicking culture. Chasing, mimicking, just terrible."

Emerging Christians were disappointed that their earlier religious experiences failed to cultivate a satisfying spirituality. As one man said, "You'd think that going to a Bible school would strengthen your faith." They also felt dismayed by the experiences they saw in others. Taylor described friends who "have been terribly, terribly hurt by the traditional church," and added, "we've observed far too many deconversions." Felicia talked about her disappointment in seeing young people leave the church, "seeing students say, 'This is completely not relevant to me or my life,' and walk away." She found it "heartbreaking." Another man described his involvement in an Episcopal church. As he got more involved in ministry and the choir, he said:

> I was shocked to discover how many Episcopalians didn't believe any of it, but they still thought it was fun to do. That scandalized me. Why do you dress up in all these funny clothes and spend all this money on bells and candles and everything else if then you get together over coffee and say, "I don't believe in God, but this is fun to do." And it's OK to say that. One of the leaders said, "I don't come here for the teachings. They could be teaching Druidism, and I'd be fine." I began to see the danger of a structure that is so wedded to tradition and formalism that it lost the life beyond that.

Emerging Christians frequently said that their religious backgrounds simply failed in their essential purpose. The result is a cumulative moral criticism of established religious institutions.

## "Oh Jeez, it's terrible, we're going to become a megachurch!"

A frequent target of criticism was the megachurch. Andy said, "We're tired of CEO, self-help gurus, 'how to conquer everything in three easy steps' pastors." Another man said, "People have been let down by mainstream churches and are sick of the 'rock and roll' type church. Have your skit. Very much show." In contrast to her prior experience at a megachurch, Savannah said, "I was valued for my talents [here] and not just for having my butt in the seat and being a number." Another woman said, "[Our leader] doesn't stand up on the big, old stage. He says his stuff from our level and then comes down and sits on the floor with us." Yet another woman summarized, "One of [our pastor's] visions is that we *not* grow to be a megachurch."

The style of megachurches is especially rejected out of a belief that megachurches manipulate people, creating neatly packaged services that depend more on marketing than truly experiencing God. Mason said: "We don't want to be the megachurch with the booth out in the parking lot where they bombard you and give you the little packet and take you to the visitors' booth, and you fill out the forms and they put the red tag on your back and everyone knows you're a visitor." One man said it was important for him to be in a church "where I could bring people—not in order to manipulate them." A former worship pastor said:

> I was starting to see how music can be extremely manipulative. It can be used to make people feel a certain way. If I play that next chord or this slight move of the hand, it became this puppet thing. At that point I was like, I don't know if this is for me.

Another member told a story of a pastor who told him outright he knew when he was manipulating an audience, saying the right words, doing the right thing at the right time. "Watch this," he told him, and over the next hour the pastor proceeded to demonstrate rhetorical tricks that reliably brought the audience to respond in anticipated ways. Stories like this told by Emerging Christians manifest an utter disdain for highly programmed, and market-driven techniques.

People repeatedly said megachurches treat people as projects. One man said, "When we were in our 'church shopping phase' people would come up to you, they don't know anything about you, they were there because I was the 'seeker.' I wanted to give them a spiritual resume and tell them, 'No, no, I'm a Christian, I've done all this stuff, I've read all this, you don't need to do that, I just want to see what your church is like.'" Emerging Christians also felt that in many churches they had attended, establishing relationships with others was merely a tool for getting people in seats and being counted as saved members. Tony Jones has described the stereotypical megachurch's seeker-sensitive approach as "a bait and switch . . . it's a means to an end of closing the deal."[5] This reflects an underlying critique of the mainstream church (whether called "traditional mainline," "evangelical," or "megachurch"): these settings may proclaim acceptance at the front end, but commitment to being a diligent Christian within these settings involves a move toward homogeneity. The definition of what it means to be a "proper" Christian is set to a particular mold, one that Emerging Christians chafe against and ultimately reject.

Emerging Christians also frequently compared the sermons of megachurch pastors to the sermons in their current emerging congregations. Noah said in his past churches, he felt the sermons were too general and dumbed-down; in contrast, "Sermons get a lot more theological as opposed to what I'm used to. Sometimes I struggle with that. I haven't studied theology that much, so I can get lost. But on the other hand a lot of them will be really powerful."

A woman said of the preachers in her emerging congregation, "They ask a real question of the text, they don't just manipulate us emotionally into a catharsis." Another man said, "There's discussion after the sermon. There's actual discussion. It's not an end product that we're supposed to package up and take out." A recent college graduate who had left a conservative, evangelical church explained, "What kept me coming back was the refreshing message that would be shared every week, focusing more on a biblical story than on trying to create a neatly packaged anecdote that we can directly apply to our life in the present day. It was more getting back to the life of Jesus and the circumstances of the time."

Overall, Emerging Christians react against the "tidiness" in the structures of megachurches. For them, such clean lines indicated masks and manipulation. Joel said, "A lot of congregations you would visit there would be a mechanized system that you follow to become a part of the community, and it's very programatized." A pastor's son and former worship leader said, "Whenever anything gets hyper-established, it loses something. This place seemed to be OK with mess. And that was good."

The rejection of megachurch models even creates among Emerging Christians consternation about visible attendance growth in their own congregations.[6] As one person stated, there were "so many people saying, 'Oh Jeez, it's terrible, we're going to become a megachurch!' and others saying, 'Calm down, it's OK.' It's a very common fear among members of the church." Growth is not considered a worthy goal. As one man asserted, "We don't focus on growth." Lilly added that there are "no big membership drives or anything." Another woman expressed it like this: "What if you grow and grow and grow? Aren't you worried that you won't be able to continue to be as intimate as you get more people?" In another church, a member said, "It's a fear of losing this intimacy."

## "It's confusing even for us who are in it."

When we asked participants about their own or their congregations' connections to the ECM, we almost always got ambiguous responses. They knew what their church was not but were not as likely to provide a label to describe their congregation. Only a few emphatically identified their congregations as "part of the emerging church" or said "we're emergent" or that there are "other emergent places." This is further reflected in the survey data where only 37% of the respondents used the term "Emergent" to describe their congregation.[7] However, we found there were some who actively sought an emerging congregation, with many connecting to their current congregation because they had been attending an emergent church elsewhere before moving to their current residence. Savannah said of her past church, a rural congregation, that "it was definitely very into the emergent, postmodern thing," and when her family moved, "we were trying to find a church like that." Rick said, "When we first started coming to the church, like a hawk I was looking for the signs that this was a postmodern expression of the faith. There was an attempt here to do things in a different way. I recognized from the get-go that there were a lot of people here that had no clue that there were some subversive things going on, some radically different things being practiced."

Felicia explained that she and her husband had been attending "a church within a church type thing"—an emerging congregation that had an established relationship with a denominational church, which is often found (as mentioned in chapter 1). Although this "church within a church" was "groundbreaking in our lives at that time," she said:

> Eventually the larger church that was hosting us said, "No way. This is too threatening." *Their* words. They told me, "This is too weird" and "too Catholic." The candles—the pastor couldn't take it. They shut us down.

Like refugees, Felicia and her husband sought another emerging congregation.

But many participants did not know their congregation is part of the ECM or only discovered it after some time. People are unsure even of what "emerging church" means. As Tony Jones said to a group of ECM congregants, "It's confusing even for us who are in it." Susan said:

> I was at work, and we were talking and they said, "What does that mean, 'emergent church?' I was like, 'I don't know. I can't explain it.' They said, 'How is your church different than my church?' I said, 'I can't explain it.'" I've been here for eight years, and I struggle with how to explain how this is different than the churches next door.

Kevin found his church by googling "post-modern church." Claire also found her congregation through an Internet search of churches in the area. "I wanted to leave the conservative background, but I was scared of taking a new step. From the website it seemed fine, but a little progressive from what I was used to." Yet another man said:

> I didn't really have an idea of what the emerging church was until I got here. But then when I started talking about the ethos, I realized that this is the stuff I've been thinking about in the back of my head but

never able to articulate. It was being expressed here, and it felt completely like coming home.

Another woman said, "I realized afterwards that it was an emergent church."

It is common to attend ECM gatherings and sit next to someone who "hadn't heard of emergent." It was amusing to hear Tony Jones speak to a group of people attending an emerging congregation, saying in a didactic manner, "This church is part of the Emerging Church Movement, even if you don't know it, and this church is well known, even in the UK." He further described the church as a "reluctant member of the movement." Another man explained how he gradually came to see that he belonged in his emerging congregation. A musician and lifelong Methodist, he said, "The first day I came, I went home and wrote a song about how [this church] was going to hell. Then I stuck around and got to know [our pastor] and then got involved with the leadership. I liked him a lot, so I stayed. Once I got to know everybody, I understood more what was going on, and it really resonated with me." The consistent theme is: people didn't know the ECM existed, but once they did, they recognized it as fitting them.

Among our interviewees, it appears that the bigger the congregation, the less likely any individual attendee is aware of their congregation's connection to the broader ECM. One woman said it is possible people in her congregation "would have heard about it, but they wouldn't know what it meant." Jake said during his interview that he was in the midst of "figuring out my role in this emerging church world." Some brush aside the lack of solid connection to the movement because it is relatively new. It is not something one reads or talks about in order to understand it but is "experienced." As Lilly explained, "Especially having a lot of young people here who may not have gone to church much, or are maybe very cynical about it, or don't have a real strong theological, biblical base to go off of, why would they think emergent was any different than Baptist, or Presbyterian, or anything? I mean, it could mean anything to them." Indeed, connection to the ECM seems irrelevant to most grassroots participants. One man said, "We've been talking about the emergent group and kind of aligning with this emergent thing. That's really odd to me. It's a community, and we are what we are, and it changes from year to year."

### Learning from Leaders: "So you're reading a Brian McLaren book…"

When participants do make direct connections with or identify with the ECM, it is most often through exposure to prominent leaders. In the United States, this usually means Brian McLaren. This tendency may be behind Phyllis Tickle's identification of McLaren as a kind of Martin Luther of the

ECM.[8] Blake is, among many, who said he and his wife "started reading Brian McLaren." Russ said that he "had been reading some McLaren books, and that's how I got introduced to emergent." Amber said, "I'd been reading a bunch of Brian McLaren's books, and I started being uncomfortable with pretty much every church around me and wasn't finding any home there, so I came and immediately felt at home here." One woman said about her pastor, "He points us toward people like Brian McLaren and all of those guys."

Comments about "reading Brian McLaren" are so common that Tony Jones joked to a group of ECM congregational members, "So you're reading a Brian McLaren book, you google emerging church [in your city] and [this church] pops up [Laughter]." Conversations with members at McLaren's Cedar Ridge Community Church while he was still the head pastor revealed they frequently connected to the church through his writings. Brooke said, "My roommate told me that she randomly found this book in the bookstore and that I had to read it. I thought she was nuts because she was so excited about it. [Laughter] But then I read *A New Kind of Christian*, and it changed the way I saw a lot of things." As a student at the University of Maryland, she saw that the back of the book indicated McLaren had taught classes there. "So I did a little research, found out it was about 15 minutes from an apartment I was considering, and lo and behold . . . started going there the Sunday after I moved in." Similarly, and shortly after moving to a new state, Elaine was talking with her neighbor: "She gave me a book that Brian had written. I showed it to my husband, and his jaw dropped because he had read a chapter of the book for a seminary class. We both read the whole book. And we were going, 'Wow, this needs to be said, this is such an obvious truth we've all managed to overlook it, and somebody's got to start talking about it.'" Kevin stated, "Someone said, 'You should read this book by Brian McLaren,' and as I was reading, I said to myself, 'I already thought of all this, Brian McLaren. You're behind the times.'" Another man said, "I read McLaren's first book and thought, 'Oh my God, there must be a certain number of people who will buy it, so there must be a small set of people who feel exactly what I do.'"

Another woman related how she discovered McLaren's books at a transitional time in her life, in her last year at university, and her first year of "post-college adulthood." She said that "after all my Southern Baptist indoctrination" she wanted to "just flip it all off and be like 'I'm done with all this theology and doctrine and church.'" She began talking with family and friends and said that she began to be turned off by churches' homophobic stances. She concluded, "I was just going through that season that a lot of people go through. I think reading Brian McLaren's books are a big part of that."

What's significant about McLaren's books is that they encourage and facilitate the sort of deconstructed experiences that people undergo when they begin participating in emerging congregations. Sometimes McLaren's books prompt people to leave the churches they are dissatisfied with and to search out what we would call an emerging congregation (whether that congregation chooses to take on that label or not). His books encourage people to consider an alternative approach to Christianity. This was the case for Joseph. Sporting thick, dark hair, long sideburns, and a friendly manner, he answered questions with long, involved explanations that often used stories from his own experiences with the church. For example:

> My dad was going through a midlife crisis/faith crisis, started reading a lot of Brian McLaren's books, passed them on to me. I started reading them and really grappled with them and just really loved the engagement that I got from them . . . When I started reading Brian's books, it sparked a lot of different thoughts in my head, some rather outrageous thoughts . . . Some of them started to sound a little bit more like things that I had already faintly heard in my own head, especially about the honesty, authenticity, and spirituality of saying as a Christian I uphold axioms A, B, and C. Why do I do that?

Although Joseph's story is one of many affirming that McLaren appeals to people of different generations, in his own life he linked his reading of McLaren to facilitating his journey into a more adult faith. He continued:

> Perhaps it's just the crisis of faith that every person goes through when they start to get into adulthood. Starting to think about: Why do I hold to the things that I hold to? I started to realize that a lot of things that I held to more or less tenaciously as an older child were things that didn't necessarily resonate with me personally and spiritually but were just things that I grew up with . . . So I found Brian's books very freeing because I was now allowed to say, "Let me think about this issue. Let me think about this doctrine and how important I really think it is to the Christian faith." Things like that. As well as facilitating that questioning process by the questions that he himself asks in his book . . . Whether or not I necessarily agreed with what he printed, Brian's books forced me to think about my faith, which was a new experience for me.

Of course, we are not reducing Emerging Christians' religious orientation to agreeing with or finding spiritual resources in books by Brian McLaren. But like so many of the resources (printed, online, relational) in the ECM, McLaren's works inspire people to pursue their individualized religious journeys in what they experience as intellectually freeing and authentic ways, while at the same time encouraging them to not give up entirely on Christian communities.

There is also a great deal of evidence found online of affinity to McLaren's approach to Christianity among people who do not publicly identify with the ECM. Examples can be found through comments on McLaren's personal blog. One person in April 2012 wrote:

> I am a former Christian fundamentalist who first discovered the Emerging Church discussion several years ago (at the behest of many of my friends). The message and discussions of the EC greatly reso-nated with me and has greatly changed much of the way I now view my own faith and the way I view others . . . all for the better. I have read several of your books, and several others from other authors/teachers associated with the EC and almost always greatly learn from them. However, I have been a lone ranger as an EC "fan" within my own circle of friends. And I have never really "come out of the theological closet" for fear of backlash.[9]

Remarks like these suggest ECM sympathies are broad and certainly not re-stricted to those who participate in emerging congregations or who explicitly label themselves as Emerging Christians.

### "We get gawkers every week coming in from all over the country."

Some people become aware of their connection to the ECM because their congregations get visitors because they are known to be "emerg-ing churches." In one congregation a member said, "We get gawkers every week coming in from all over the country. Those 15 guys in neckties, they're United Methodist pastors, you know—all seminary class." Another man said, "They come in here and this is one of their stops." Another woman said she talks to people several times a day "about what we're doing," about "the new emergent church or the new growing church—the new young person church—whatever you want to call it." At the same time, she gets frustrated: "They always wanna think of it in theological terms," and fre-quently finds she needs to correct them, saying, "Please don't think that it's a new theology because the theologies of those churches are going to vary quite widely." They keep thinking, "'OK, a new page of theology–who's the new Martin Luther?' No, no, no, no. Don't think Martin Luther. This is Hudson Taylor reaching China." By citing a missionary famous for adopt-ing Chinese dress and customs to evangelize the nation, she describes the ECM as an attempt to reach a culture still foreign to the gospel of Jesus. She said, "The point of this is not a new theology."

## "To out myself as an emergent church member would be a very big no-no."

Of course many in the ECM, particularly the leaders who write books and speak at conferences, are articulating new theologies, which we explore in chapter 4. These theologies are often diametrically opposed to conservative theologies, especially when it comes to the nature of truth and the nature of God. But many within the ECM are unaware of such theological wrangling and struggle to understand how their congregations work or what they stand for. As one man said, "Emergent churches, well, they kind of believe what they want to believe." However, some Emerging Christians said that "critics" would be surprised at the general orthodoxy of their congregations. One woman said, "I've got a conservative, evangelical Baptist brother pastor, and he's like, 'I don't like that whole emergent thing,' and I try to explain to him, 'No, no, it's really sound, and there's even room for disagreement within that.'" Another man said "anti-emergent people" would be surprised to experience their congregation and discover it was an emerging church. Claire said her church is a place she feels comfortable bringing "friends who aren't Christians . . . as well as my friends that are conservative Christians." While ECM congregations vary greatly in their theological persuasions, many ultimately hold surprisingly orthodox views (at least within their leadership structures), much to the chagrin of more radical Emerging Christians who fiercely desire to cut themselves off from their conservative past and to profoundly undermine the standard systems of Christian belief and practice.

As members come to understand their identification with the ECM, they become more cautious about claiming that connection when they speak to others. One woman said she finds herself "nervous" in telling other Christians, "I attend an emergent church," so she keeps it to herself. "They're Presbyterians and they're Calvinists, so to out myself as an emergent church member would be a very big no-no because it's just they're so orthodox that it's not allowed, I guess." Indeed, there are reports of conservative Christians who show up at ECM gatherings because they see emerging congregations as mission sites in their own right. One congregational leader said, "It was funny because we'd always have a couple of fundies drop in just to make trouble." She illustrated with this story:

One time in particular, we had these two Calvinists that infiltrated on purpose to try to save us, you know? They were trying to teach us "the truth," and then they realized that we were already predestined to go straight to hell. So they left. I basically said, "I'm glad that you're here and I affirm the way you apparently see the world, but if you come to this group, you have to be open to hear what other people think about the world, too, and about God, and you can't assume that we're all going to be like you when this is over." They weren't going to have that, so they left.

Members may come to love their emerging congregations, but they simultaneously come to avoid explicit references to their congregations when among more conservative Christians. For researchers, such avoidance of self-labeling further obscures the breadth of ECM participation.

## Emerging Christianity as a Form of Strategic Religiosity

Philip Harrold has argued that the ECM's "association with postmodern deconstruction makes insiders and outsiders alike wrestle over the movement's tentative definitions of identity, meaning, and purpose."[10] As we have reviewed here, the ECM's focus on deconstruction and deconversion has meant the movement is often reduced to what it *is against* or what it is *leaving behind*, with very few other defining characteristics to hold it together. As one Emerging Christian said, it's "Christianity for people who don't like Christianity." While we see deconstruction as central to the religious orientation of Emerging Christians, what makes that orientation coherent is that it is strategically formed in community with others and framed out of resources established by the Christianity they critique.

Emerging Christians nurture a shared "deconstructed" religious orientation by participating in reoriented religious communities that draw on long-established and well-understood structures of institutionalized Christianity. As Alan Jamieson observes, "They are made up of exiles, refugees, and outcasts of established churches."[11] The ECM strives to avoid inauthentic, "standardized" spirituality and aims to cultivate new religious orientations, some of which start with reading books like those by Brian McLaren, others which expand by following the path of friends who have become "church exiles" or finding a group of strangers with similar doubts and questions, and still others who uncomfortably forge their own way in shedding and subsequently reorienting their religious lives.

Their move toward ECM structures (broadly conceptualized as pluralist congregations) might be understood as an escape from standardized agency—or what Emerging Christians experienced as the oppressive structures of fundamentalist piety. Emerging Christians question the roles faithful believers are supposed to step into without question; specifically, the layout of belief and behavior dictated by institutionalized, conservative Christianity. So while much of modern society is based on the positioning of individuals to play out their agency in particular ways, Emerging Christians are finding newly legitimated ways to move out of such expectations and to form new structures to support alternative ways of enacting religious agency.

Emerging Christian are not simply a striving for an "authentic" self, they are enacting a type of "legitimized" religious self.[12] What appears on the surface to be a freewheeling heterodoxy reacting to the established institutions of contemporary Christianity is, on more investigation, a strategically framed religious self that is enabled, and often nurtured and sustained, through congregational involvement. Emerging Christians continually balance the dual demands of deconstructing their individual faith and investing in cooperative congregational relationships. Rather than cultivating communities in which they can lose themselves or find a means to adopt a larger collective identity, Emerging Christians join emerging congregations that promote a religiously individualized self, one that strives for a type of nonconformity that commingles ambiguity and conviction.

In short, the concept of strategic religiosity reinforces that the ECM does not exist as a free-standing religious form; rather, all the activities and beliefs of Emerging Christians exist within an overarching religious orientation that is strategically deployed. This shared orientation, a simultaneously critical and respectful orientation toward existing forms of Christianity, is a base from which their new religious orientation and congregational behaviors are shaped. Our use of the term "orientation" rather than the more sociologically conventional "identity," and the emphasis on Emerging Christians' strategic enactment of religiosity, allows us to more fully grasp the dynamism, responsiveness, and diversity present in their approach to living a "religious" life that accommodates varieties of identities under a more general set of principles.

Analysis of the ECM reaffirms that social institutions—whether those be pub churches, arts collectives, online networks, or more conventional-looking congregations—are necessary for the construction of religious agency.[13] In sum, Emerging Christians are attempting to renegotiate the rules of the broader system of Christianity. In the process, they actively negotiate their own religious selves.

# 4

# Faith as Conversation

I'm not here because we all think alike, because we definitely don't, but because I'm free to think how I think, and somebody will challenge me on that. I can be myself and say what I think and why I think it. Everybody may go, "yeah, we completely agree," or "no, we absolutely disagree," but nobody's going to ostracize me or ask me to leave the church.

—Hailey, *on what keeps her in her congregation*

People in the Emerging Church Movement (ECM) can't stop talking. They talk and write continually both face to face and through social media. They have even taken to calling their movement a "conversation."[1] Key thinkers and leaders associated with the ECM, such as Rob Bell, Brian McLaren, Tony Jones, and Peter Rollins, have portrayed faith itself as conversation. This conversation includes questioning the idea that faith means articulating and intellectually assenting to a set of beliefs. For Emerging Christians, conversation is essential to the continual process of working out how to live like Christians in the "real world." While it has been the leaders and public figures of the ECM who have most forcefully articulated the idea of "faith as conversation," all participants in our research spoke about how important conversation, dialogue, and storytelling are to their faith and how their congregations provide a unique arena for this. And our immersive fieldwork affirms the centrality of conversation in ECM gatherings.

The discourses of people in the ECM can be understood as a conversation/dialogue/storytelling process that is important *in and of itself.* At the same time, the content of those discourses is significant, because we can discern the ideas that compose their distinctive religious orientation by analyzing what Emerging Christians say. Accordingly, in addition to our interview respondents, we draw on the work of key thinkers associated with the ECM to identify the major themes of conversation that are important. In this chapter more than the others, we utilize published works by key authors, because we consider such sources as providing exceptionally focused reflection on important themes in the conversation. Their published works draw explicitly on the broader intellectual streams associated with postmodernity, thus allowing us to see more directly how the ECM reflects and engages with this context. At the same time, we include narratives from participants in the ECM that illustrate how those who do not have high-profile leadership positions are engaging in the conversation. Their lived experience within the ECM encourages them to keep talking and to continually ask questions.

The literature on institutional entrepreneurialism, specifically how institutional entrepreneurs use discourses, helps explain the effectiveness of the "faith as conversation" approach of the ECM—which Philip Harrold describes as "a rather disorderly arena of discourse."[2] The aim of Emerging Christians' conversation is not to settle on established positions or to reach a point where all can agree and therefore stop talking. *Ongoing conversation is in itself a mechanism or a strategy to maintain a plurality of identities and positions within emerging congregations.* Their religious orientations are formed around the process of conversation, which constitutes an ongoing process of institutional change. Like institutional entrepreneurs in other fields, Emerging Christians are engaging in "meaning work" that includes theorizing, mythologizing, valorizing, and demonizing to undermine previously held assumptions and beliefs and to justify change.[3] Grounded in a commitment to intellectual freedom and asking questions, Emerging Christians are developing distinct ways of thinking about the nature of truth, doubt, and God. These ideas are disseminated through congregations, which can be understood as organizations that "order the intrinsic flux of human action, to channel it towards certain ends by generalizing and institutionalizing particular cognitive representations."[4] The development of these ideas in turn sustains the ECM by affirming the autonomy of individuals while helping them make sense of their faith in contemporary social contexts.

ECM "talk" is therefore a strategic point for investigating shifting patterns in religious affiliation in the context of pluralism, secularism, and new civic identities. Ideas are not merely "ideas" for the ECM; rather, the attempt to actualize values with integrity promotes the concrete conversations and practices of emerging congregations. This discursive aspect of the ECM also provides an excellent entrée for understanding broader aspects of institutional entrepreneurialism. *Institutional entrepreneurs are insiders from a particular institutional field who attempt to change existing institutions and to justify their own innovations.*[5] *Religious institutional entrepreneurs are those who accomplish such work within religious organizational fields.*

## Religious Institutional Entrepreneurs
## and the Use of Discourse

Scholarship on institutional entrepreneurship has continually emphasized the role of key individuals in processes of institutional change. A proponent of the approach, Paul DiMaggio, suggested institutional entrepreneurship as "a way to reintroduce actors' agency to institutional analysis." As Bernard Leca, Julie Battilana, and Eva Boxenbaum note in their review of the literature, this implicates the concept in classical sociological debates about "structure versus agency."[6] However, critics have claimed that institutional entrepreneurship errs too much on the side of agency, drawing caricatures of institutional entrepreneurs as autonomous "heroes" disembodied from the constraints of their context.[7] We disagree with this dismissive reading, convinced that more recent work has located institutional entrepreneurs firmly within their constraining contexts and demonstrated how individual agents are both enabled and constrained by the existing institutions they are trying to change.[8]

While institutional entrepreneurs have been studied in a variety of organizational fields, there has been very little work on entrepreneurs in the religious field.[9] This is surprising, given the recent sociological conceptualization of the religious field as a "market," which seems to invite the innovation of entrepreneurs.[10] Parallels also could be drawn between the charismatic "prophets" of Max Weber and the depiction of institutional entrepreneurs as charismatic "heroes." Both prophets and heroes spark innovation through the force of their personalities operating within particularistic social contexts. The failure to investigate what insights institutional entrepreneurship brings to the sociology of religion may in part be due to a tendency for sociologists to regard religious identities and institutions as especially robust and immune to change. It may also be due to a Western tendency to think about religion in terms of fixed creeds, which by definition are not up for renegotiation, which may tempt sociologists to discount or fail to investigate religion's internal contradictions—not least of which includes adherents' disregard for or lack of knowledge of so-called doctrines. It also downplays the strategic religiosity of religious actors (see chapter 3) and how profound reorientations, both subtle and dramatic, are ongoing aspects of religious life.

We suggest that institutional entrepreneurship provides a fruitful lens for the understanding of strategic religiosity and larger patterns of religious change. A great deal of research on institutional entrepreneurship focuses on discourses, seeing entrepreneurs' ability to "make meaning," to "frame" new ideas, and employ "discursive strategies" as key to instigating change.[11]

Institutional entrepreneurs are able to rework already existing "institutional vocabularies" consisting of commonly understood words, expressions and meanings, similar to the ways Weber's prophets reinterpret religious traditions. Such work requires "expert theorizers"—like Bell, McLaren, Jones, and Rollins who we analyze throughout this book—who exhibit high levels of reflexivity and creativity.[12] Researchers drawing on a critical realist framework further suggest that the capacity to operate as an institutional entrepreneur comes through the process of reflexivity, the ability to look back upon oneself and cognitively disembed oneself from one's institutional commitments.[13] Indeed, prominent representatives within the ECM like those named here have in part defined their posture toward ministry among Emerging Christians as the intentional provocation of reflexivity. The emphasis on reflexivity echoes the work of Anthony Giddens and Ulrich Beck on the inherent reflexivity of individuals within modern society, who must renegotiate their identities and behaviors in light of new information.[14] As Battilana, Leca and Boxenbaum note, "Some researchers even propose that institutional entrepreneurship is mainly a discursive strategy whereby institutional entrepreneurs generate stories, discourses, and texts."[15]

## Institutional Entrepreneurship and the Limits of Discourse

Many studies of institutional entrepreneurship conclude what ECM participants regularly put into practice: that storytelling is one of the most effective ways people "make meaning" in support of institutional change. Examples include the extemporaneous stories, or "small narratives" that entrepreneurs share in their everyday conversations with employees, customers, and suppliers.[16] Other examples are the more scripted narratives told in formal presentations to audiences such as bankers, venture capitalists, and media representatives. Examples of the written mode include the story segments, or "minimal narratives,"[17] that appear on promotional materials such as company brochures, websites, and product packages, as well as the fuller narratives that appear in documents like annual reports, business plans, and IPO prospectuses.[18] Stories, or the "narrative way of knowing" they reflect,[19] have primacy over the scientific and paradigmatic modes of thinking in everyday processes of sense making and communication.[20] Stories are also very engaging, as they appeal to both cognition and emotion.[21] These characteristics of stories may explain their central role in organizational life,[22] as well as in entrepreneurship.[23] As anyone who has been around ECM churches or read the works of ECM leaders knows, Emerging Christians explicitly value "storytelling" as a key mode of communication.

However, there is more to religious institutional entrepreneurialism than merely "talk." In an influential working paper, organizational theorists Leca, Battilana, and Boxenbaum write that the discursive aspect of institutional entrepreneurship has been overemphasized and point to studies that stress the importance of entrepreneurs' skills, resources, and social position. The social skills of institutional entrepreneurs include the ability to motivate the cooperation and activism of others by facilitating "communities of practice."[24] Such skills include creating new networks and alliances. Institutional entrepreneurs usually already occupy key positions in social networks, thus possessing "a high level of 'reach centrality,' defined as access to a large number of field members through a limited number of intermediaries."[25] They enjoy high levels of "social capital"; thus, they are able to command the trust of others in their networks and to garner information and support.[26] Cooperation is so essential to institutional entrepreneurship that the research suggests "that institutional entrepreneurs have unique political and social skills."[27] Certainly we can detect such skills and reach centrality among key figures in the ECM.

Entrepreneurial discourse therefore involves social skills and network centrality. Such discourse does not have an independent impact but always operates within a social context. Some scholars rightly emphasize the importance of the contexts in which institutional entrepreneurs are embedded, analyzing how they operate in response to external and internal factors. Institutional entrepreneurs may become convinced of the need for change by external factors such as "social upheaval, technological disruption, competitive discontinuity, and regulatory changes that might disturb the socially constructed, field-level consensus and invite the introduction of new ideas."[28] Others who have studied the ECM recognize external factors as important. For example, while Josh Packard does not conceive of Emerging Christians as institutional entrepreneurs, he does outline some of the external, cultural factors that he judges to have influenced their work for change.[29] Institutional entrepreneurs also may be convinced of the need for change by factors internal to their institutions or organizational fields. In the case of Emerging Christians who challenge contemporary institutional Christianity, this includes the perceived ineffectiveness or irrelevance of congregational structures, environmental changes in orientation toward spirituality and religion, and people's personal disillusionment when life doesn't work out the way the preacher promised it would. For example, Packard and his coauthor George Sanders describe internal factors that stimulate change when they describe Emerging Christians as establishing "lines of flight" to free themselves from the suffocating effects of late modern "corporatization" in churches. Evidence of corporatization in churches includes the licensing of worship music and the subsequent distribution of royalties for artists . . . the reliance upon professional market consultants and the implementation of "regular programming evaluations" to assess worshippers' attitudes and satisfaction with the services . . . the incorporation of retail outlets into the physical architecture of churches . . . the deployment of a wide variety of consumer goods that are readily accessible to the casual church-goer . . . the development of synergetic strategies of promotional marketing . . . the generation of brands and branding . . . and the deliberate attempt by religious organizations to appeal to "today's consumerist ethos" . . . just to name a few.[30]

Forms of discourse are developed and shared among Emerging Christians. Public conversations in ECM congregations, alongside books, conferences, and websites, are among the resources available that "provide vocabulary and narrative frameworks for the emerging church."[31] Moreover, "personal narratives contained therein are defined primarily in terms of revulsion, rejection, and turning-from an originative context, usually the 'institutional' church."[32] As Matthew Engelke observes:

> Emerging church literature can be jarring to read. Despite their rhetorical self-deprecations, emerging evangelical writers can sound pretty self-satisfied about how different they are. It is therefore especially important to keep in mind that what emerging evangelicalism most promises to break with is "conservative" evangelicalism—or, at least, the stereotype of conservative evangelicalism.[33]

Just as Engelke describes, institutional entrepreneurs' embeddedness in their context means that they must regularly refer to the institutional order they are trying to change, either to delegitimize it or to demonstrate how their desired changes do not depart too far from it.

Emerging Christians' frequent critique of contemporary institutional Christianity serves to delegitimize and distance them from the religious orientation they believe they left behind (usually evangelicalism). But institutional entrepreneurs must also simultaneously work to legitimize new or changing institutions by connecting them with taken-for-granted beliefs and values, not only in their own organizational field but also in society at large.[34] As religious institutional entrepreneurs, Emerging Christians do this by claiming that the changes they advocate facilitate a more authentic living out of the gospel and that they help people make better sense of postmodern, pluralist contexts.

## The "Conversation" as Religious Institutional Entrepreneurship

We see the "conversation" of the ECM as a paradigmatic example of the type of "meaning work" that has been so central to studies of institutional entrepreneurship. Indeed, the *Encyclopaedia of Religion in America* defines the ECM as a conversation. Tony Jones cites this as the "best definition of the ECM." Written by Warren Bird, the definition in the *Encyclopaedia* is as follows:

> The emerging church movement is a loosely aligned conversation among Christians who seek to re-imagine the priorities, values, and theology expressed by the local church as it seeks to live out its faith in postmodern society. It is an attempt to replot Christian faith on a new cultural and intellectual terrain.[35]

Reimaging and replotting constitute the main types of discursive work described in studies of institutional entrepreneurs.[36] Institutional entrepreneurs' first step is to frame the problem at hand (diagnostic framing) or suggest a solution (prognostic framing).[37] The second step is arraying events and experiences in cognitive packages that justify and legitimate change.[38] Much of *The Deconstructed Church* is taken up with Emerging Christians' diagnostic framing of what's wrong with contemporary institutional Christianity, including their critiques of "modern" religion in various guises, including evangelicalism, megachurches, and mainline denominations. Significantly, Emerging Christians believe that within these existing expressions of Christianity, there is *not enough space for conversation*. So it is not surprising that their prognostic framing valorizes conversation as key to overcoming the perceived shortcomings of existing religious institutions. Emerging Christians thus think of discourses (conversation) as in and of themselves a strategy for instigating almost continual change. This is in contrast to institutional entrepreneurs in other fields, who tend to think of discourses as a strategy for bringing about and justifying a desired change—and then institutionalizing that change.

For Emerging Christians, dialogue simply means listening to others' points of view or positions *without trying to change them*. "It's not about forcing a conclusion," said one participant. This way of thinking about dialogue contrasts to what Emerging Christians see as evangelical dialogic practices: the evangelical has the "right" answers and the purpose of dialogue is to convert others to that point of view. It also differs from a traditional ecumenical approach to dialogue, which is focused on discovering points of commonality. Participants instead describe the process as a form of pedagogy in which people strive for mutual understanding. It involves "a lot of listening." And it assertively challenges the more directed, exacting forms of dialogue they've experienced in their past.

Emerging Christians practice narrating their lives but do so in the public venue of their congregations where strangers listen. Sharing unpretentious and uniquely private experiences also inspires others to talk as everyone struggles to concretize their subjective experiences as distinctly spiritual experiences. Ulrich Beck writes that such monologues "make it possible to immerse one's own life in the space of the other."[39] In short, as speakers reflect on their inward experiences, they generate engagement among their listeners, prompting them to craft their own biography in a way that foregrounds statements on the nature of spiritual life.

As such, Emerging Christians seem comfortable embracing the tensions in what appear to be mutually exclusive positions. They not only intend to create "safe spaces" for nonconforming dialogue, but they also celebrate when it is achieved. In *The New Christians,* in a section titled "After Objectivity: Dialogue," Jones describes a Jewish-Christian dialogue between "some of us emergent Christians" and "a group of young and innovative rabbis."[40] Jones explained that he and Shawn Landres, the director of research at Synagogue 3000, agreed that they would not "predetermine what they can agree on and then talk only of those things."[41] Jones writes:

> No one held back, which ultimately led to more candor and openness about what we really believe. And that, in turn, led to deeper friendships, since openness and authenticity are such important qualities in making friends . . . In one small group, the question was raised about whether rabbis from older, established synagogues might bless and assist young rabbis who are attempting to start something new. After some discussion among the Jewish members of the small group, Tim Keel, pastor of Jacob's Well in Kansas City, spoke up. He told the story of Eli and Samuel, found at the beginning of 1 Samuel, and of how the very old prophet, Eli, and the young boy and prophet-to-be, Samuel, formed a mutually beneficial and nonhierarchical relationship.
>
> When Tim finished, silence ensued. Then a rabbi quietly said, "*Yasher koach.*" Shawn told me later that's a Yiddish version of the Hebrew *yishar kochachah,* which means, "More strength to you." He also told me that it's a traditional expression of appreciation and respect for an interpretation of Torah.
>
> It was a moment of beautiful truth.[42]

When it comes to storytelling, Emerging Christians most often take two approaches: (1) grounding the interpretation of the Bible in careful attention to its "stories" or narratives; and (2) telling stories themselves through dialogic fiction (such as McLaren's *A New Kind of Christian, The Story We Find Ourselves In,* and *The Last Word and the Word After That*),[43] original parables (for which Rollins is well known),[44] or stories of their personal experiences. Presenting the Bible as a series of stories, or "storifying" the Bible, is a deliberate move away from what Emerging Christians see as modernist ways of reading the Bible.[45]

Modernists read the Bible like a history or a science textbook that contains mainly empirical facts and laws and has no internal contradictions. This way of reading the Bible has led to Christians using it to claim that their particular interpretation is the one that is right and true. As Nadia Bolz-Weber, who was raised in the conservative Church of Christ and is now pastor for House for All Sinners and Saints in Denver, writes:

> The Bible had been the weapon of choice in the spiritual gladiatorial arena of my youth. I knew how, wielded with intent and precision, the Bible can cut deeply, while the one holding it can claim with impunity that "this is from God." Apparently if God wrote the Bible (a preposterous idea), then any verse used to exclude, shame, harm, or injure another person is not only done in the name of God, but also out of love and concern for the other person. I had been that person on several occasions, lying spiritually bleeding on the ground, while the nice, well-meaning, and concerned Christians stood above me and smiled in condescension, so pleased with themselves that they had "spoken the truth in love."[46]

But for Emerging Christians, the Bible becomes a collection of narratives that can speak to different people in different ways. As Rollins puts it: "The Bible itself is a dynamic text full of poetry, prose, history, law, and myth all clashing together in a cacophony of voices."[47]

For the leaders in the movement who preach and teach through their sermons, lectures, and books, the emphasis on narratives has led to an effort to demonstrate the gospel through stories—not to *tell* people about the gospel through three-point sermons or a series of bullet points. It has also resulted in preacher-performers like Bell, whose use of storytelling is exemplary in his sermons, films (the NOOMA video series), and books (for example, parts of *Love Wins* read like free-verse poetry). James Wellman describes Bell as "a postmodern evangelist—a slam poet, Billy Graham type, who beguiles with words, images and ideas about a beautiful Jesus, whose stories transfix and transduce words into flesh, making incarnation the arbiter of all value."[48] Wellman writes how in an interview with Bell he observed: "It almost feels like you're more in love with just the process of communication than with whatever you want to call it, the gospel." Bell responded: "My experience, I had seen people talking about the gospel, preaching the gospel, being true to the gospel, and it sucked." This led Wellman to conclude that for Bell, a primary "communication principle" is to *"show rather than tell."*[49] (Emphasis in original.) And it is stories that *show* best of all.

Similarly, Engelke's study of the British and Foreign Bible Society demonstrates how key members of its staff, influenced by theological and intellectual currents within ECM, approach the Bible "not so much as a book to be read as this story to be lived," as captured in a phrase used often within the organization—"doing Bible." Engelke explains:

> In this rendering the Bible is a full-body experience, a way of life and a way of living that melds body and mind. Reading is not only, or even primarily, a cognitive activity; it is also a sensual experience. What we think of as "the Bible"—leather, glue, paper, ink—is but one of its many forms. During meetings, Ann used to ask the Advocacy Team, "How are you doing Bible?" *Doing Bible.* It was never "How are you applying biblical principles to your work?" or "How do the Scriptures relate to this activity?"[50]

Emerging Christians also encourage people to draw their own conclusions from stories. No one is forced to agree on a particular interpretation of a story.

The ECM's storytellers are also fond of suggesting different meanings for biblical parables, such as Kester Brewin's inversion of the prodigal son parable in which the father is *not* seen as a loving, god-like figure.[51] Rollins has been most innovative in adapting a classical biblical form of story, the parable, and using it in his videos, lectures, and books—including an entire book devoted to parables, *The Orthodox Heretic and Other Impossible Tales.*[52] Also, in an inversion of the dispensational evangelicalism that has been so influential in the United States (as well as in some churches in Northern Ireland),[53] Rollins wrote a parable called "The Rapture," which was produced as a Chick-style tract.[54] Rollins's parables are simultaneously biting and satirical in that they usually have embedded within them critiques of theologies. But they can be playful, with an unexpected twist at the end meant to catch the attention of listeners and readers and to push them toward thinking in different ways.

In a manner that echoes the traditional "testimonies" of being converted or "born again" within evangelicalism, Emerging Christians are encouraged to share stories about their personal experiences of faith with others, publicly or in small groups.[55] However, as Harrold has noted and we describe further in chapter 3, these are stories laced with disillusionment or "de-conversion."[56] Sharing these stories can have a cathartic effect for the tellers, when they realize that others have been through the same experiences. Lindsey Mitchell, who is involved with Ikon, related how she felt increasingly constrained by her conservative church upbringing, where she was expected to wear a hat to church and her contributions were limited to making tea for the men. Conflict with her congregation came to a head when she began working at a nursing home and was required to work Sunday shifts, causing her to miss worship. Mitchell said this failure to attend church got her "chucked out." But she found kindred spirits when a former chaplain at Queen's University said that he was attending the launch of one of Rollins's books. Mitchell went along and got talking with some of the people involved in Ikon, whose personal stories resonated with her own.[57] As speaker Kathy Escobar once shared, "When I told my story, other people started telling their stories."[58] As Emerging Christians share their experiences, their stories beget more stories.

## The "Conversation" as Collective Institutional Entrepreneurship

Looking at key ECM figures like Bell, McLaren, Jones, and Rollins, we find that their personal characteristics "fit" those of the institutional entrepreneurs described in the literature. But our research also reveals that almost all those who participate in ECM communities are entrepreneurs to the extent they actively work to build and maintain their communities. Indeed, we found many rank-and-file Emerging Christians participating in "the conversation" have not read or listened to these leaders and are completely unaware of the wider ECM. This resonates with recent research on *collective institutional entrepreneurship*, as well as research that claims that "social movements can act as institutional entrepreneurs."[59] We agree with Battilana, Leca, and Boxenbaum, who argue:

> Agents without any grand plan for altering their institutions, or even awareness that they are contributing to changes that diverge from existing institutions, might thus end up acting as institutional entrepreneurs. We thus define institutional entrepreneurs as change agents who, whether or not they initially intended to change their institutional environment, initiate and actively participate in the implementation of changes that diverge from existing institutions.[60]

Broad range religious change therefore involves broad participation in institutional change, a collective institutional entrepreneurship, regardless of the degree of conscious awareness.

In sum, through their discourses Emerging Christians are collective entrepreneurs in their corporate attempt to craft an approach to spirituality that is simultaneously private yet communal. Sharing their private stories in public spaces corresponds to an attempt to connect their "particular existence and the *universal* individual, the *universal* God of one's own, that struggles to express itself."[61] ECM congregations are sites in which a collective religiosity emerges that allows freedom for the distinctive biographical experience of each individual. Beck writes of such religiously individualized people as distinctive to our modern societal context: "In a world morally devastated by the madness of terrorism, you chose to ask for something more, over and above the collective religiosity that constantly preached conformity. You acted just as if one could assume responsibility for one's own life, including its religious dimension."[62] For Beck, "This idea overturns the order of faith that has survived for millennia through every vicissitude."[63]

While institutional entrepreneurs in other organizational fields may have the goal of institutionalizing their innovations, the ECM maintains a much more ambivalent approach toward institutions in and of themselves. For Emerging Christians, participating in the conversation stymies any desire to "institutionalize" their religious innovations. Packard and Sanders borrow the concept of "nomads" from Deleuze and Guattari to describe this aspect of Emerging Christianity, writing:

> The nomad exists in stark contrast to corporatization, whose function is to categorize, compartmentalize, and contain. Where corporatization lends itself to the creation of a religious "product" that is uniform, stable, and predictable, the nomad's efforts target transgression. Antithetical to corporatization, then, the Emerging Church frames itself as an open-ended conversation—an activity that is typically inclusive but malleable.[64]

So Emerging Christians' commitment to ongoing conversation can be understood as a strategy for maintaining an almost constant process of change.

## The Priority of Intellectual Freedom and Asking Questions

The open, fluid nature of the ECM conversation places few demands upon people to believe the same things. When we write about Emerging Christians strategically developing a religious orientation that includes distinct ideas, we want to emphasize that we do not see these as a checklist of beliefs or philosophical orientations that people sign up for. Our research demonstrates that Emerging Christians share distinct approaches to the nature of truth, doubt, and the nature of God, yet these approaches are rooted in a context that values intellectual freedom and asking questions. This is a context in which the institutional entrepreneurs of the ECM thrive, as their conversations deconstruct "conventional" Christianity and simultaneously provide discourses for resisting institutionalization. Indeed, it could be said that for many within the ECM, the purpose of conversation is to generate more questions. In *Love Wins*, Bell asks an astonishing 350 questions.[65] Many of our interviewees spoke of how when they were previously integrated into evangelical subcultures, excessive questioning was discouraged and people were encouraged to "let go and let God."[66] It might have been expected that after more than ten years with him as pastor, Bell's Mars Hill congregation would have been accustomed to asking questions. But Wellman relates that the publication of *Love Wins* prompted people to push their questioning further: "Across the board, from those I interviewed at Mars Hill, the reaction to Bell's theological provocations created a sense of relief. Bell's congregation had permission to ask questions they assumed forbidden: 'Oh, are we allowed to do that?'—'Yes!'"[67]

The eagerness of people in the ECM to ask questions may stem in part from their origins in evangelical subcultures, where a practice of "existential questioning" is more widespread than outsiders often assume. Claire Mitchell and Gladys Ganiel have argued that although "evangelicals are sometimes caricatured as sheep-like creatures following literalist interpretations of the Bible or charismatic preachers, questioning is actually deeply embedded in their subculture."[68] Evangelicals' questions may range from trying to discover "God's will" for their lives to contemplating the cosmic meaning of everyday and world events. Their questions are usually asked within a context in which belief in a providential, interventionist God is taken for granted. In some ways, this is the sort of environment that Wellman describes when he analyzes Bell's evangelical upbringing and immersion in the evangelical subculture at Wheaton College. Bell's father, and those he met at Wheaton, encouraged him to ask questions. But as a matter of course, people in the ECM take questioning to a level that makes conservative evangelicals uncomfortable, including questioning the idea of a providential, interventionist God.

Emerging Christians' desire to ask questions is often rooted in personal experiences in which the "pat answers" that were supplied to them by their churches did not ring true in their lives.[69] This is characterized by Doug Pagitt as a process of moving "from 'Amen' to 'Uh-Oh,'" in which his experience of faith did not gel with the answers he had been given. Mitchell and Ganiel's *Evangelical Journeys* contains myriad examples of these experiences, ranging from how evangelicals started asking difficult questions when traveling outside their home culture, attending university, making friends with someone

"different" (such as from a different religion or of a different sexual orientation), studying sociology, and so on. Many of the books written by leading
figures in the ECM contain biographical vignettes, where the authors explain
how the faith with which they were originally presented either discouraged
them from asking questions or provided them with unsatisfying answers. By
sharing these stories in their books, lectures, films, and blogs, leaders of the
ECM let people know that they think that it is OK—even healthy—to question what they have been told about their faith. As Ikon's Lindsey Mitchell
said: "Ikon doesn't really preach. It poses questions and explores them. It
provokes thought, which is great . . . [because] sometimes people don't think
enough, they just sort of mamby-pamby out rehearsed responses."[70] Similarly,
Liam relished the intellectual freedom in his emerging congregation, which he
contrasted to other churches he had attended. He said:

> People here are very spiritually interested. They ask interesting ques-
> tions. They talk about interesting things. They have a genuine inter-
> est, and they want to grow spiritually. And they will go places, discuss
> things, talk about things that in other churches it's like, "Oh, you don't
> go there." Whereas here there is no place that you "don't go," you just
> go there.

Similarly, a focus group conversation with people from another emerging congregation illustrates how asking questions promotes the intellectual freedom
that Emerging Christians were unable to find in other congregations. One
woman said, "It's a place where my faith can grow, but nobody's telling me
what to believe." She said, "In every other church I've been to is this attitude
that the preacher has of knowing it all and this is the way it is, and these are the
three points that you need to remember." Hailey said:

> I'm not here because we all think alike, because we definitely don't,
> but because I'm free to think how I think and somebody will chal-
> lenge me on that. I can be myself and say what I think and why I think
> it. Everybody may go, "yeah, we completely agree," or "no, we abso-
> lutely disagree," but nobody's going to ostracize me or ask me to leave
> the church.

Disagreement is not a basis for fragmenting the congregation. Instead, the atmosphere allows for further individual expression where not only one's views
are heard but also personal identities are asserted and affirmed.[71]

In short, disagreement can fuel the continued construction of one's orientation as an Emerging Christian. Another woman added:

A big reason that most people are here is because you can be your-self. You can have different beliefs and thoughts than the person sit-ting next to you and they're not going to tell you that you're going to hell or that you're wrong . . . When I graduated from college, I came here about a year afterwards, and I went through this period of my life where I didn't know anything anymore. I didn't know who I was. I didn't know what I believed. I had grown up and had everything laid out for me by my parents or by the church in high school. So every-thing had very clear answers to all the questions you could ever have in life, there was an easy answer to it.

She went on to describe how she "almost self-destructed" but explained she was able to come through the experience because the people in the congrega-tion around her supported her and did not condemn her for asking questions. "I could listen to a sermon and totally disagree, and I felt like that was OK not to agree with something that was being said." The value of asking questions is reinforced in many emerging congregations when sermons end with questions or leaders invite questions during services. Nicole said, "I was so impressed that people were questioning and being allowed to answer in different ways. It was a free place to question, so that really sucked me in." Another woman said, "I really love to be in a place like this where there's room for questions."

Sociologist Grace Davie famously wrote of "believing without belonging,"[72] but what we see in the ECM are people characterized by what Ulrich Beck de-scribed as "belonging without believing" and "multiple believing with belong-ing," that is, hybrid beliefs—even contradictory beliefs—combining with the purely conventional membership of a church.[73] One man said he appreciated the intellectual freedom in not having to "constantly think about, you know, am I making the checklist of things I'm supposed to believe." Another man said: "Here, one of the first things I noticed is that it was OK to end sermons with questions. Which just makes sense. I started to feel like if it's not messy and screwed up, I don't know if I trust it."

Emerging Christians not only ask questions, they assert that other Chris-tians are failing to ask the important questions. McLaren complains that this has happened with his writings. In the conclusion to *A New Kind of Christi-anity,* he describes the reception of a previous book, *Everything Must Change,* while he was on tour promoting it:

I remember returning to my hotel room night after night with a strange uneasiness. As I tried unsuccessfully to drift off to sleep, I would realize that the same thing had happened once again. During the Question & Response session, most questioners simply ignored the four crises I had talked about. Instead, they focused on arguing fine points of theology with me—all within their conventional paradigms. It was as if they said, "Oh yeah, yeah, a billion people live on less than a dollar a day. But you're decentralizing our preferred theory of atonement!" Or "Yeah, yeah, yeah, we're in danger of environmental collapse and religiously inspired catastrophic war, but you seem to be questioning our conventional ways of reading the Bible about homosexuality!"[74]

The "four crises" that McLaren references above are (1) the crisis of the planet (which is ecological), (2) the crisis of poverty (which highlights the gap between rich and poor), (3) the crisis of peace (in which the gap between rich and poor contributes to cycles of violence), and (4) the crisis of religion (in which the major world religions are *not* actually inspiring people to address the first three crises but are in fact contributing to the crises). Scot McKnight's review of *A New Kind of Christianity* conforms to the pattern McLaren observes, quickly moving on from the four crises to focus on what he sees as the two major themes of McLaren's book: a critique of the Greco-Roman narrative, and a proposal for a new way of reading the Bible.[75]

Reactions to Bell's *Love Wins* further illustrate how Emerging Christians and conservative and/or neo-Reformed evangelicals disagree on what are the most important questions. Wellman notes that while in many ways Bell's *Jesus Wants to Save Christians* (co-authored with Don Golden) is a more radical book than *Love Wins* in its sociopolitical critique of the American "empire" and the churches' role in sustaining it, it was *Love Wins'* hint at universalism that stirred the biggest controversy of Bell's career. Emerging Christians recenter away from doctrinal disputes toward broader, substantive themes with consequences for redefining "Christian" beliefs and imperatives.

## Broad Themes in ECM Conversations

Emerging Christians experience their congregations, communities, and collectives as safe spaces where they can ask difficult questions and where intellectual freedom is encouraged. This intellectually open posture is very much part of Emerging Christians' distinct religious orientation, and by encouraging creativity and debate it resources their ability to act as collective institutional entrepreneurs. In this process the ECM conversation nurtures individual autonomy and places responsibility for spiritual development primarily upon individuals. This near-constant dialogue involves a struggle for self-coherence in a group context. Yet the result of this process is not solely focused on singular individuals. Rather, the process of conversation means that people are engaged in a process of collective institutional entrepreneurship, developing relatively coherent, unified, and distinctive religious orientations around areas such as the nature of truth, doubt, and the nature of God that can be shared and mutually affirmed. Many of these ideas are developed organically among emerging congregations in services and in conversations over coffee or in a pub. But they are also absorbed through engagement with popular books written by leading figures in the ECM, many of which we draw on to illustrate the conversational trends.

## What is Truth?

"What is Truth?" is Pilate's question at a crucial moment in the story of Christ's crucifixion. It is also a question that people in the ECM ask. What is emerging from their conversations is a conception of truth that is experiential and "embodied" in the example of Jesus. Coupled with this, Emerging Christians reject what they see as "modernist" conceptions of truth. For them, modernists conceive of truth as a set of objective propositions about the world as it really is. Modernists are said to pair "propositional truth" with the idea that the facts we discover can help us construct an all-encompassing, overarching narrative that explains everything. Emerging Christians contrast their approach to truth to this modernist paradigm. Drawing explicitly (or in some cases seemingly subconsciously) on postmodern insights and philosophies, they argue that the failure of Christians to engage with postmodern approaches to truth is hindering the church and the healthy development of individual Christians.

For Emerging Christians, what is more important than adjudicating between competing "truth claims" is discovering truth through stories and lived experiences. And the real test of what is "true" is whether it empowers you to live as a better person. Jones locates truth in the incarnation of Christ, as encapsulated in his hypothetical "statement of faith":

> We at First Christian Church acknowledge that God's coming to earth in the person of Jesus Christ and recounted in the Gospels turns upside down what we used to think about concepts like "truth." For in him, "truth" walked around, talked to people, and even cried and bled. We're left with a faith that, while deep, is also paradoxical and difficult. As a result, we've committed to leaning on each other as we collectively try to follow Jesus. We're confident about some things: Jesus' coming to earth was good news, it's still good news, and there's more good news to come. You're welcome to join us anytime.[76]

The degree to which leaders and participants in the ECM speak about the impact of postmodern philosophy on their conceptions of truth varies. Rollins, for example, is trained in postmodern philosophy at the doctoral level, and his popular writings reflect this background, often drawing explicitly on it. Engelke observes that within the Bible Society's staff, only one person (Parliamentary Officer Dave Landrum) had a passion for postmodern philosophy and "arcane academia," noting that "he could also get excited by the mention of, say, Zygmunt Bauman, in a way that none of the other team members did. The MPs called him 'Discourse Dave.'"[77] Others, like Ikon's Stephen Caswell, see insights from postmodern philosophy as a way to explain their personal experiences. Caswell said:

> I don't read continental philosophy. No more than maybe a few articles. I think Ikon primarily has been driven by people's experience, and then we've realized [our experience resonates with continental philosophy]—largely with the help of Pete, spending all this time reading these books. But our experience fits the ideas, rather than the other way round.

Phyllis Tickle argues that postmodern philosophy has provided two key insights that impact on ECM conceptions of truth. The first insight has to do with philosophers' deconstruction of "all written texts" and their challenging the idea of "the ability of language to convey anything without prejudice."[78] For Tickle, this has translated into leaders aligned with or sympathetic to the ECM becoming anxious about seminary training, due to "the very real fear that formal training in academic theology might somehow entrap one in a spiritual and intellectual prison constructed of words."[79] This meant they sought secular, liberal arts educations, where they studied at least some contemporary philosophy, which then influenced the way they looked at the world and thought about how Christians should live and the church should be organized. Similarly, in a section of his book titled "Language Trouble," Bielo identifies a general mistrust of language within the ECM, arguing that the ECM has developed a "language ideology that emphasizes the limits of communication."[80] Analyzing Rollins's *How (Not) to Speak of God*—the very title of which immediately places the "truth" of language and communication in doubt— Bielo concludes:[81] "Rollins articulates a clear and consistent posture toward language: it will always fail if the task is to use language to adequately communicate divine realities. This fundamental suspicion of language does not result in despair, but in a call to creativity and 'excess' (of which irony is a premier example)."[82] This approach feeds into a sense among Emerging Christians that it is impossible to discover a whole, objective truth. As one man said, "We don't want to be a church with a take-home message. We want to be a church where we present what truth we can, and people get out of it what God wants to put into them on that day." This illustrates how Emerging Christians conceive of truth as experiential.

Tickle's second insight focuses on postmodern philosophers' dual emphasis on the deconstruction of overarching metanarratives and the influence of context on written texts. This feeds an outright rejection among many in the ECM of the idea that the Bible can be thought of as providing an overarching narrative about God, the universe, and our place in it. It has also led to a rejection of reading the Bible like a manual for living in the contemporary world. The Bible then becomes "true" for Emerging Christians in a much different way than it is "true" for "modern" Christians, especially evangelicals. For Emerging Christians, one can come closer to truth through seeking to understand how context shaped what was written, through close examination of the micronarratives of the Bible. As Pagitt says: "The gospels are not generic, abstract truths. They are embedded stories. They are filled with culturally relevant language, images and symbols that made them ring true in the hearts of their listeners."[83] Similarly, in his treatment of "Scripture in the Emerging Movement," McKnight recognizes that people in the ECM have been influenced by the postmodern "linguistic turn," arguing that in some cases this has led to a throw-up-the-hands conclusion that God can never be known or spoken about or intellectual arrogance. McKnight then advocates reading the Bible as "wiki-stories of the story," a method that echoes postmodernism's emphasis on microstories and truth as story. He summarizes his approach like this:

> The ultimate truth is "the Story."
>  The written truth is made up of "wiki-stories."
>  The oral truth, our interpretation of the wiki-stories, our plots of the wiki-stories, is "church tradition."[84]

For McKnight, the advantages of his wiki approach are that it conveys the ideas that God chose to communicate with people through *language* at various times and contexts;[85] God needed a variety of stories to tell the full Story;[86] and wikis are in and of themselves reworkings of stories by new authors, so that a story "never has a final, unrevisable shape."[87]

One of the most radical approaches to truth can be found in Rollins's *The Fidelity of Betrayal*.[88] The book is framed by Rollins's retelling of the biblical story of Judas, the betrayer of Jesus. Rather than accepting the commonly held view that Judas was greedy and evil, he considers four alternative readings, raising the possibility that Judas's betrayal might have been an act of faith. This discussion, coming in the first chapter, sets up the defining argument of the book: Christianity is not a set of beliefs about God, but a critique of *all* religion. It is especially a critique of religions that align themselves with power.

The central task of Christians, then, is to interrogate their own religious beliefs and institutions, discerning how they exclude or oppress the poor and the outcasts. Along the way, Rollins critiques the "modernist" approach to apparent inconsistencies in biblical texts, which he sees as explaining the inconsistencies away. Rollins says there is an alternative approach that accepts the "inconsistencies" in the Bible as windows into the mystery of God. They are "holes" that testify to events that are greater than any words on a page, words which up till now readers might have assumed were attempts at factual description. He urges Christians to reject any reading of the Bible as final and to wrestle continually with the meaning of its texts. This is why Rollins does not advocate a single interpretation of the Judas story, saying that it is better to be open to competing interpretations. Consistent with this approach, a woman said she "really appreciated" that people were not forced to adhere to one, literalist interpretation of all Bible texts in her emerging congregation. She said, "In discussions or on Sundays, we can say—you know, that's crap. Noah and the Ark? Please."

Rollins also critiques the modern Western way of approaching truth as an *object* that can be discovered, analyzed, and comprehended. Rollins believes this approach creates too much distance between believers and the source of their faith, gives scholars and theologians too much power to determine truth, leads to the separation of knowledge and practice, and reduces Christianity to a set of comforting claims that make people feel good about themselves. The practices of emerging congregations' small groups also encourage people to stop thinking about truth like an object, for example by inviting people to share their own interpretations and insights from biblical texts. Wyatt, in another emerging congregation, described it this way: "I was struck by how open the dialogue was through the rest of the time I was there. It was something that I've always wanted to find in a church. I wanted to go to church, but I wanted to go to a church in a place where I could have an open dialogue and be up front." Rollins also contends that truth is more like the Eastern concept of enlightenment, in which a person's whole orientation is changed. Truth is embodied in believers and in their responses to God.

Ultimately this conception of truth gives individual experience precedence over "articles of faith" or doctrinal "truths." So Rollins does not necessarily regard traditional Christian articles of faith as factual statements; rather he judges their value by how they motivate people to love one another. Rollins's concern is that articles of faith have at times helped create a proud caste of Christians who claim knowledge of God but actually have limited experience of the divine. For Rollins, the test of what is "true" is either passed or failed in the way that people live. British journalist Jo Ind puts it this way: "So I started to think of truth, as being Christ himself, as in 'I am the truth' rather than 'These words are the truth.' In other words, something is true if it evokes love, goodness, peace."[89] Such an approach is illustrated by the experience of another woman from an emerging congregation. In contrast to her previous congregation, she described how relationship and experience trumped seeking after an elusive "objective" truth:

> There was always an underlying sense elsewhere for me that people were really worried about everybody, like worried about what exactly everybody believed. Maybe a senior pastor, you got this feeling from them if my flock—if they don't believe all the right things and then . . . Jesus comes back or everybody dies, if I taught them the wrong things, then we go to hell. It was all about being scared or worried about people. If I had a question like, "I don't really understand Jesus?" You know, like, "Oh my God! We have to save her!" There's nothing more liberating for me than being able to say I don't have to justify my own personal theology to anybody—and even to myself. I do not have to say, "You have to pick certain things to believe and then you just have to have those." It's OK to not have bullet points anymore. It's OK to just always be exploring what could be and just not having to justify it.

Beck's conclusions on the trajectory of modern religiosity reflect this approach, saying, "It is the 'credibility of his or her quest' that confers personal authority, not any efforts to conform to pre-existing truths. This de-institutionalization and subjectivization of religious truth is frequently the product of church teachings themselves which regard the obligation to go in search of subjective truth as the mark of the success of their pedagogic efforts."[90] In short, for both Beck and for Emerging Christians: "In religious matters there is no truth apart from the personal truth that one has acquired through one's own efforts."[91]

## Can We Doubt?

"To believe is human; to doubt, divine."

That's the tagline of Rollins's website and the subtitle of his book, *Insurrection*.[92] The ways Rollins and Emerging Christians think about truth are inextricably linked with their insistence on embracing *doubt* as an authentic and even necessary aspect of faith. Among "post-evangelicals" in the United Kingdom, this is in response to an "unthinking creedalism and biblical literalism."[93] As the philosopher John D. Caputo writes in *What Would Jesus Deconstruct?*, "A faith insulated from doubt fuels fanaticism and high-handed triumphalism and is in love with itself and its own power."[94] For Emerging Christians, doubt is linked to the general postmodern mistrust of language and its ability to convey truth, as explored in the previous section. Their doubts also extend to what they had been told by their former faith leaders they *should* believe about their faith. This can mean embracing doubts about big questions such as the nature of the resurrection and the nature of God. It also includes a willingness to admit that there is much about life, faith, and God that people simply cannot know with certainty.

Emerging Christians' embrace of doubt can also be considered a reaction to what they see as "modern" Christianity's conception of doubt as an enemy of faith that should be resisted. Wellman explores how Bell resists "the coercion of certainty" found within much of evangelicalism, concluding, "Bell suggests that faith characterized in forms of certainty is akin to the religion of the Pharisees. For the authors of the gospels, it can't get any worse than that."[95] Or as Alyssa puts it when describing her pastor's approach, "Doubt is okay." She said:

> [Our pastor] is very intelligent and he comes across that way speaking. Things are just presented in a way like, "We are not going to coddle you or think that you're just going to blend into what we say." It's an interaction. I've felt like I've been able to ask questions, and that doubt is OK. I don't have to feel like I know exactly everything, but it doesn't mean I don't have faith. I know I'm growing all the time and learning new things, but I've grown a lot because I've been able to argue and delve into things and ask, "Exactly why do you think that?"

Emerging Christians also describe doubt in terms of a willingness to live with tension, ambiguity, and gray areas. For Judy, that means not pressing leaders of the congregation to articulate what they believe about salvation or universalism. Recall that in her story told in chapter 3 she links doubt to intellectual freedom, emphasizing individual autonomy in people's ability to make up their own minds:

> I've never pressed [my leaders] "what do you really believe about this?" And I love it that they're comfortable leaving some gray area, saying, "It's a bit of a muddle. I'm just trying my best. But here's what seems right to me. Here's what makes sense. Here's what creation is telling me." It seems so right to me, the honoring of common sense and the mind that God gave you.

Rollins has been developing ideas around doubt since his first book, *How (Not) to Speak of God.*[96] But in an interview between he and Bell, Rollins explained that a "fundamental problem with my first book," is that while it encouraged people to embrace doubt, it did not really develop what it would mean to live with these doubts.[97] Rollins aimed to remedy this in the chapter of *Insurrection* titled "I don't have to Believe, My Pastor does that for Me." He claims that when people affirm that it is OK to doubt, it doesn't necessarily lead to any changes in their behavior. People still go to church and sing songs and hear sermons that affirm belief, providing security that everything will be okay. But Rollins sees this as people using the structures of the church—the structures of religion—to prop themselves up.

Rollins's assessment resonates with Dietrich Bonheoffer's thesis that Christians have created a "God of religion" who functions more like a psychological crutch to give them what they want and to make them feel good about themselves.[98] But Rollins wants his readers to "get rid of the need to believe."[99] Drawing on the example of Mother Teresa, Rollins says that she lived as a Christian even though her private writings have now revealed how she spent most of her life "beneath the shadow of a profound sense of God's absence."[100] Similarly, in Jay Bakker's *Faith, Doubt and Other Lines I've Crossed,* there is a chapter called "Doubting Faith" in which he draws on the work of theologian Paul Tillich to argue that doubt "is an important element of the spiritual life."[101] Bakker explains, "Doubt has caused me to grow in faith," arguing that it requires great courage to admit your doubts and through that courage (and in fellowship with others) he has been strengthened.[102]

Beck seems to echo the experiences of Emerging Christians when he writes, "In their nomadic search for religious transcendence, individuals are both believers and unbelievers at the same time."[103] For example, Ikon's Pádraig Ó Tuama, who is Catholic, recounted a story his mother told him that portrayed doubt as a part of faith rather than an enemy of faith:

> I remember as a ten-year-old being told by my mother about St. Thérèse of Lizieux . . . In her last hours before she died she went through a spiritual trauma. She was upset, and she was saying she didn't believe in God. She was asking what was going to happen to her, and she died like that . . . I don't even know if my mother has that story correct; I have never bothered to verify it, but it was a story that was told to me about a figure of tremendous sanctity within religion and within the church who was honored and who lived with tremendous anxiety and doubt. And that had always remained with me: doubt was never an enemy . . . And then Stuart Henderson, a great poet from Liverpool, in one of his poems says: "I believe doubt is a process of saying, excuse me, I have a question."[104] And when I read that . . . I recognized my

younger self that heard that story and thought I will never apologize for doubt again.[105]

In another emerging congregation, a man described how he had come to accept doubt, linking it to an experience of grace: "If I have doubt or some kind of fear, I don't have to run from it. I can face it and accept that God will be there instead of just denying it until it's absolutely undeniable . . . Recently I have felt like being [in this congregation] has helped me come to this place where I understand grace better." Among Emerging Christians, the insistence on certainty found in more conservative churches is viewed as a "faith-limiting atmosphere."[106]

A blog post from Briton David Masters, who describes himself as a "rogue theologian, freelance maverick, peace-loving anarchist and wannabe clown," further illustrates Emerging Christians' suspicion of a faith without doubt.[107] Masters writes of being on a panel discussion where he was asked, "What would happen if I was given proof of God's existence?" His initial reply to the panel was "being given absolute, incontrovertible proof for God's existence would massively influence my faith, of course it would. And I'm not sure it would be in a good way. I'm tempted to say it would destroy my faith." He used the blog to explain this reply in more detail:

> If I *know* I'm right, if I'm 100% certain, then I have nothing to learn. I don't need dialogue. Instead, I'm tempted to enforce my beliefs on others, whether that's simply by refusing to listen to them, or worse, by physical, structural or cultural violence.
>
> I want to be a person who can have a genuine, engaged conversation with anyone. This desire is central to my faith. Having all my doubts removed would destroy my faith. I know this seems counterintuitive, even paradoxical, but it's how my faith works.

Masters's post not only illustrates the ECM's embrace of doubt, it also links it to the ECM's ideal of conversation.

Embracing doubt can be difficult and uncomfortable, as Rollins acknowledges and McLaren attempts to convey in the dialogue between the characters in his early books, *A New Kind of Christian, The Story We Find Ourselves In,* and *The Last Word and the Word After That.* The substance of these books is an extended dialogue, which reveals how the characters have struggled with their doubts and have indeed struggled to come to a place where they accept that certainty is the enemy of faith. In another section of *Insurrection* titled "When God Became an Atheist," Rollins claims that Christ's cry on the cross of "My God, my God, why have you forsaken me?" is "a profoundly personal, painful, and existential atheism, based not intellectual doubts about God's existence but the felt absence of God."[108] Bakker takes a similar view of the crucifixion.[109] Rollins takes his line of thinking further in *The Idolatry of God: Breaking the Addiction to Certainty and Satisfaction.*[110] Here, he argues that Christians' attempts to find certainty in explanations churches give about the nature of sin, God, and the crucifixion/resurrection have turned God into an "idol" that we manipulate to try and satisfy our desires. For Rollins, it is better to "embrace suffering, face up to our unknowing and fully accept the difficulties of existence."[111] Bakker adds that doubt is best experienced in community:

> I find it divine to doubt. But that doesn't mean doubt is not hard and scary. It can shake your foundations—and that's why we have one another, why we have community. We can go through those days of doubt together . . . That's why Jesus and the writers of scripture talk about the importance of being in a community, the importance of gathering together—even in twos and threes—because often you just need a person who will listen, someone you can lean on and trust.[112]

As Rollins puts it in *Insurrection,* the ability to embrace doubt and enter into an experience of the absence of God is what it means to identify with Christ's crucifixion. Emerging Christians have reframed doubt as a natural, healthy, and even central part of faith—welcoming it rather than attempting to banish it, as many within evangelicalism have tried to do. Bakker captures the spirit of this well when he writes, "I am no longer concerned with eliminating doubt— my faith has become the life partner of my doubt, and I love how cute they are together."[113]

In the embrace of doubt, Emerging Christians tap into a more general willingness to live with the tension of uncertainty that is part of the contemporary Western context. Even more, the freedom to doubt affirms the autonomy of individuals, or as Frederick Buechner put it during a lecture at Harvard University: "Without somehow destroying me in the process, how could God reveal himself in a way that would leave no room for doubt? If there were no room for doubt, there would be no room for me."[114] For Buechner, as for Emerging Christians, doubt affirms that the individual is actively involved in their faith. Brandon Ambrosino, an Orthodox gay Christian, during the 2013 season of Lent wrote, "I am giving up God for Lent to make room for God."[115] Similarly, Dave Tomlinson wrote, "The assumption is often made that those who struggle with doubts and questions, those who drift away from the Church or even mainstream Christianity, are in some way spiritually substandard; that they lack the grit or piety to pursue the Christian faith. Yet the reality is quite often the reverse: it is the doubters, the people who have outgrown the hand-me-downs of religious certainty yet who continue to ask the questions, who are on a genuine faith journey."[116]

## Who is God?

Among the most controversial areas that Emerging Christians have expressed doubts about is the substitutionary theory of the atonement, a cherished doctrine within many expressions of Reformed and evangelical Christianity. Tickle writes that this is "the bitterest—or at least the most divisive" of all the questions people in the ECM are asking.[117] The substitutionary theory posits that because God is just and holy, He will not tolerate sin. For God, the cost of human sin is death. But by dying on the cross, Christ pays the debt of human sin and acts as a substitute for sinners, taking the wrath of God upon himself. One ECM pastor called this "the 'Jesus-died-on-the-cross-to-pay-for-your-sins' bullshit."

In a 2003 book, *The Lost Message of Jesus,* Steve Chalke and Alan Mann likened the substitutionary theory to "cosmic child abuse," a claim that prompted a harsh backlash for its emotive language as much as for its criticism of the theory.[118] McLaren has been among Chalke's defenders, and both Bell's and Rollins's books reject the substitutionary theory. Tickle concludes that for Emerging Christians there "is more unanimity than in some other areas of belief" that the substitutionary theory should be rejected because "the concept of an omnipotent and omniscient God who could find no better solution than that to the problem of sin is a contradiction of the first order."[119] That said, there is no agreement among Emerging Christians (typically, there is an ongoing conversation) about what might replace the substitutionary theory, though Tickle suggests a turn to Orthodox interpretations as one likely development.[120] Doubts about, and ultimately the rejection of, the substitutionary theory of the atonement reflect the way Emerging Christians think about the nature of God. In contrast to what many in the ECM see as a "modern" view of God—an authoritarian, judgmental, and interventionist father figure—is the ECM's Trinitarian, incarnated, and even at times absent God.

The nature of God is the main theme of Bell's 2013 *What We Talk About When We Talk About God.* Lamenting that "God appears to be more and more a reflection of whoever it is that happens to be talking about God at the moment,"[121] Bell compares the conceptions of God he has encountered to an Oldsmobile—outdated and about to be "left behind."[122] Picking up on the ECM's familiar critiques of "modernist," Reformed, and neo-Calvinist conceptions of God, Bell argues that this God seems to come from another era, and that continuing to think about God in these terms will ensure that

Christians are actually working *against* the way God leads people forward through history.[123]

Bakker's *Fall to Grace* argues for a "revolution" in the way people think about God. This involves moving away from what he sees as "law," as opposed to "grace"-inspired understandings of God. Bakker contrasts his grace-inspired view of God to that of conservative charismatics like Pat Robertson and Reformed evangelicals such as John Piper. Citing broadcasts of Robertson's *700 Club* television show, he notes that in 1998 Robertson warned the city of Orlando, Florida, "You're right in the way of some serious hurricanes, and I don't think I'd be waving those [gay pride] flags in God's face if I were you." And in 2010, Robertson blamed the earthquake in Haiti on "'a pact with the devil' in 1804 to get out from under French colonial rule." Similarly, in 2009 when the Evangelical Lutheran Church in America (ECLA) voted to allow gay and lesbian clergy, Piper blogged that a tornado damaged the building where the ECLA was meeting, claiming, "The tornado in Minneapolis was a gentle but firm warning to the ELCA and all of us: 'Turn from the approval of sin.'"[124] Bakker has a succinct summary of what he calls this "violent vision of God": "Follow the law, or God will annihilate your ass."[125] Or as Bolz-Weber puts it, "The image of God I was raised with was this: God is an angry bastard with a killer surveillance system who had to send his little boy (and he only had one) to suffer and die because I was bad."[126] Bakker acknowledges the violent images of God in the Hebrew Bible but argues that even in the Hebrew Bible the "tender and beautiful" images of God outweigh the violent ones. For him, the "trajectory" of scriptures "points inexorably from judgment and punishment in the distant past through time toward forgiveness and all-encompassing love." Bakker then uses the language of God as "Abba" or "daddy" to describe the "fatherly" aspect of God's character. This tender Father-God is presented by McLaren in *A New Kind of Christianity,* which Bakker acknowledges.[127]

Overall, people in the ECM see *change* in the presentation of God in the Bible, often interpreting this as a reflection of the way the writers of scripture understood God rather than a change *in* God's nature. In contrast, their critics (especially evangelicals) believe it is wrong, or even heretical, to think that God (or the Bible's presentation of God) could evolve or change.

Emerging Christians also emphasize the Trinitarian nature of God. Of course, Trinitarianism is something that Western Christianity has not *lost,* but some Emerging Christians contend that evangelicalism's presentation of God as a judgmental father has obscured the importance of the Trinity and what it says about the *relational* nature of God. Tickle argues that both the charismatic/Pentecostal movements and Greek Orthodoxy have influenced ECM conceptions of the Trinity: charismatics and Pentecostals have reintroduced the importance of the Holy Spirit, while the Greek Orthodox conception of *perichoresis* has reintroduced the idea of God as relational in and of him (or her) self. Tickle claims that the term *perichoresis* "certainly occurs with frequency in Emergence conversation" and that its English meaning is akin to "the perfect and harmonious being-together-ness of things and parts when they are in dance."[128] Irish theologian Cathy Higgins traces the influence of the Eastern *perichoretic* conception of the Trinity on ancient Celtic monastic ways of interpreting God, arguing that *perichoresis* is an apt "metaphor for Trinity" for churches in "postmodern" contexts. She writes:

> The ongoing task of the twenty-first-century faith community is to live and celebrate *perichoresis*. The embodied presence in the wider community, human and environmental, is to be a living sign of *perichoresis* . . . This means a ministry of mutuality, collegiality, team ministry, in which diverse gifts work together in the dance of life that is community . . . This is why the prayer of great thanksgiving in the Celtic Eucharist gave thanks that earth was part of heaven.[129]

Emerging Christians think of God as a community, seeing their lives with others as reflecting the nature of God. Indeed, many Emerging Christians have been influenced by Jurgen Moltmann's theology and his "Trinitarian thinking." Jones applies Moltmann's Trinitarian emphasis on community to the "relational ecclesiology" of the ECM. Picking up on Moltmann's idea that the Trinity is a "community free of dominion," Jones argues that the communal, egalitarian nature of God should be reflected in the church, concluding, "Moltmann believes that the church should be an egalitarian community of mutual love, both formed by and exhibiting the perichoretic love of the three persons of the Trinity."[130] Similarly, British theologian Michael Moynagh, who has been deeply involved with Fresh Expressions, writes of the "communion" or "community" of the Trinity in an attempt to emphasize that "the essence of church lies in relationships rather than practices."[131]

The ECM has moved away from an emphasis on the judgmental father God in the heavens to foregrounding the accepting son Jesus who lived on earth. Many Emerging Christians see God's incarnation in Jesus as a mirror on the nature of God, and what is reflected back to them is a radical but loving prophet who acted on behalf of the poor and marginalized and was willing to suffer alongside them. This also represents a decisive turn away from a "Jesus is my boyfriend" God or a God who exists to give people certainty (about this life and the next) and to satisfy their individual needs. Rather than seeking certainty and satisfaction from God and thereby turning God into an "idol," Rollins claims that Christians should live so that they subvert the social, economic, and political systems that keep people divided or oppressed. With this move, Rollins shifts much of the responsibility for "changing the world" away from an interventionist God and to communities of people who strive to live like Jesus. In *Pastrix: The Cranky, Beautiful Faith of a Sinner & Saint* (published in the United Kingdom as *Cranky, Beautiful Faith*), Bolz-Weber provides examples throughout of how she thinks God works in the world by sending others with a message for her; she writes: "But when God comes to me in the form of a friend who will be just enough of an asshole to tell me the truth, then it really is as if my heart had been ripped out of my chest and replaced with something warm and beating."[132] As a woman from one congregation put it, "There's a general embracing of a philosophy which is: we are in the world, we can be in the world, live in the world, and love God as well."

The idea of an interventionist God is thus not jettisoned altogether. But Emerging Christians understand God's intervention as consisting of having lived authentically as a human as Jesus, so now it is up to Christians to figure out what that means in their contexts. Such a view of God allows some in the ECM to identify as Christians while experiencing what we have called the "felt absence of God." For them, there is no expectation that God will intervene, like a magician, to save them from depression, anxiety, or difficult circumstances. With Rollins, they see this as a more empowering, and thus more hopeful, vision of how to think and live as Christians.

## Keep Talking—Interrogating Conventional Christianity

For Emerging Christians, the worst course of action they could take would be to settle on established positions for their movement—to stop talking. As Jones writes in *The New Christians*:

> Emergents hold that by talking to others, they get closer to the truth. That's why emergents are virtually obsessed with dialogue—they talk to Christians of other stripes, to dead Christians (via books), to non-Christians, and to one another. They talk on the phone, attend conferences, frequent coffee shops, read and comment on blogs, and buy lots of books . . . One becomes a better interpreter by sitting at a dinner party, engaging in a conversation.[133]

In the context of Emerging Christians' understanding of themselves, described in chapter 3, we see how the discursive practices of the ECM conversation can be considered a paradigmatic example of collective institutional entrepreneurship. The ECM's ongoing conversation is a mechanism that works to sustain a plurality of identities and positions within emerging congregations, which in turn allows for a strategic rebuilding of personal religiosity. At the same time, the ECM conversation has helped Emerging Christians develop ideas that justify their desire to change institutions, provide them with resources for making sense of their faith in pluralist contexts, reaffirm their individual autonomy, and legitimate their attempt to redefine what constitutes a "successful" congregational innovation.

But the emphasis on conversation frustrates many critics of the ECM, who see it as a way of avoiding difficult choices about what to believe or how to answer life's most challenging questions. They know that interrogating conventional Christianity is actively encouraged in many of the resources provided by ECM leaders. For example, McLaren's *A New Kind of Christianity: Ten Questions That Are Transforming the Faith* is one of many books which stress that conventional Christianity is afraid to ask questions while the ECM is willing to confront "hard questions" head on. It could be considered ironic, then, that some of the most strident critics of the ECM take its leaders to task for a *failure* to engage with what they see as the tough questions. D. A. Carson titles a subsection of his book critiquing the ECM, "Failure to Face the Tough Questions, Especially if they are Truth-Related."[134] For Carson and others from a neo-Calvinist or Reformed perspective, the "tough questions" have to do with issues like the truth of other religions, homosexuality, the substitutionary theory of the atonement, whether heaven and hell are literal places, and how the "inspiration" of the Bible should be understood. Critics have also asked people in the ECM to draw up "a doctrinal statement that lays out clearly what they believe." Leaders of the ECM responded by enlisting LeRon Shults, professor of theology and philosophy at Adgar University in Norway to write an "anti-statement of faith (irony noted)" that was posted on the Emergent Village website in May 2006 and reproduced in Jones's *The New Christians*.[135] Shults argues that constructing a statement of faith would be "disastrous" because a statement of faith "tends to stop conversation. Such statements can also easily become tools for manipulating or excluding people from the community. Too often they create an environment in which real conversation is avoided out of fear that critical reflection on one or more of the sacred propositions will lead to excommunication from the community."[136]

Some participants in the ECM are unsettled by the ambiguity created by the inability to answer these questions or resolve these tensions—they are worried that without some clear boundaries around faith and practice, their congregation or community risks sliding into meaninglessness. They spoke of friends leaving their emerging congregations due to frustration with the lack of boundaries. As one woman said:

> I've heard other people in the community [her neighborhood] accuse me of going to a church that's new age-y and wishy-washy or whatever. But ultimately, this is about the gospel. I don't think you can

leave a sermon and not know that this is about the gospel. [And] I don't think a healthy community can exist where everyone is forced to think exactly the same thing. Either that community is going to fall apart, or it's just going to be extremely superficial. So that's one thing about this community is that there is a little bit of wiggle room. There's a little bit of freedom to say, "Well, we're still in this community together but I don't think exactly that." I think in a lot of churches you would be asked to leave or become so uncomfortable you would simply want to leave.

It appears that ambiguity is a necessary and strategic aspect of Emerging Christians' religious orientations. Using the term "messiness" rather than ambiguity, Packard and Sanders explain: "Messiness then, is pure potential; it is process rather than product. Messiness (as represented by fluidity, contingency, provisionality, etc.) is critical for the Emerging Church because that is what distinguishes it from other corporatized and consumer-friendly churches."[137] The presence of ambiguity especially communicates to people the value placed within the ECM on intellectual freedom and asking questions. Ambiguity further encourages people to join the conversation, even as Emerging Christians develop particular ideas around the nature of truth, doubt, and the nature of God.

Institutional entrepreneurship does not completely explain the ECM, but it does provide insight on the effectiveness of discourses (conversation) as a means of facilitating change. Furthermore, collective institutional entrepreneurship emphasizes that the broader practices of Emerging Christians who actively participate in discourses through pluralist congregations maintain and reproduce the "movement" regardless of their connections to the more visible leaders and authors. Their foundational practice of talking through their faith (as well as their lack of faith and their critique of "the faith") helps us understand how the ECM's emphasis on conversation can be so effective in motivating people to change—or create alternative—institutions that create social spaces in which they believe their faith can be more authentically expressed. In this process, Emerging Christians are collective institutional entrepreneurs, using religious discourses to interrogate conventional Christianity and to create congregations where they can not only say what's really on their minds, but they can also more freely craft their legitimate, "messy," individuated religious self.

# 5

# Deconstructing Congregational Practices

> Early on we called it "liturgical eclecticism." We took a lot of stuff
> from the Book of Common Prayer, a lot of Catholic stuff. We felt
> free to borrow not only from our specific traditions but also from
> the whole tradition of the church.
> —A pastor, *describing the liturgy of his emerging congregation*

What is most striking about the renegotiated practices of the ECM is how they legitimate, and help create, *pluralist congregations* (as explored in chapter 2). This does not necessarily mean that emerging congregations are diverse in terms of ethnicity, socioeconomic, or religious background. Rather, pluralist congregations strive to be open to all and to provide an environment to enact a *strategic religiosity* (as explored in chapter 3) where a range of religious practices is both acceptable and legitimate. Such practices reinforce the ECM's "inclusive" ideal and provide mechanisms for sustaining a plurality of positions and practices within their congregations. Pluralist congregations also ensure that individuals' intellectual freedom and autonomy in pursuing their individualized religious paths are respected even within a corporate setting, thus fostering a kind of *cooperative egoism* (chapter 7). This is a complex deconstructive process involving significant renegotiations of practices in preaching, pastoral leadership, public worship, and the physical spaces and locations of "church."

We therefore characterize Emerging Christians as *collective institutional entrepreneurs*. While much of their work as *religious institutional entrepreneurs* (chapter 4) has been narrative—that is, participating in "the conversation"—their discursive work has been accompanied by a deconstruction and renegotiation of congregational practices. This process of deconstruction is embedded in the conversation, in that their new or altered practices must be continually justified with narratives. At the same time, their discourses set their new practices in deliberate contrast to evangelicalism, seeker megachurches, and mainline congregations. This contrast is described by them as a matter of conviction—intellectual and spiritual. But that weight of conviction exists alongside a continued need for some type of institution to actualize those convictions. Through their pluralist congregations, Emerging Christians craft participatory gatherings that allow individuals *multiple paths* of spirituality by permitting diverse engagement and responses to congregational activities. This capacity for hybridity in turn reflects the *heterogeneity of the religious organizational field,* from which Emerging Christians have been eager to draw new (to them) practices or to reimagine old ones. Furthermore, the pluralist structure of emerging congregations facilitates the *heterogeneity of religious identities* within a broadly defined religious orientation. Thus we see how newly shaped beliefs (heterodoxies) depend on the creation of new forms of organization (alternative congregations). As Paul DiMaggio has argued, "Recruiting or creating an environment that can enact their claims is the central task that institutional entrepreneurs face in carrying out a successful institutionalization project."[1]

## Disdain for the Megachurch and the Mainline

The ECM has two dominant conversational partners in its reshaping of congregational practice: the "seeker megachurch" and the "solemn mainline" experience.[2] A reaction to formalism, performance, and rote is implicit in the criticism of both. Criticism of the seeker megachurch is most pronounced in the United States, where it has become a dominant expression of Christianity. Indeed, Packard's analysis of the ECM comes close to reducing the movement to a counteraction against megachurches.[3] In contexts like the United Kingdom and Ireland, where there are not significant numbers of megachurches, Emerging Christians critique existing religious institutions, including mainline denominations and evangelical congregations.[4] As seen in the example of Ikon in Northern Ireland, evangelicalism need not produce megachurches to invite critiques of its practices.[5] That said, even in the United Kingdom and Ireland, Emerging Christians are well aware of American megachurches and seeker services, having seen their own (almost always smaller) evangelical congregations attempt to adopt these American techniques.

The seeker megachurch is abstracted among Emerging Christians to represent forms of church life that strategize weekend "shows" to woo and entice unbelievers.[6] One woman said, "I came from a megachurch, and I *hated* it." For her and others, the megachurch is seen as a charismatic, senior pastor–oriented service buttressed by a never-ending series of gimmicks (sketches, videos, giveaways) to persuade crowds in manipulative fashion under the guise of "winning people for the gospel" by "becoming all things to all people." One woman said, "I remember walking in every week and expecting to be wowed." Emerging Christians frequently state that meaningful spirituality does not require "a huge, expensive church." Frequent targets for criticism are slick, mall-styled megachurches with five-point sermons and large carbon-footprint campuses.[7] The strategies of megachurches are repeatedly characterized as cherry-picking elements of mainstream, consumer-driven, pop culture in a play for "relevance."

On the other end, staid and repetitive services that work familiar (often denominationally specific) processes are equally off-track for the ECM. The mainline churches are believed to be more committed to perpetuating custom and cliquish power structures than genuine spirituality. The notion of "preserving dead traditions" is refused; what one ECM leader described as "all these things that had been done in the past that's old and stale and bad." A woman with a PhD in history said, "Over the years, it didn't wear well. Ultimately, it bored me to tears." Our respondents report that in mainline congregations newcomers are only welcome if they fit into existing conventions, and clergy are seen as expending all their energy in ministry appeasing entrenched, older constituents who resist any form of adaptation. As one man said, "I began to see the danger of a structure that is so wedded to tradition and formalism." While the seeker church model may throw away all forms without consideration of their meaning and potential contribution, from the perspective of the ECM, an excessive attachment to ritual practices is both slavish and equally thoughtless. For Emerging Christians, both seeker and staid models are formulaic, having devolved religious devotion to strict rubrics, and thus have lost the base meaning, formation, and conversation necessary for the construction of significant and formative corporate worship.

Accordingly, it could be assumed that emerging congregations would have dispensed with many of the congregational practices of the churches they critique. But over the course of our research, we encountered many church leaders and observers who, after visiting emerging congregations to investigate for themselves, are disappointed that this is not often the case. Seeking radical changes in liturgy, they seem sad to discover there is still congregational music, corporate prayer, forms of preaching, tithing, and even church announcements. When finding the elements of Christian church worship from their own congregations, they are prompted to ask, "What's different?"

The ECM remains bound to paradigms of congregational worship that have developed over the past 2,000 years. Emerging Christians remain largely committed to prayer, singing, scripture, and teaching in corporate settings within structured time limits. What's different in the ECM is the careful reconsideration each element of the meeting receives before implementation. Every moment of every ECM meeting is layered with intended meanings that might be missed or misunderstood by the casual visitor. As Alan Jamieson writes, "'Emerging forms of church' may well share some of the features of established church, but they are intentionally focused on new forms of organization."[8] Of course, this also is the case in seeker megachurches and mainline congregations where careful considerations are embedded in all liturgical aspects. But in the ECM there is a fresh reconsideration that throws out obligations to all previous practices and includes a ready willingness to adopt previously unknown, unacknowledged practices from other times and traditions.[9] They also frequently subvert familiar practices by implicitly harking back to more conventional Christian experiences while simultaneously critiquing them. As one ECM leader colorfully said, "We have to shake the shit out of it."

ECM liturgy is structured to shake people out of their ordinary and familiar experience of church to create a fresh and distinctly unformulaic response to God in worship. Spontaneity is valued—not the spontaneity of spirit manifestations in prophecies or supernatural ecstatic actions, but in the unforced, free response of individuals to speak and relate to each other, to God and to one's self. Rather than tightly structuring activities or strategically planning for individual reactions, the ECM strives to create open spaces for reflection and response. Emerging gatherings also aim to have people depend less on the expertise of professionalized religious laborers (both paid and volunteer) and more on their own messy, unanticipated, and decidedly untamed responses. Further, women are seen reading scripture, giving public talks, and even bearing the brunt of leadership. Thus ECM practices attempt to minimize patriarchy, which is also a direct challenge to what Emerging Christians see as the patriarchal practices of many expressions of evangelical (or even mainline) congregations.[10] The purposes of gatherings are, then, not to "convert" or "lead" people to God through established recipes but to create open opportunities to see, hear, and respond to God. Some emerging gatherings combine a curious juxtaposition of performance and dialogue, of Christian symbols with antiritualistic presentation, while others feel more traditional in their approach. Nevertheless, at the center of the liturgy in all settings is an attempt to foster conversation that mixes clear structure with potentially awkward, unknown space for personal interactions and unguarded reflection by one's self.[11]

What is most interesting is how each aspect of an ECM meeting is contextualized to accentuate the demand for individuality, while at the same time using the historically rich resources of Christian institutional practices: a double contextualization of ancient and contemporary. This aspect of the ECM is often referred to as an "ancient-future" orientation or conversation,[12] or as Dan Kimball described it in the title of his 2003 book, a "Vintage Christianity" that draws on ancient practices to enrich contemporary Christian life.[13] Bielo considers the interplay between ancient and future so important to the dynamics of the ECM that "ancient-future" makes it into the title of two of the chapters in his book.[14] Ritual practices are intended to relate to all ages of Christianity so that practices do not become unmoored from the flow of Christian community experienced across time. This is a type of ecumenism, but an ecumenism that does not self-consciously identify with the historical ecumenical movement. Also the range of practices and alternative Christian traditions is inevitably limited by education and experience. Forced to choose from an array of alternatives, Emerging Christians quickly default to practices most accessible to them. This leads to imitation and diffusion from other influential ECM communities (like Solomon's Porch in Minneapolis) and dependence on recent publications of prayers or worship manuals or volumes on "spiritual practices" in which the authorial or editorial choices are obscured. Even an ambitious attempt to contextualize liturgy within the full range of church history will tend to be channeled through the unique networks of information (e.g., colleagues, conferences, colleges) that shape yet still constrain perspective.[15] In practice this means that the ECM is still heavily influenced by evangelicalism, while at the same time remaining critical of it.

## Areas of Deconstruction

We find four key areas in which the ECM deconstructs practice to allow and even create room for the strategic deployment of a self-possessed and nonconforming religiosity in the midst of a pluralist congregation: in its approaches to preaching, leadership, worship; and in the physical location and make up of their meeting spaces. Again, this is more than making superficial changes to services, what one member called "just a veneer over a regular kind of traditional church." One man said, "Some of the 'emergent churches' say they're postmodern models but just change the musical style or put candles out." Another man next to him quipped, "I call them fundamentalists with goatees. [Laughter]" One woman insisted she and her husband were not interested in gimmicks. "Did we just want to become part of a hipster church? If something's cool and stylish, is that enough? What's actually gonna be different? What would make this unique and special?"

### Preaching–"Am I being talked to or preached at?"

Tony Jones, writing as a theologian and an active participant in the life of Solomon's Porch, describes a typical service:

> Worship, scheduled for 5:00 pm, usually starts closer to 5:15. The music is both composed and performed by members of the church. After a song, there's a call-and-response invocation, also written and

led by someone in the church, and after some more music, Doug
[Pagitt] stands to welcome everyone, making a special point to welcome visitors. A member of the community is then interviewed about
her life, and she tells about her struggles with sexual abuse at the
hands of a former boyfriend. For the sermon, Doug sits on the afore-
mentioned stool and, for about forty minutes, guides the congregation through two chapters of the Gospel of Matthew, often referring
to the "Tuesday Night Bible Discussion Group," which helped him
prepare the sermon. At the end, he hurriedly leads a short discussion
on the Bible passage as the children are ushered back to their parents
by volunteer childcare workers.[16]

Pagitt is typical of what we call a "communitarian" preaching style, as Jones
writes, he refers to traditional preaching as "speeching"—in favor of his own
"implicatory dialogue."[17] This style is not the accepted norm in most churches
in the West. Preaching—proclaiming and explaining the "Word of God"—
was at the heart of the Reformation of the sixteenth century. The Reformers
brought the expository sermon to the center of Christian life. This is reflected
in the relatively long length of time devoted to the sermon during Protestant services, and in the architecture of many European and early American
churches, where the preaching pulpit is large, ornate, and elevated.[18] The
preacher delivered his sermon front and center, with a largely silent and passive audience who did not, except on rare occasions, challenge his message or
his interpretations of the Bible.

 Communitarian preaching subverts the Reformation-style model of a
preacher speaking at an audience. Those gathered are not considered audience members but participants. Dressing down and adopting an unassuming
manner, the leaders—if there is one or a handful identifiably present—are
facilitators of conversation. Communitarian preaching is conversational and
not confrontational. Everyone is given an opportunity to share their thoughts
without the obligation to do so. One man said, "There was a regular Sunday
service, but it wasn't like preaching. It was more like being in a junior-level
college religion course with more speaking than actually preaching, and when
I left, I just thought, 'That's kind of cool.'" Communitarian preaching more
closely reflects certain approaches to adult education, where the "teacher" is
seen as a facilitator of conversation rather than an expert on high.

 Emerging Christians contrast communitarian preaching styles favorably in
relation to their previous churches. As one woman said during a focus group:

 In the church where I grew up, it would have been very much, "This
 is what the Bible says," and the pastor would tell us some completely

unrelated story and then he'd say, "This is what the Bible says," and that was the sermon. [Laughter] There was really not much you could get out of it. But at [this church] they really do look at the ideas behind it, and they let you draw your own conclusions.

These are the types of interactions that many Emerging Christians have become accustomed to in their workplaces and their university classrooms, and they feel that the experience of church should not be any different. As Isaac said, in choosing a church he considers, "Am I being talked to or preached at?" Isaac went on to describe a sermon in his emerging congregation: "All we did was look at the same scripture, but it was a very Q and A. It was very interactive. People from the congregation talked." All this ties either into the attempt to create interactivity or to apply a belief in a communitarian hermeneutic (a separate and important theological nuance).[19] Yet it is not intended to be openness without boundaries. One member insisted, "They're not being wishy-washy. Their sermons are challenging."

Given the ECM's roots in evangelical Protestantism, it is not surprising that in their practices Emerging Christians critique the ideal of the elevated, expository preacher *and at the same time* place a great deal of importance on verbal communication in their meetings. By whatever name (one member called it "the theology lecture"), preaching is important, and the use of scripture remains central to most gatherings, even when scripture can take a very subtle, even covert, aspect of the service. Gerardo's observations at Solomon's Porch affirm Jones's observation that "the Bible is referred to as a 'member of the community' with whom we are in conversation, and the communal interpretation of a text bubbles up from the life of the community."[20] In some cases, perhaps only one verse is read—rather stated—in the whole time, but the thoughts and considerations play with themes and events recounted in scripture. For example, "who is my neighbor" discourse on the "Good Samaritan" can be used in reflections on marginality and justice. Greek words like *kenosis* (self-emptying) can inspire reflections on more abstract, existential themes. Alternative Bible translations can be introduced to again provoke the unfamiliar in the seemingly familiar. The Psalms or the Genesis creation story can be invoked when discussing the environmental crisis. Sometimes a book is absent (just paper, on screen, or from memory), but other times "the book" is exaggerated, a massive tome used for a prop to evoke a theatrical element in the service. The press of the ancient and the pull of the contemporary are always present in the use of the Bible. In all cases the Bible is present while attempting to keep a doctrinaire, dogmatic insistence at bay.

*Provocative preaching* is strikingly different from communitarian preaching. The provocative preacher, at least initially, delivers an uninterrupted, energetic monologue, with the intent to shake familiar notions, move to unexpected rhetorical spaces, and push listeners to reflection. One man justified the style this way:

> When you codify a story and it's 2,000 years old and it's told over and over again, one thing that gets lost is the element of surprise. "Oh yeah, Jesus was crucified and put in a tomb and rose from the dead," all that stuff. There's nothing surprising about it anymore. We need to be able to come back to the text and keep asking the question: Is the conventional reading of this not the right one? In fact, is the opposite of the conventional reading worth considering?

The style of Peter Rollins's preaching (described in chapter 1), in which he takes on the role of religious *provocateur,* is an example of this. As Katharine Sarah Moody writes, Rollins evokes "rhetorical figures such as the prophet, the pirate, the heretic, and the trickster, who disrupt and disturb, creating openings for the incoming event of the other, for the transformation and conversion of current structures, and for the possibility of a new world, of new ways of thinking and being otherwise."[21] Other prominent examples of provocative preachers include Jay Bakker, formerly at Revolution Church in Brooklyn, New York, and now at Revolution Church in Minneapolis;[22] Erwin McManus of Mosaic in Los Angeles;[23] and Rob Bell, founding (and now former) pastor of Mars Hill Community Church in Grand Rapids, Michigan.[24] If we include writing as a form of preaching, Tony Jones's consistent stream of blog posts regularly provoke conversation and often outright controversy.

The provocateur in the ECM is not comfortable being the functional representative of the faith on behalf of the faithful, but sees him- or herself as the point of instigation to mobilize others into taking a stand somewhere. The provocateur, what V. I. Lenin defined as "the agitator,"[25] moves away from easing anxieties to raising them, from a comforting tone to removing a too easy smugness, and from giving assurance to urging individual initiative and risk taking. The enemy for these provocateurs is rarely "the world" (which is treated sympathetically) but rather the capital "C" Church that has corrupted rather than modeled the way of Jesus, pursued power over servant-hood, caused pain more than pleasure, and exploited rather than inspired the masses. The preaching by the provocateur is an act of justice to restore that which was lost; to proclaim evil present in the seemingly holy; and to redefine a path of godliness that denies the name godliness because of its sanctimonious, distancing, and (from their point of view) ultimately destructive connotations.

Nearly all the ECM leaders—the primary "preachers" we've spoken with— believe they talk too much. Yet they can't seem to get away from occupying the provocative, vision-sharing, direction-defining moment given to them by those who come to hear them, and by the very structure of congregationalism inherent in most forms of the ECM (which prompts speaking by a charismatic leader as an anchor point to gatherings).[26] While ECM leaders who occupy prominent roles stress nonhierarchical and highly relational modes of leadership, they remain charismatic leaders who attract and maintain followers. By charismatic, we mean Max Weber's definition of central figures who speak and act in ways that resonate with the needs and desires of followers as they call for value rational ways of living, provoking followers to vision-centered morality and ideal-motivated relationships inside and outside the congregation.[27]

These two types of preaching, communitarian and provocative, can be understood as alternative practices developed in the aftermath of the deconstruction of the long or staid monologue sermon. People in the ECM do not view that style of sermon as communicating much worth to the Christian community; rather, they see more authentic Christianity emerging from the unhindered conversation of the wider community or engaging with the difficult propositions of the provocateur. One woman said, "The difference is they don't lead you down this straight path like you find in an evangelical church or a Catholic Church where you can predict what kind of theology path they're going to lead you down. Here, you're never quite sure what path they're going down. [Laughter]"

## Leadership—"It doesn't seem like there's a hierarchy."

The ambiguous position of leaders that is reflected in forms of preaching extends to other aspects of emerging congregations, including decision-making and the oversight of congregational activities. For Packard, one of the primary ways in which emerging congregations resisted institutionalization was through their "flat" leadership structures and their ambivalence toward ordained clergy.[28] In many of the congregations he studied, ordained participants were either employed only on a part-time basis or were careful to spread their responsibilities among others in the congregation. This allowed for a more egalitarian form of congregational government and acted as a mechanism to resist decrees coming from distant denominational institutions.[29] Tickle also notes the prevalence of part-time clergy in emerging congregations, with those taking on this role believing that it is important that they keep secular employment—in the spirit of missionary-apostle Saint Paul, who was after all a tentmaker.[30] Tony Jones acknowledges this deliberate flattening of leadership in the title of his book, *The Church is Flat*.[31]

The ideal of flattening the church is a response to some Emerging Christians' previous experiences of church, which featured what they now see as unhealthy relationships with senior pastors. This especially was an issue for those from evangelical or charismatic backgrounds, where pastors are often treated like "stars" and attract followers through the force of their personality. That said, there is considerable variety in the roles taken on by leaders in emerging congregations. In some congregations, the role of a pastor or team of leaders is still central in providing the preaching and teaching that draws people in. Some leaders even exude a guru-like quality in attracting followers.

But even when leaders are prominent in their congregations, members contrast the style of these leaders with pastors in their former churches. For example, Stephen said about his previous pastor, "I felt like he was preaching more to glorify himself instead of God. Whereas here at [our church] it's evident that it's not about that." Celebrity and self-centeredness is universally condemned, while current pastors are viewed as thoughtful, unaffected, and personal. Janice said hearing her pastor was what initially brought her to the church, and she finds him to be an "effective" and relevant speaker. Theresa described her pastor's speaking as "so profound, it really spoke to my heart." In a focus group conversation, Rod said, "I am big on the messages because they're usually challenging. They make sense. And that's what kept me going back." Vicki responded by saying, "[Our pastor's messages] spoke to me. And he answered a lot of questions that I didn't even realize I had in my head. He was talking to me, and he made me thirst for more."

Furthermore, people perceived their current pastors as "genuine," "authentic," and "humble." Rick said, "[Our pastor] has such a gift of being so transparent, but just so refreshing. Nothing against former pastors, but I just need to see someone who can really be genuine—you know, he can be human." Rather than being showy or ostentatious, Lilly characterized her church leaders by saying, "They all keep a low-key profile . . . You don't have the Sunday bulletin that has senior pastor, music minister, Sunday school director. That's all gone." One member made a point of saying there are no "holier-than-thou" leaders at their church. Other comments focusing on the "humility" of pastors included Andy, who said, "He's a humble guy. Tortured, but humble." Jane said, "I was struck by the fact that the pastors didn't seem to take themselves too seriously." Another man said, "I hate to use the word, but they were authentic. I mean, they were just real guys." Micah said, "It was just a real, genuine approach to living the life of what we call 'a Christian' that I hadn't seen in a very long time, if ever, in leadership."

In some of the congregations visited, the leaders were in a sense "famous," or well known within the ECM, but did not play up that aspect of their ministry. It appeared many people were unaware of their pastors' books and speaking engagements. In a focus group conversation, Isaac talked about "the humility of leadership" of his "famous" pastor in contrast with his experience elsewhere: "I've visited some other churches around here where the pastors were well-known authors, and they were mentioning where the book was on Amazon." Others in the room were surprised by this, saying, "No . . . come on," along with murmurs of astonishment. Another member added, "I don't think I've ever really heard [our pastor] talk about *his* books." In another focus group, a member said, "A lot of the people in the church don't even realize how well known [our pastor] is." Others chimed in, "Right, that's true." A former receptionist at her emerging congregation said, "There would be these people coming in all the time to see [our pastor] and would call asking, 'Is [he] going to be talking this Sunday? Could I actually see him?' Meanwhile people who have gone to [our church] for years don't realize how much he's doing."

The ideal congregational structure repeatedly described by Emerging Christians is decentralized, egalitarian, spontaneous, and relational, with low overhead and an energizing atmosphere. At the same time, people in some congregations worried that they relied too much on their pastors. One woman said, "If something happened to him—oh God, what would we do?" Another woman said, "There's a huge percentage of people who just come on Sunday mornings, and [our pastor] is a huge part of that, and how many of those people would leave if [he] was gone?" She added, "He's half of the service . . . It's hard because you don't want to have that dependency on him. At the same time he's the one who had the whole idea for the church and a general feeling of which way to take it. How can he not be a huge part of it?"

Ikon has gone further than most groups in trying to minimize dependence on leaders. In an interview with Rollins in *Christian Century,* he said:

> Paradoxically, I say, "Ikon doesn't care about you. Ikon doesn't give a crap if you are going through a divorce. The only person who cares is the person sitting beside you, and if that person doesn't care, you're stuffed." People will say, "I left the church because they didn't phone me when my dad died, and that was really hurtful." But the problem is not that the church didn't phone but that it promised to phone. I say, "Ikon ain't ever gonna phone ya." Pete Rollins might. But if he does, it will be as Pete Rollins and not as a representative of Ikon. Ikon will never notice if you don't come. But if you've made a connection with the person sitting next to you, that person might.

Later in the interview, Rollins went on to say, "Ikon is like the people who run a pub. It's not their responsibility to help the patrons become friends. But they create a space in which people can actually encounter each other." Rollins's interview illustrates how at Ikon people strive to shift responsibility from leaders and an institutional church, which is somehow seen as having a duty to support people during times of trauma and stress ("the church . . . promised to phone"), to individual Christians who should love each other enough to offer their personal support.

But Ikon's Sarah Williamson pointed out that issues arose around "pastoral care" due to this approach to leadership. As Ikon's gatherings and small groups were at times deliberately provocative, it was thought that Ikon could be upsetting people and then leaving them without any means of support to work through difficult issues. Williamson admitted that her frustration around the lack of pastoral concern from Ikon even led to her leaving the Cyndicate (the name for Ikon's core planning group) for some time.[32] As Williamson explains:

> It was the analogy of a doughnut, which is Pete's analogy, that Ikon is like the center of a doughnut—yeah, non-existent. So Ikon is a gravitational force which kind of brings people together and is nothing in itself. So people in Ikon, they care for each other, but Ikon as an organization does not care for you. I totally understand philosophically why that's a very interesting point. But I think I have significant reservations about it.

Ikon's ideal of nonmembership emphasizes that people are not expected to be committed to Ikon, or to use it or its (nonexistent?) leaders as spiritual or emotional crutches.[33] Rather, they are expected to be committed to others—whether in Ikon or not—and to express their care by taking responsibility for their individual responses to others.

While this approach has clear drawbacks, Ikon is removing the responsibility for care from clergy and church institutions to individual Christians. While Ikon's choice was deliberate, people in one congregation described a similar value when recounting the loss of their lead pastor. They found his unplanned absence to be empowering. One congregant described it as a "community-led community," saying that as the community pulled together it "showed our true colors" and "showed we weren't a pastor-oriented community like every other church in the world is. The pastor's not there, nobody knows what to do. But we're like, 'Well, we don't have somebody to talk to us every week, so let's pull ourselves up by our bootstraps and make it happen because we love each other and we love this place.'" Experiences like these introduce the viability of valid congregational life without a centralized leader.

Other Emerging Christians described how the flattening of their congregations led to more personal involvement in decision-making and genuine friendships with their pastors, experiences they contrasted with their previous congregations. One woman said, "It doesn't seem like there's a hierarchy of people. They're us." Another woman said the leadership does "not talk down, but just [says] 'We're in this together. This is what we want. Do you agree? OK, let's work on this together.'" Another woman said, "To me it is that idea of the dialogue, the fact that the leaders say, 'Here this is what we want to do. Here's our heart, here's our plan, what do you guys think?' And there's always that sense of 'we are on this mission together,' and 'you're invited to do what we're doing right now.' The fact that we have the chance to speak up. I feel like I can walk up to [our pastor] or e-mail him and go, 'That was cool, what was that?' And there's going to be a dialogue. That's really unique." As another woman said about her pastor, "A lot of people feel they have a relationship with [him], including everyone at this table, which is an alien concept for a lot of people. 'A relationship with your pastor, oooh.' That's incredible."

Most Emerging Christians recognize that this apparent decentralization results in certain people in their congregations holding more influence in decision-making. Lilly said, "We don't announce everything from the pulpit that's going to happen like small groups or other little groups. We have our own way of communicating and getting words out." Yet, one astute member said, "The net effect of some of these aversions—at least organizationally—is it's always the really strong personalities that drive the church and sometimes drive it off in one direction before the community corrects it because we haven't spent very much time actually developing ground rules." One man said, "It's radically exclusive, but a benign dictatorship." He continued, "There's discomfort with confessions of faith because that begins to be exclusive: 'We believe this unlike those other people.' But I wonder too if it isn't partly a distrust of the community. Like saying, 'We don't trust the community to develop a confession. We want to be controlling the agenda from the pulpit.'" Another woman in the conversation said, "We are not a democracy. We don't have membership. We don't have a vote. I don't even know who's on the board. And I've been here for three years!" Tony Jones talked in a focus group about the power relations of emerging congregations. He said there is a recognition that speakers take a privileged position in their talking, for example by speaking uninterrupted for up to thirty minutes during their gatherings. Even if they say, "You can disagree with me," they have command of the platform. One college professor even described how a good teacher can create an environment in which individuals appear to have freedom to make decisions, but they are being "facilitated." Elaine said, "Lack of central control is something that I've noticed about this church." Following up, Stella said, "Sometimes it can be an issue, because you don't know who is in control." Vicki said, "We may not be organized from time to time, but we're never without somebody offering to volunteer, or offering to help, I mean it's just a family unit, that's all, that's what I think of it as."

In short, the ambiguity of structure in emerging congregations, under a supposed egalitarianism, leads to a type of oligarchy that concentrates influence and decision-making to an elite few. This affirms Robert Michels's famous "iron law of oligarchy," a surprising conclusion that resulted from a groundbreaking study of egalitarian-minded activists who formed a volunteer organization.[34] He demonstrated that certain people had the time and opportunities to work for the organization, and by virtue of their availability and the evolution of their insider status, a small group eventually had enormous control over setting agendas and determining organizational decision-making. In sum, all organizations, even those highly committed to nonhierarchical relationships, become ruled by an oligarchic structure due to the demands of keeping the organization functioning.

So, emerging congregations achieve varying levels of "flatness" in their leadership. "Leaderless" congregations are never truly leaderless because some people will inevitably assert themselves and assume more power in decision-making and shaping congregational activities. That said, emerging congregations demonstrate a high degree of self-awareness in their attempts to subvert the hierarchical leadership they have experienced in evangelical or mainline congregations. From behind-the-scenes decision-making to public worship, emerging congregations strive to distribute power and get everyone involved.

### Public Worship—"Everyone can respond to God in their own way."

Traditionally, liturgical practices are designed to draw people into an experience of worship of God—and this also is part of their purpose in emerging congregations. Liturgy refers to how a religious group publically worships and is often equated with ritual, which in the context of public congregational worship consists of the repetitive, meaning-filled elements that make up liturgies. Evangelicals historically believe themselves to be nonliturgical; for example, evangelicals have often contrasted their forms of worship with the supposedly more ritualized Roman Catholic or Anglican worship. Of course, the form and structures of evangelical services follow patterns that constitute a liturgy of its own, whether or not evangelicals are comfortable calling it by that name.

There is no such thing as a "typical" liturgical experience in any emerging congregation, with practices varying widely within congregations as well as across different congregations, groups, and collectives. Yet we agree with Bielo that a curious mix of sacramentalism and ahistoricism characterizes the liturgy of the ECM.[35] Sacramentalism is evident by the seriousness and theological import given to classic rituals of baptism, corporate prayer, and the Lord's Supper. At the same time, these rituals are stripped of their various native contexts and "re-traditioned" into experimental gatherings. As Phil Snider writes, "The emerging moment helped Christians from a variety of contexts to (1) encounter wider Christian traditions that have come before and

(2) consider ways to reappropriate these traditions in creative, authentic, and culturally accessible ways."[36] Pastor Nadia Bolz-Weber, a prominent voice in ECM circles, exhorts, "Let's be innovative with the traditions that have been passed down to us and consider ways we might be caretakers of them in culturally appropriate ways."[37] Bolz-Weber speaks out of her own experience at House for All Sinners and Saints in Denver, which is affiliated with the Evangelical Lutheran Church in America and so follows a liturgical calendar.

The ECM's historical connections with evangelicalism mean that its reconstruction of liturgy is in many ways a reaction against the implicit liturgies of evangelicalism, as well as a "discovery" and incorporation of the liturgical practices of other Christian traditions.[38] This process is captured well in the title of Doug Gay's book, *Remixing the Church,* in which he describes how Emerging Christians have retrieved ancient Christian practices, including utilizing the church calendar, set prayers, ritual action (such as observing Ash Wednesday, Lent, and Easter Vigil), images and icons, spiritual exercises, and spiritual rules (as developed by monastics, such as the Benedictines). Both Gay and Bielo locate this process within the ECM's "ancient-future" conversation. Bielo documents this "staying connected to church history" through "closer attention to the annual church calendar than conservative Evangelicals have required; designing multisensory worship experiences; performing monastic disciplines; integrating pre-Reformation theologians into public and private reading rituals; and rethinking the role of materiality in worship events."[39] Dave Tomlinson labels himself a "progressive orthodox" and asserts, "My interest lies in finding expressions of Christianity that are both rooted in the originating sources of the Christian faith and which also make sense to people today."[40] Ikon's gatherings provide some of the more dramatic examples of subverted rituals. Almost every Ikon gathering prominently features a ritualized element near the conclusion of the event (although the format of the "ritual" is different every time), often including distributing a physical object that people can take home with them. Ikon's "transformance art" performances create multisensory experiences involving words and the movement of people's bodies through physical space, all of which are in implicit dialogue with conventional Christian liturgy.

Seeker megachurches have striven to make liturgies simple and understandable to the "unbeliever" or the "unchurched."[41] But seeker churches do not make all aspects of their services, such as communion, open to the uninitiated. Mainline churches try to focus people's minds and spirits on worship. Like evangelical congregations, they reserve some aspects of their services, like communion, for those who have been confirmed in their church. In contrast to both seeker and mainline services, Emerging Christians' liturgies are open, designed to cater to a pluralist congregation that makes everyone—even atheists or unbelievers—feel welcome to participate.[42] Times of "open re-sponse" are a common feature in ECM services, a general time in which those present are given options of what they may do as part of the liturgy—including the option to sit in their chair and do nothing. Even more, drawing people into an experience of worship does not need to be the primary purpose of emerging liturgies. Rollins has explained that Ikon's public events should not be under-stood as worship but rather as "transformance art," carefully crafted experi-ences that may disturb those present, guide them through an experience of the absence of God, and ultimately provoke them to live like Christians outside the walls of the church. Overall, the reworking of ritual practice is common among emerging congregations, particularly the practice of communion, or Eucharist.

In short, emerging congregations are characterized by intentional efforts to keep the atmosphere open for the ambiguous, the uncommitted, and the unbeliever. It is not unusual for even the most ardent and faithful of those at-tending to accentuate the "questions" and experiences of doubt at the same time as they participate in recognizable rituals. And the ECM allows, even encourages, the full engagement of even the most complete nonbelievers in ways that are stereotypically understood to be "religious." Recall in chapter 3 the liturgical inclusion of Judy's atheist husband who regularly participated in communion at their church. Emerging congregations allow for a personal, strategic enactment of religiosity that is dynamic, responsive, and diverse.

Variety is also important for allowing individuals to experience God in their own way. For example, in a focus group conversation one woman said about her emerging congregation:

> We have all these very experiential things. Our services aren't just the pastor up front talking at us. We have the prayer path, and we have these spaces you can go to if you just need to be with Jesus alone. There's all these very experiential things set up to really draw you into communion with God.

Following this, Joseph explained the variety of liturgical elements in terms of providing different paths for different individuals to experience God:

> If you bring all those elements together [i.e., prayer labyrinths, art, different types of music, different types of expression, etc.] and mix them up, then you've got a greater chance of somebody saying, "You know what? Music doesn't really do it for me. But if I can go and take communion and then go and say a prayer while I light a candle . . . " Then you've created a path for someone to follow in their worship of

God. And you've created something for them to do and something for them to incorporate into their life that they didn't necessarily have before.

In scheduled "gatherings," actions and sequences of events are explained briefly with small "how-tos." For things left unexplained, insiders hospitably cozy up to guests to guide them through welcome times, corporate prayer, serving of the elements of communion, or after-service functions. New people move in and out smoothly, and those that stay often take up key roles in future services. The ECM may appear to be an insiders-only zone where sometimes abstract theological and philosophical ministry points are debated; but in their public gatherings, Emerging Christians attempt to hold onto aspects of marginality, elevate simple human connections, and allow for those most recently incorporated to remind longer-term members what it is like not to belong to the group.

Given evangelicalism's comparative neglect of communion, it is perhaps no surprise that much of the subversion of ritual in the ECM has focused on communion practices. We see the practice of communion as the most conspicuous example of a subverted ritual. Jones describes it as "the first and most notable concrete practice in the eight ECM congregations that I studied."[43] One of Ikon's early gatherings was a parody of a communion celebration. Advertised with a poster from an Alpha course that portrayed what one Ikon participant called "smiling, happy people," Ikon concluded the event with a communion "service" featuring champagne and chocolate cake—indicating that the evangelical emphasis on being "happy" and their sweeping the dark and doubting aspects of Christianity under the carpet ultimately undervalued the most serious of Christian sacraments. Evangelical churches often have communion quarterly or once per month compared to the weekly or daily practice of communion in other traditions. Emerging Christians have reworked communion not only in terms of frequency (with many ECM groups having communion more than once per month) but also in *how* communion is distributed.

For Emerging Christians, serving communion is a strategic place for mixing what can often be a serious, somber time with highly ritualistic aspects ("Take this bread," "Take this cup") and reference to the passion of Christ. Whether grape juice or wine (and Emerging Christians tend to think of grape juice as an unnecessary sanitization of Jesus's inaugurated practice, a prudish and childish caution against the dangers of alcohol, so wine is much preferred), the more surprising element is what is used for bread. Sliced bread from the supermarket is much too crass for the sacredness of the moment, so artisan baked bread is preferred. Indian naan bread is often used, and Jewish matzo wafers can provide a historical ambiance. Sometimes communion is done individually through pulling pieces of bread and dipping them into a chalice of wine at two or three tables distributed around a room. Other times people are asked to "serve each other" by handing bread to others for breaking or even breaking off pieces for others. Shared cups are not common (too many health issues) nor are preloaded plastic cups (which evoke supermarket disposable packaging that demeans the importance of the moment). Instead, the act of breaking bread and the act of pouring wine to drink add to the communal activity. There is often no need to wait on each other before consuming; it is not unusual for conversation to break out, and communion can become a moment for catching up or meeting someone new. The ritual of communion is most often surrounded by an ancient aura, and words, vessels, and physical elements of communion can reinforce an ancient ambience; yet the same can say "today" just as loudly through the incorporation of conversational and unfamiliar words. A sense of the contemporary can also involve the use of everyday, common vessels to drink and to hold or pass the elements, and to use bread and wine recognizable from a restaurant or a Whole Foods grocery store. In most cases, communion is much more informal and chaotic than in evangelical or other Christian churches, and laypeople have a much more prominent role in distributing and partaking of it.

How communion is carried out is not set permanently, and leaders frequently talk about how they "tried something different" at various points in their ministries. At Solomon's Porch, communion is shared along with corporate prayer in which words are read that call on attendees to draw closer to God, prepare their lives for service, and commit to a pleasing way of living. Mars Hill in Grand Rapids utilizes prayers from saints across history, read together during the service, and mixes traditional hymns with wholly original music as a background for a leader-structured call and response. "Low church" Christians find this unfamiliar, while "high church" Christians find the unconventional wording awkward. Those with little, distant, or no Christian background accept it as another aspect of church, all of which for them is new and unexpected and becomes familiar and normalized through steady attendance.

A woman who said, "I'm a Catholic," described her experience of communion in an emerging congregation this way:

> I have to have communion every week . . . when communion actually took place, I was just in awe, you know, how everybody did different things, and it was a very solemn moment . . . You can have a different feeling or you can do a different thing that you want to speak to God with. It's not going to be the same every week and you can approach it in a different fashion each time that you come. Unlike being

a Catholic, and you go and you get your bread and your wine, and you have your silent time to pray. This was just awesome to me.

Others talked about how they appreciated the open-ended nature of communion in congregations, in which people were invited to partake, abstain, or become engaged in other activities during the communion period. As Stacey said, during communion "there are prayer stations. There are prayer counselors. There are candles, so if you just want to have a meaningful time with the Lord there." Another woman described it as "many ways to respond to the call of God." She said:

> You can go to a prayer station. You can make your financial offering as a gift of worship. You can come up and serve yourself or someone else communion, or you can go to the stations in the back and be served by a minister. Or you can just stay sitting in your chair and be alone with God.

The element of choice underlines individuals' autonomy in worship, allowing wide avenues of response and negating any pressure to conform. Isaac said:

> We have this open-ended period of time . . . Where are you and what are you ready for? Do you want to have prayer? Do you want to do your offering? Are you worried about somebody and you want to do a prayer request? Do you want to do communion? I grew up in churches that did communion once a month, so communion every week kind of feels a little bit weird to me, but I love the fact that I can choose when to go, and I usually try to do it once a month or something . . . So that free time in the middle where you're sort of mulling the sermon, you might be moved in some way, you might want to reflect, you might just want to pray. I do mostly just sit and hang out. And then the music starts again, but it's sort of slow, actually it starts during that, and then you start to join in and that sort of leaves on a sort of an upbeat. That whole arc of beginning to end is just to me the perfect sequence.

Elaine summarized, saying, "I really fell in love with the communion time because everybody can respond to God in their own way." Another woman said that in this free-choice communion format, "there's no threat to my ideas. There's no being called out wrong if I don't phrase something correctly or if I don't use the proper terms or whatever it may be."

It is this freedom, openness, and inclusivity around who may partake of communion, how often, and in what manner that makes this ritual the most "subverted" of the practices undertaken in emerging congregations. It is a moment in ECM gatherings that allows the widest range of enactment of one's religiosity. All other Christian denominations or congregations have strict boundaries around who may or may not receive communion, which encourages uniformity—rather than the plurality for which emerging congregations strive. Scheduling and style of partaking are also firmly set. So through an examination of the practice of communion we can see how a certain hybridity happens in the liturgy of ECM services. One leader said, "Early on we called it 'liturgical eclecticism.'" He said, "We took a lot of stuff from the Book of Common Prayer, a lot of Catholic stuff. We felt free to borrow not only from our specific traditions but from the whole tradition of the church." In another church, Blake said, "This church is doing stuff like liturgy and daily prayers and the church calendar, which was really foreign to my Baptist background." He enjoyed it. And in yet another church, one woman said, "Every now and then, we'll say the Apostle's Creed. [Our leader] almost does it as a reminder, 'By the way, this is how we're connected in some way to historical church.'"

In sum, the varied liturgical practices of the ECM can be understood as deconstructing the liturgical practices of other Christian traditions, especially evangelicalism, with its noisy denial of liturgy and its relative downgrading of communion.[44] At the same time, the deliberate attempt to promote inclusivity and openness reinforces the ideal of the pluralist congregation. The intention is to allow for what Matthew Guest and Steve Taylor describe as "a less prescriptive and more multidimensional engagement."[45] While the liturgical time has a structure, it is one intended to feature expansive opportunity for approaching one's own sense of their religious identity—however indeterminate that may be.

## Location—"The space doesn't feel like church."

Public spaces such as restaurants and art museums or transitional spaces like storefronts and empty warehouses are examples of buildings repurposed for congregational use in the ECM. Such spaces are rented or essentially borrowed, such as in the use of coffeehouses or art galleries; alternatively, permanent spaces are often refurbished spaces, for example, old churches, unused barns, or renovated warehouses. One man described his congregation, saying, "The space itself was very different from anything that I associated with church." There is an intentional effort to reconstruct spaces to move away from pews, altars, or elevated pulpits. If such spaces are not available, they are created. One woman described their gathering place as "like a coffee shop." In another sanctuary, a high, industrial ceiling simultaneously evoked the ambiance of a cathedral and a gymnasium for one participant. Sharon said about another building, "It was very loftish and we were really excited because it just looked like a loft. That was it. We were like, 'That looks like a loft.'"

Both architecture and seating arrangements push away stereotypical notions of church in order to emphasize egalitarianism, artistry, and dialogue. The arrangement is simple more than stoic. Outer walls are often where welcome tables, prayer/communion stations, and storage are placed. Low lighting (sometimes with votive candles) promotes a contemplative mood. For some, these arrangements are unsettling. Hailey said, "It freaked me out walking in at first because I was like, oh my gosh, it's dark. There's nothing like—no pews. There's all these couches." For others, the lack of "churchy-ness" was critical to the decision to join their congregation. One man said, "The space that we're sitting in now doesn't feel like a church room to me, and that's important to me because I don't have much interest in the other aspects of what I grew up in as far as church is concerned."

For Emerging Christians, the locations and physical spaces in which their preaching and worship take place matter a lot. They see these physical places and spaces as extensions of the values they wish to live out; values that include being open and inclusive, cultivating community, promoting social justice, and so on. Emerging Christians are very intentional about where they locate themselves geographically, how they then organize and decorate the spaces they inhabit, and what secular cultural resources they bring to their gatherings. Bielo explains that the geographic location of "New City," a "church plant" in Oakley, Ohio, was chosen for very specific reasons:

> Their church would be in Oakley, a middle-class urban neighbourhood six miles northeast of downtown Cincinnati. Why this neighbourhood? Josh's official Church Plant Proposal announces on the opening page, "approximately 60,000 people live within seven minutes of Oakley Square," a fact Josh and other launch team members committed to memory. Josh "strongly encouraged" the entire launch team to leave their current residence and move to or near Oakley. The model of evangelism and social engagement typical of Evangelical megachurches . . . is to return to suburbia following a day's labor in the city. Following his training at Princeton and his consumption of missional resources, this model was flawed and the move from Mason to Oakley was not just a good idea; it was necessary.[46]

As New City shows, the ECM situates itself as an urban phenomenon, and the city itself is among its most valuable religious resources: highly urbanized locations allow ECM groups to select among a variety of meeting spaces from which to correlate the sacred and the profane and thereby accentuate God's immanence. Indeed, the ECM does not seem to be present in rural locations—although some isolated individuals may share some of the orientations and ideas of their emerging counterparts in cities. More importantly, the ECM is actively antisuburban, with many Emerging Christians deliberately moving *out of* the suburbs and exurbs and into inner cities as a lifestyle choice. This can be seen in the example of New City, as well as in the lives of new monastics, who, like Shane Claiborne and the Simple Way in Philadelphia, choose to live together in community in deprived areas of inner cities. This self-conscious urbanness is one way in which Emerging Christians see themselves as living out the gospel—identifying with the needs of the poor and disadvantaged rather than serving the economically privileged who populate the suburbs.

Emerging Christians' propensity to select from a variety of meeting spaces in urban areas also means that they are reluctant to have their gathering spaces resemble iconic church buildings. Our previous descriptions of pub churches, conferences, online networks, and neo-monastic communities (chapter 1) stress that Emerging Christians most emphatically do not organize their Christian lives around traditional church buildings. They meet in a variety of locations, on various days of the week. Emerging Christians also may eschew Sunday morning services and prefer Sunday evening or midweek gatherings to facilitate the demands of their busy lives. The use of public, secular spaces is particularly significant since they intentionally serve to reduce the distance between a transcendent, inaccessible God and to encourage an orientation toward the immanent ubiquity of God. It also avoids highly institutionalized expectations or "prompts" regarding the propriety of their religious actions while "at church."

Conscientiousness regarding the physicality of ECM gatherings does involve not only the *outside* geography and architecture but also what happens *inside* the building. The way Emerging Christians organize their meeting spaces is different from traditional churches. Solomon's Porch is noted among emerging congregations for its "seating in the round," where they arrange comfy couches in concentric circles around a central stool for the "preacher."[47] Other groups that meet in pubs gather around small tables, facilitating intimate conversations. Still other ECM groups vary the types of spaces they interact in. Thinplaces, "a loosely knit community of ancient-future worshipers in Cincinnati," organizes around three events: a biweekly "artwalk" in a local museum, a weekly journaling group, and a monthly "maproom."[48] Maproom could be likened to an art installation, where people are invited to visit various stations to meditate on a theme. Ikon gatherings, described as "transformance art," are similar to maproom. In recent years, Ikon gatherings have migrated from place to place throughout Belfast, including the crypt of a nonsubscribing Presbyterian church, unused police barracks, the MAC art museum, and the Black Box bar/music venue—the places were selected depending on what type of physical space was required for the event.

ECM communities that meet consistently in the same physical space are intentional about how they decorate it. At Solomon's Porch, original art, mostly from the congregation, is displayed on the walls. On the far wall is a large cross—perhaps the only vestige of the original architecture of the refurbished church where this self-described collective meets—but around the bottom of this wall and creeping up both sides of the cross are a series of portraits, varied head-and-shoulders images of men and women from the congregation. Although never stated explicitly, the casual placement of parishioners' portraits immediately stands out as a reappropriation of images of historic Christian saints. Every evangelical learns through Bible study that Paul addressed the "saints" in his New Testament letters, and by that he meant ordinary believers gathered in the congregation. All Christians are "saints," and Solomon's Porch is creating a prominent place for the display of their everyday saints, giving their pictures a special, even sacred, space next to the cross at the focal point of the interior. The use of artists from the congregation to freely create portraits of their friends and fellow members in this way is a type of contextualization of contemporary culture assimilated into the experience of the church.

Contemporary churches, especially evangelical expressions like the seeker megachurch, have incorporated readily accessible cultural resources in the form of music styles (i.e., Christian rock), conversational preaching, current Bible translations, use of sketches and audiovisuals, and more intentional use of graphic arts. In contrast, Emerging Christians have been highly critical of what to them seems an attempt to create a segregated "contemporary Christian culture" that smacks of derivative consumerism.[49] They also see this as taking a half-step toward the world in order to mask old-school orthodoxy. For Emerging Christians, this type of false "relevance" is far from the realness and authenticity that they yearn for. It is like putting the King James Bible in a "cool cover" with some graphic inserts as highlights. For Emerging Christians, the spaces they create and inhabit are intended to help them live an everyday, nonreligious life, stripped of any seemingly false rituals or cute reminders of crosses, doves, fish, Bible verses, or slogans like What Would Jesus Do? (WWJD?) and "God Doesn't Make Junk."

A particularly interesting case is Mars Hill Community Church founded by Rob Bell. While the church is technically a megachurch due to its multithousand attendees, the church building is located in an abandoned indoor mall, which most would characterize as simply ugly.[50] It certainly does not look like a traditional church. The building has no signs either on the street or on the building to direct attendees. Inside, a near-empty, square platform occupies the middle of the main auditorium, and white, plastic chairs radiate in rows into a larger circle. Except for occasional images on screens above the platform and sporadic art displays in the halls, Mars Hill avoids any exhibition of Christian symbols or artifacts. Despite its rapid growth and healthy revenues, Mars Hill maintains a very plain, low budget, and even antichurch attitude toward decoration and ambiance. Although the church gained the resources to refurbish, or even rebuild, their site, the defunct retail outlet has taken on a character of its own in defining the values shared by members of this church.

The practices of Emerging Christians—as city dwellers and as creators of alternative Christian spaces—can be understood as an active deconstruction of the practices of suburban seeker megachurches and solemn mainline churches. In selecting urban spaces and profane (as opposed to churchy) settings, emerging congregations communicate their core ideas about the immanence of God—that (S)he is to be found in the ordinary places and experiences of life—and the desire for an unrestrained response to God. Emerging Christians avoid a sacred-secular divide and attempt to find the sacred *in* the profane. This means that Emerging Christians see their location in these cities and spaces as vital to their ability to live out Christianity as they understand it.

## Embodying Critiques of Conventional Christianity

At first glance, the practices of emerging congregations appear as eclectic, mix and match, even anything goes approaches to Christianity. But it is not simply the case that Emerging Christians pick from the practices that they like without regard for how these practices will have an impact on their personal development and on communal, congregational life. Rather, in their approaches to preaching, leadership, liturgy, and the physical locations and appearances of church, ECM congregations are embodying their critiques of evangelicalism, seeker megachurches, and mainline congregations. In their diverse and varied practices, we can see Emerging Christians' deconstruction of these expressions of Christianity worked out and strategically reassembled into something new, while still rooted in Christian traditions. This is the work of collective institutional entrepreneurs, reinforced by the discursive work of "the conversation," as discussed in chapter 4.

Paul Tracey, Nelson Phillips, and Owen Jarvis write that new organizational forms are created "when institutional entrepreneurs combine elements of established institutional logics and their associated practices and organizational forms to create a new organizational form underpinned by a new, hybrid logic."[51] Resulting changes in organizational forms thus often appear as hybrids, forms combining new and old elements.[52] We certainly see this process reflected in the practices of emerging congregations, including pub churches, neo-monastic communities, religious arts collectives, and other more recognizably congregational expressions. As Michael Lounsbury and Ellen Crumley have demonstrated, innovative practices emerge from spatially dispersed, heterogeneous activity by actors with varying kinds and levels of resources, in which actors are distributed across multiple dimensions including space, status, and time. At the same time, actors are united by shared cultural beliefs that define the field.[53] Lounsbury and Crumley's more distributed notion of collective institutional entrepreneurship emphasizes that innovation is dependent on shared social frameworks, which can be discerned in the many-sided, religiously individuated membership of the ECM.

All the practices found in emerging congregations are chosen carefully and strategically, with a view to embodying the ideals inherent to the wider conversation. The result of this is what we call a "pluralist congregation," where practices are deliberately open, inclusive, and drawn from a variety of traditions—all in an effort not only to make people feel comfortable but also to allow them to *choose* which religious practices *work best for them*. More than mere "theological minimalism that allows the efficient adaptation of the content of exhortation to the demands of modern individualism for self-fulfillment and personal realization,"[54] we find that what we call "strategic religiosity" in the ECM is an attempt to allow multiple paths of spirituality through heterogeneous responses to congregationally stimulated devotion. In this, the individual autonomy of each person's religious journey, and their personal religious identity, is respected. At the same time, the practices encourage a sense of corporate responsibility, with people expected to participate in preaching (in the communitarian style), decision-making, various aspects of public worship (the liturgies and rituals—although always free to choose which ones), and communion. In these ways, the practices of emerging congregations help people accommodate apparently contradictory priorities: exercising individual religious autonomy while participating in a collective congregational life.

# ‖ 6 ‖

# Following Jesus in the Real World

It's like life, more so than just church. This is just what you do.
—Dakota, *on living a more holistic Christian life*

Emerging Christians often describe themselves as "postcreedal," stressing that true religion is not doctrinal but lived practice, as one person said, "doing stuff." For Emerging Christians, Christianity is something that is "lived out" in the "real world." The test of whether people are Christians is not if they assent to specific intellectual beliefs and doctrines. What matters is the way they live their everyday lives outside of official church spaces. This has been identified as a shift in emphasis from orthodoxy (right belief) to orthopraxis (right practice).[1] It is also reflects Emerging Christians' conviction that there is no distinction between secular and sacred spheres of life—for them everything, including the mundane world of work—is sacred.

Of course, the conviction that Christianity should permeate how one lives one's life is not unique to the ECM. The evangelicalism in which much of the ECM has its roots has long had as one of its central assumptions the idea that faith should inform every aspect of the believer's life. But many in the ECM see evangelicalism or institutional religion as forcing people to conform to predetermined ideas of what a Christian should look and live like, thus hindering their ability to live authentically and holistically in the world.[2] Furthermore, the conventional church is believed to have disqualified itself by its many concessions to contemporary power structures. As John D. Caputo writes, "The deconstruction of Christianity is not an attack on the church but a critique of the idols to which it is vulnerable—the literalism and authoritarianism, the sexism and racism, the militarism and imperialism, and the love of unrestrained capitalism with which the church in its various forms has today and for too long been entangled, any one of which is toxic to the kingdom of God."[3]

As discussed in chapter 1, the ECM has roots in evangelistic mission—an attempt to bring a so-called lost generation back to church. This is the case in both the United States, with the activity of the Leadership Network in the

1990s, and in the United Kingdom, with the Church of England's *Mission-Shaped Church* report and the Fresh Expressions project of the Anglican and Methodist churches. The term "missional," which is increasingly being used by people within the ECM to describe their communities (sometimes deliberately replacing the term "emerging church"), captures something of this evangelistic thrust. Within the ECM, there is a spectrum of ideas about the extent to which the purpose of the church is to evangelize others. Some emerging congregations are deliberate "church plants," while others within the ECM strenuously resist the very idea that they should be evangelizing others. Emerging Christians contrast their approaches to what they see as the aggressive and inauthentic evangelism methods of evangelicals and seeker megachurches, often expressing a great sense of relief that they no longer feel pressured to engage in such practices. There is deep appreciation for the perspectives and integrity of those who are not Christians, as exemplified in Frank's words, who said, "Now I can see the beauty of God in someone who might not even claim to know him."

In this chapter, we focus on the ways in which people in the ECM live beyond their occasional congregational gatherings. We observe that people within the ECM do not agree on the extent to which they *should* be living their lives to try and convert others. We argue that some in the ECM choose lifestyles that they see as inherently political, believing that this is the best way for them to live out their Christianity. For them, Jesus's mission was a *political* one on behalf of the poor and marginalized, so they seek to emulate Jesus by identifying with disadvantaged communities or working for peace and reconciliation. We explore in more depth the different ways in which people in the ECM are trying to live out these (evangelistic and political) ideals through conventional political engagement, forming neo-monastic communities, creating Temporary Autonomous Zones (TAZs), and choosing careers that enable them to work for social justice.

For some, "living differently" requires immersion in the structures and relationships of ECM communities. Church is not intended to be a sacred space isolated from the rest of the world, but rather the relationships fostered at church become the occasion to experience those relationships more continuously and thereby have faith become an ongoing, regular aspect of everyday life. Sadie, like many, said, "We see each other all the time. I kid you not, three or four times a week, maybe more, maybe five times a week." For others, it implies a move toward a "religion-less Christianity," where religious institutions and meetings become ever less important as people focus on loving others outside the walls of churches. While we cannot demonstrate that being involved in the ECM makes people live better or more authentic lives, their distinct practices of living are integral to their religious orientation, a key way in which they deconstruct and define themselves against other expressions of Christianity such as seeker megachurches (in the United States), sectarian denominations (in Northern Ireland), and churches aligned with conservative political agendas in the United States, the United Kingdom, Ireland and beyond. These practices have erased distinctions between sacred and secular in their lives and helped them to set their personal, individual religious journeys in a context in which corporate, real world religious practices are understood as central to their religious orientation. So, while involvement in pluralist congregations is important, congregational involvement is not the sole focus of an Emerging Christian's religious orientation.

Emerging Christians find various openings for relationships with people outside their congregations and engagement with loftier concerns that extend beyond congregational ministries. Rather than being *individualistic*, the religious practices of Emerging Christians are *individuated* through a highly conscious embrace of broader relational commitments and larger social values. Emerging Christians intertwine the sacred and the secular through immersive community living, larger missional projects, and various ethical and political involvements, and they find ongoing opportunities for the intentional deployment of a renegotiated, legitimate religious self.

## Mission, Witness, and Appreciation of Those Who Are Not Christian

It could be argued that the very existence of ECM groups is evidence that they wish for others to join with them in their way of life. Bielo identifies emerging evangelicals with the term "missional" and emphasizes their evangelistic priorities. In his book of eight chapters, two have the word "missional" in the title and two others have "church planting" in the title. Bielo links emerging evangelicals' focus on mission to the influence of British Anglican Lesslie Newbigin, a missionary in India who subsequently argued that the way to convert the secular West is—like a foreign missionary—to seek to understand the culture and to adapt one's missionary techniques to it. Bielo writes:

> Emerging Evangelicals have applied Newbigin's missiology as a methodological critique of conservative Christian evangelism. They decry a wide range of common witnessing practices: street preaching, handing out Bible tracts, delivering finely tuned conversion speeches, using hyperlogical apologetics, and using weekly congregational events as the entrée to church. For those self-consciously striving to

be missional, these methods suffer from several problems: a failure to understand the shift in American public consciousness from modernity to post-modernity; an inability to effectively use the mediums and idioms attractive to a post-modern audience; and the lack of meaningful, lasting personal commitments. Being missional means seriously cultivating relationships—not before or after conversion attempts, but in place of them. To accomplish this goal, they advocate mimicking the acculturating foreign missionary: settling into a locale and becoming intimately familiar with a place and its people.[4]

Similarly, the Church of England deliberately links the Fresh Expressions initiative with mission, defining it as:

A fresh expression is a form of church for our changing culture established primarily for the benefit of people who are not yet members of any church. It will come into being through principles of listening, service, incarnational mission and making disciples. It will have the potential to become a mature expression of church shaped by the gospel and the enduring marks of the church and for its cultural context.[5]

Likewise, a 2010 edited volume focusing on neo-monasticism in the British context identifies mission as a priority. In the introduction to the book, Graham Cray (who chaired the working party that wrote *Mission Shaped Church*) writes:

The greatest mission challenge facing the Church in the UK is the growing majority of the population who have not been involved in local church, even as children. There is no quick fix strategy for work among those who have no experience of church and little knowledge of the Christian story... New monasticism offers the possibility of important frameworks of support for those deployed on such a mission... Teams can sustain the integrity of their witness, walking the tightrope between irrelevance and syncretism, through a shared rule of life that emerges as they immerse themselves in their new context.[6]

Neo-monastic communities are not the only examples of new missional structures. New structures range from small, house churches to cell groups to independent congregations to congregations backed by traditional denominations. Bielo writes that he was convinced of the missional thrust of the ECM when his research participants kept talking about "church planting."

Although Bielo says that he did not originally see church planting as a focus of his research, his participants were so keen to talk about it that it became one of the central themes of his book. Bielo observes that church planting is not new—it is something that evangelicals have been doing for years. But what is new is that "Emerging Evangelicals have made church planting a craft to be mastered" and "being a church planter has become an organizing identity." For Bielo, church planting is a "cultural critique of conservative Evangelicalism, most notably . . . the suburban megachurch."[7] At the same time, Bielo records that some of the church planters he spoke with were very similar to modern evangelicals, particularly in their conservative attitudes toward women's roles in the church and in their use of expository preaching, rather than the dialogic style of preaching we describe in chapter 5. Many of his research participants were from the Acts 29 Network, which adheres to Reformed, Calvinist theology. For him, this represents a tension between modernism and postmodernism among emerging evangelicals. For us, the inclusion of Acts 29 and other communities associated with the "new Calvinists"—they of the "Jonathan Edwards is my Homeboy" T-shirts featured on the cover of Collin Hansen's 2008 book, *Young, Restless, Reformed*[8] —is a conflation of two distinct movements or orientations in contemporary American religion: the ECM and neo-Calvinism.[9]

Bielo's inclusion of these Reformed church plants skews his analysis of emerging approaches to mission. A neo-Calvinist mission or church plant will ultimately articulate and embody very different theological ideas about what it means to be a Christian in the world, and what doctrines Christians should believe, than the congregations or communities that we identify with the ECM. In his work on congregations in the Pacific Northwest, Jason Wollschleger describes Redeemer, a congregation that superficially looks like part of the ECM due to practices like meeting for theological discussions in a pub. Indeed, some informants he contacted before beginning his research thought that Redeemer *was* part of the ECM. But on closer inspection, Redeemer fits very much into neo-Calvinism, forbidding the ordination of women; practicing closed communion; and following the liturgy of a small, conservative denomination, the Presbyterian Church in America.[10]

In contrast to neo-Calvinist congregations, with their emphasis on traditional doctrines and practices, the Dock initiative in the "Titanic Quarter" of Belfast is an example of a "church plant" that embodies many of the values described by Bielo and articulated in *Mission Shaped Church*. In the years since the peace agreement in Northern Ireland, there has been a push for economic development in the previously largely derelict part of the city that is home to the Harland and Wolff shipyard, where the *Titanic* was built.[11] This has included the Odyssey (a shopping mall and sports arena), apartments, hotels, businesses, a campus of a third-level educational institution, and a signature building that houses the Titanic Belfast visitor attraction. Titanic Belfast opened for the centenary of the launch of the Titanic in 2012.

Amongst this flurry of activity, no church buildings have been built. But a group of Christians from various denominations have established the Dock, officially a limited company with charitable status, with the intention of buying a boat that will be moored permanently in the area and serve as church or chaplaincy for people from all denominations and none. The Dock has a Board of Directors and a Board of Management, which include people from Catholic, Church of Ireland (Anglican), Presbyterian, Methodist, and independent church backgrounds. At the time of this writing (December 2013), a Church of Ireland minister, Chris Bennett, oversees many of the activities at the Dock, assisted by chaplains from five other traditions, who volunteer in addition to their other duties with Methodist, Catholic, Presbyterian, Congregational and Nazarene churches. In naming their denominational affiliations, the Dock website reads: "or as they prefer to be known (because who boxes people up like that any more?), Chris, Karen, Finian, Brian, Wesley and Richard."[12] Given Belfast's religiously divided and violent past, the ecumenical makeup of the Dock leadership is significant, as is its appropriation of the discourse of a "Shared Future." *A Shared Future* is the title of a 2005 British government policy document recommending more meaningful interaction among Northern Ireland's divided communities. The Dock's mission statement reads:

> In these days of Shared Future, it is the churches' challenge to find out what it means to share ministry in this place—to lead by example in breaking down barriers, connecting people, and building community cohesion.
> The purpose of "The Dock" is to provide a shared space, achieved through the permanent mooring of a boat within the Titanic Quarter area, on which a "Shared Future" expression of church may be based.[13]

The Dock has not yet purchased a boat but has established the Dock Café and organized other activities including Dock Walks, which happen on Sundays at 3:33 p.m. In 2013, the Dock also began a monthly evening gathering on board the recently refurbished visitor attraction, the *Nomadic,* a boat that was used to ferry passengers from the shore to the *Titanic.* The Dock Walks seem to be an alternative to a church service, described on the Dock's website this way:

> The Dock Walks are a new way of doing church, on foot, in the midst of the rich heritage and the exciting new development of Belfast's Titanic Quarter. We walk, talk, drink coffee, and as we walk through the

TQ we stop to pray or listen to scripture, meditations or music. The route, the people, the weather and the conversation are never exactly the same!

No-one is put on the spot, made to speak or pray out loud. And we don't sing, or preach, or walk around with sandwich boards. . . .

There's something great about going for a walk. It's a way to meet new friends, breathe fresh air, see the great outdoors, and give thanks to the Creator of it all.[14]

Dock Walks embody something of the ECM's missional ideal: rather than expecting people to "come in" to a church building, the church is "going out" and walking in the neighborhood. It is not clear to what extent the Dock has been influenced by developments within the ECM. It also is not clear to what extent the Dock is attracting people from all denominations, especially the Catholic Church, or how it might deal with potentially divisive issues in the future, such as sharing Eucharist or communion.

People in congregations we have identified as neo-Calvinist would have serious difficulties with missional communities like the Dock, which with its commitment to interdenominationalism seems unable to articulate a unified theology that would be consistent with all the Christian traditions represented therein. But for people in the ECM, that's not the point. *Living* is the point, as is also illustrated in Wollschleger's study through his analysis of the Church of the Apostles, a self-consciously emerging church in Seattle connected to both the Evangelical Lutheran Church in America and the Episcopal Church. Apostles and its African American pastor, Karen Ward, are well known in the ECM; they are featured in chapter 2 and in Tony Jones's research.[15] Wollschleger describes Apostles' approach to mission as "simply serving those around them without efforts to proselytize," and "being community in the neighbourhood" by offering its building space to the community and participating in hands-on service projects.[16] Apostles' approach resonates with the term "witness," as described by Ikon's Jon Hatch: "A witness is someone who is called to testify and answers questions. A witness doesn't go around volunteering information. Christian living is living differently from the world and then answering questions when you're asked why."[17] The concept of witness includes a crucial element that is not immediately obvious in discussions about mission. That element is the ability to accept people as they are—without trying to change or convert them. This is not easy to do, in practice, or to understand, in sociological theory.

Grace Yukich has identified a sociological dilemma when what she calls "inclusive religious groups" make such claims: there is a tension between the need that all groups have to construct boundaries between themselves and "others" (without boundaries, they would not be groups, after all) and their claims to inclusivity. She writes, "A lack of research on the topic suggests an assumption among researchers that 'inclusive' groups using boundary work are merely hypocritical and not *really* inclusive."[18] In her study of the Catholic Worker movement in New York City,[19] Yukich gets around this dilemma by arguing that "concrete practices of inclusion outweigh boundary drawing in groups like the Catholic Worker."[20] Primary among those concrete practices of inclusion are the Catholic Workers' commitment to hospitality to strangers. In the urban inner cities in which their community houses are intentionally located, these strangers are often poor. Yukich argues that this commitment to hospitality manifests through "sharing food as inclusion,"[21] "sharing space as inclusion,"[22] and "sharing spirit as inclusion" (including inviting everyone to mass and practicing open Eucharist, which would be forbidden by the hierarchy of the Catholic Church).[23] Through these practices, Catholic Workers live "with people with different ideals and practices regarding war, violence and consumerism than they did."[24] It was because they encountered people who were different from them in the real world, rather than merely theorizing about them in an abstract way, that Yukich sees Catholic Workers overcoming her sociological dilemma.

Indeed, encounters with those who they perceive as radically different in their beliefs and practices are what many Emerging Christians strive for.[25] Some people from Ikon said that Ikon had helped them live, or at least helped them realize that they wanted to live, in a way that demonstrated they accepted those who are different. Especially for those who worked in Northern Ireland's "cross community" sector, accepting the other was important. Jonny McEwen put it this way: "One thing that I think is really important, is to know that you are probably wrong. So you hold your beliefs, but you hold them lightly ... I'm involved in some cross community work as well. Even in those circumstances, I try and convey the sense that I might be wrong, and being open [to the other]."[26] So, what it means to "witness" is to be able to live with people who are different without trying to change or convert them. McEwen thinks that this type of witnessing makes it easier to have conversations about God:

> Since I gave up being evangelical it's easier to talk about God ...
> Everyone struggles to describe what Ikon is, and this leads you into
> interesting conversations that an evangelism conversation wouldn't
> lead you into ... Partly because you are apologetic and confused, it
> opens up intrigue and it doesn't create defensiveness.[27]

McEwen's words resonate with what Gladys has written on her blog about Peter Rollins's approach to mission, which she characterized as "anti-conversionism":

Rollins clearly doesn't want to convert anyone, at least not in the sense that many Christians (especially evangelical Protestants) think about conversion. He won't appeal to you to become "born again," that's for sure, although it must be granted that anyone who is a writer and public speaker like Rollins is probably trying to "convert" you to his own point of view.[28]

In a later, related post, she wrote: "It follows from this that the best form of mission is simply *being* the church—a model of peaceful, loving community that the rest of society can see (an idea I am stealing from Stanley Hauerwas).[29] This is a church so compelling that others cannot help but be attracted to it. I think this is the kind of church Rollins is seeking."[30] Both the "mission" and "witness" approaches reflect Emerging Christians' appreciation for those who are not Christians.

Unlike in evangelicalism, non-Christians are not categorized as the unsaved in need of conversion. As one man said, his family has been deeply impressed by

> the emphasis that [our pastor] and everyone has placed on being in a relationship and being in a conversation with non-Christians. [Our pastor] invited a coffee shop manager, non-Christian, very antichurch, and he gets in front of the congregation—he didn't feel threatened at all to be interviewed in front of the congregation. It's really had its effect because we talk so much about being in relationship and being missional out there among non-Christians, being in the coffeehouses, being in the art galleries—just being out there with them.

He said his elementary school daughter was talking about Jesus with a friend in the backseat of a car, and when the mom—who was "blown away"—said it was "amazing" that she was sharing her faith, the little girl said, "Where I go to church, they talk a lot about just being comfortable with non-Christians and sharing your faith." But sharing faith does not mean trying to convince others that you are right. As another man explained, it means *living in the right way.* He said:

> I feel like [our church] equips me to actually live out what I feel Christianity...should look like—not preach at people. I don't try and convert people, but I try to treat them as well as I can. I try and love them as much as I can without grabbing them and shaking them ... I feel you have to *show* Christ, not *tell* Christ.

For another woman, mission happens naturally in her small group, flowing from the way they share their lives together. She said, "They are so missional without trying. Every week we seem to get into some discussion about how to share with someone about God. People are actually living this way without us having to tell them to go 'evangelize.' I don't like that word. I just like being the church to people out there who don't like church." Similar examples were multiplied throughout our data. One man described this encounter in his Bible study group:

[A woman in our Bible study said] "I don't want anyone telling me about Christianity. I know what it is, I don't want anything to do with it." Normally [in other churches] if that would happen, someone would try to convince her or try to prove her wrong. And this was a time when for that whole two hours no one tried to convince her or say anything. And she came here for a really long time. I was shocked by that. You didn't have to try to convince someone. You didn't have to try to make them think the way you did.

Another woman said:

We had members of the community that didn't really necessarily believe in God and it was like the church didn't try to make them believe in God. They said, "Okay, well, we do [believe in God] and you can [still] hang out with us."

Others said this approach to others had helped them to become less judgmental. Frank said:

Before, I was judgmental. I was all about the whole, "get you into an accountability group, and how are you doing?" And if you're not [in an accountability group or doing well], you're not good enough. It's helped me realize how much my life was spent thinking I was better or judging people if they weren't better. Whereas now, I can see the beauty of God in someone that might not even claim to know him.

Or as Ben put it, "Another thing that [our church] has done for me is it has taken away the whole 'who's going to heaven' game. It's really allowed me to give the benefit of the doubt to people that I'm just meeting. And my first thought isn't whether or not they're going to heaven, my first thought is, 'who is this person?'"

Furthermore, some claim to detect a *deeper* level of spirituality among those who are not Christians. Blake, like many, said, "Our 'unsaved'—for lack of a better term—artist friends are much more spiritual and insightful and more interested in talking about spiritual elements of their art than our Christian artist group friends." His wife added that they are "much healthier people [emotionally] too—which is kind of bizarre."

In sum, Emerging Christians hold a range of positions on the extent to which the purpose of their lives should be trying to convert others to Christianity. Some clearly see the ECM as a missional movement, designed to draw in the unchurched and the dechurched, with the ultimate aim of adapting Christianity to local modern and postmodern contexts. This approach is exemplified in the Dock. Yet others shy away from terms like "evangelism" and "mission," preferring the language of "witness" and, they claim, deliberately not trying too hard to convince others to join them. Peter Rollins's approach to mission seems at the extreme of this position.[31]

## Following a Political Jesus

But if Emerging Christians do not agree about "mission" and "witness," they share at least a loose consensus that Christianity is inherently political. For them it is political with a small "p," identified with "social justice" causes that are believed to reflect Jesus's passion for the poor. Following a political Jesus means taking their faith outside the walls of the church and into the neighborhoods where they live. As Joseph said, living out his faith is linked to "the opportunity to just sit and think about what it means as a privileged, powerful American. What it means for me to live in a world of poverty. So just that dialogue is at least the first step in encouraging an active faith in everyday life." In comments that reflect the priorities and passions of many Emerging Christians, Joseph went on to describe in more detail what this means to him:

> There's a spirit of humility that much of Christianity lacks and that it needs to re-emphasize. The humility of: we are not the privileged. We are the servants. And we are here to love God and love our neighbor. And this is what we're concerned about in light of those commands. If we want to write articles and books and have seminars and do all that, then let's not do it about how to get the Ten Commandments back in Alabama. Let's do it about how to tackle this human rights issue over here or this enslavement issue or this poverty issue. Let's start helping people that need help. Let's actually do good, and if we want to talk, let's talk about how to do that good. If people hear Christians

being concerned about things that I really think much of the heathen world is more concerned about than we are—namely those political, human rights, economics issues that put so much of the world in terrible conditions—if people heard the church saying, yeah, that's awful and we're here to serve and do something about that, then I think they might sit up and listen . . . If we're trying to communicate truth, then we should just shut up for a while. Because the world has tuned us out, probably credibly so. We need to start looking again at what is important truth, and what we're truly called to be about.

For Emerging Christians, following a political Jesus is central to their religious orientation, allowing them to feel that their faith is authentic and holistic. Emerging Christians try to live this out through conventional political engagement, forming neo-monastic communities, creating Temporary Autonomous Zones (TAZs), and choosing careers that enable them to work for social justice.

## Conventional Political Engagement

In some cases, Emerging Christians engage in direct political activism by forming pressure groups or special interest organizations, like other groups in Western democracies do. One example was the involvement of some people associated with Ikon in the political action group Zero28.[32] Zero28, which started in 1999, had its origins in a student discussion group at Queen's University Belfast led by Gareth Higgins, who later worked as director of the Wild Goose Festival.[33] Zero28 focused on how to promote peace and reconciliation in Northern Ireland and took its name from the telephone code for Northern Ireland, 028, which they described as "the one thing that brought Catholics and Protestants together." A suggested tagline for Zero28 was "Following Jesus in the Real World," and supporters were asked to sign a pledge card. During Gladys's interviews in 2004, one supporter removed his card from his wallet during the interview and read the pledge: "To live the change I want to see through nonviolent action to achieve peace and social justice in Northern Ireland."[34] Zero28 organized activities such as public discussions and private meetings with politicians (including Sinn Féin's Gerry Adams), as well as discussions on sectarianism and Orange Order parades. In 2003, Zero28 expanded its political focus, identifying five strands of work (peacemaking, social ethics, environment, arts/creativity, and justice/poverty) and attempted to organize activities and campaigns around these themes until it wound down in 2007. Since 2007, people in Zero28 who wished to remain politically active channeled their energies to other areas, such as the Belfast Feminist Network or the One Small Step Campaign. Most shunned active involvement in political parties, with a few exceptions like John Kyle, a medical doctor who joined the small, working class Progressive Unionist Party (PUP). In Northern Ireland this could be interpreted as a shockingly radical step, due to the party's historic (and some would say all too contemporary) links to the paramilitary Ulster Volunteer Force. But Kyle understood it this way:

> I am convinced that the paramilitaries have moved on from vio-
> lence . . . And the truth is that despite the violence in which many
> of them engaged, the men of the UVF were also capable of progres-
> sive political thinking. You see, the media is all too keen to portray
> the average Loyalist as a thug, with his knuckles scraping the ground
> and his arms covered in sectarian tattoos. Middle-class Protestants
> are particularly dismissive. They forget that many Loyalist working
> class communities have had it very tough in a way that they them-
> selves have not.
>
> No, if, as a Christian, you want to change things, then you have to
> get in there and be involved with the way things actually are, instead
> of waiting around until it's "safe" or respectable to do so. Jesus associ-
> ated with all kinds of people and so can we.[35]

Conventional approaches to political engagement like forming special inter-est groups, organizing marches, or joining political parties have not been the focus of the ECM. In fact, many Emerging Christians see these conventional tactics as ineffective. Emerging Christians may not directly discourage politi-cal activism or other "prosocial" activities like volunteering or giving money to charity.[36] But many would judge these activities as simply helping to per-petuate an unjust system—like applying a band-aid to a gaping wound that is gushing blood. This is how Rollins assesses the North American church in his contribution to the edited collection, *Letters to a Future Church*. The book is based on a conference organized by the Epiphaneia Network in Toronto in which people, mostly associated with the ECM or evangelicalism, were invited to write a letter to the church, modeled after the letters of John to the seven churches in the book of Revelation. We quote from Rollins's letter:

> Today you give generously to those who are homeless, organizing gift
> days, flea market sales, and clothing collections. But surely the point
> is not to treat the homeless with dignity but rather to help create a
> society within which homelessness is no longer a reality. Indeed, in-
> stead of making the situation better, giving some spare change can
> actually be destructive in the long term, as it can help you feel that you

are doing something good when you are actually allowing a horrible injustice to continue.....

It is not enough for you to say that you are falling short of your beliefs, for this very confession plays into the idea that there is a difference between your various beliefs and your actions. Rather, if you will permit, I ask you to remember the radical Christian insight that one's actions reflect one's beliefs. That you cannot say that you believe in God if you do not commit yourself to what Kierkegaard referred to as the work of love.[37]

In the United States, some within the ECM identify with the evangelical left, exemplified by Sojourners.[38] But unlike the evangelical Christian right, the ECM has not launched large-scale political campaigns reflecting their values or political positions, though some in the ECM, on both sides of the Atlantic, have taken political stances on LGBTQ issues.

Jay Bakker, who describes himself as a gay rights activist, has been among the most prominent in this regard. While it is not the main focus of his book *Fall to Grace,* Bakker dedicates a significant portion of it to explaining how he arrived at his views on homosexuality and gay marriage.[39] This includes personal stories, as well as an explanation of how he believes Christians have mistranslated and misused the Bible to foster homophobia. Bakker argues that Old Testament references to homosexuality, such as Leviticus 18:22 and 20:13, are as outdated as Old Testament prohibitions on eating shellfish, cutting sideburns, getting tattoos, interracial marriage, slavery, and treating women like property.[40] He says that Christians who today use these passages from Leviticus to make their case, claiming a so-called biblical high ground, are in fact taking a pick-and-choose attitude toward scripture. Further, he claims that New Testament references to homosexuality (in I Timothy, I Corinthians and Romans) have been mistranslated and "actually refer to acts like male prostitution, ritual sex, and inhospitality to strangers—all things that Christians discourage, whether gay or straight."[41]

In another book, *Faith, Doubt and Other Lines I've Crossed,* Bakker challenges Christians who agree with him to ask their pastors and leaders: "Are we able to welcome and affirm LGBTQ people in our church?"[42] He recounts how pastors and leaders have told him they cannot be affirming, not out of personal conviction, but because they might lose their jobs, other staff might lose their jobs, financial donations would cease, or people would leave their church. Comparing how Christians used the Bible to prohibit interracial dating to the question of LGBTQ inclusion, Bakker says Christians have no excuse for remaining silent.[43] He recognizes that some will lose their jobs, suffer financial insecurity, be kicked out of their churches, and so on. Bakker has experienced these things, which makes his call to action more credible. After Minnesota's legalization of gay marriage in 2013, Bakker's Revolution Church in Minneapolis served rainbow-colored communion bread to mark the occasion. Courtney Perry and Tony Jones also served the rainbow bread at their symbolic wedding ceremony in 2011.[44] Brian McLaren and Rob Bell have publicly supported gay marriage, with McLaren presiding over his son's same sex commitment ceremony.[45]

Other emerging congregations have led by example simply through the presence of people of varying sexual orientations in their midst. Pastor Nadia Bolz-Weber's House for All Sinners and Saints in Denver started with eight people, "four of whom were queer." As she writes: "Our church continues to be not 'inclusive' of queer folks; House for All Sinners and Saints—its origins, its leadership, and its culture—has always been partly queer itself." Even so, in *Cranky, Beautiful Faith,* Bolz-Weber describes her difficult decision to continue blogging for Sojourner's "God's Politics" website after it "refused to sell ad space to Believe Out Loud, an organization that is helping churches become fully inclusive of all people, regardless of sexual orientation or gender identity."[46] She was condemned by the "progressive" Christians she considered her allies, who did not share her assessment that keeping channels of communication with more conservative Christians open on Sojourners was the right decision.

At the same time, there is no evidence that Emerging Christians are involved in a widespread or systematic way in LGBTQ activism. In Northern Ireland, several Ikon participants are prominent figures in LGBTQ activism (with most of their fellow LGBTQ activists unaware of their involvement with Ikon). But Emerging Christians have not been especially prominent in traditional political campaigns around LGBTQ issues in the United States, the United Kingdom, or Ireland.

This, perhaps surprising, lack of political engagement may be related to the diffuse nature and small numbers of people identifying with the ECM. But it is also linked to a deeply held view that conventional political engagement is not the only or the best way to emulate what they see as Jesus's inherently political approach.

## Neo-Monastic Communities

In 2011, Gladys had a Facebook exchange with a man from Ikon who asked:

> Is the emergent church bourgeois? What is its engagement with, understanding of, or presence in politically or economically marginalised communities? Discuss. heheheheheheh . . .

Gladys replied:

> To attempt to answer that, it would be convenient to claim the likes
> of Simple Way (Shane Claiborne) types for the emerging church . . .

He replied:

> Whether Claiborne would consider himself part of the emergent con-
> versation is open to debate, I guess.[47] He's usually the name that is
> mentioned when I bring this up, leading me to believe that he fulfils
> the same role in making the emergent movement "socially conscious"
> that St. Brigid does in making the early Irish church "feminist."

We have already noted that some within the ECM see neo-monastic communities as "missional," which implies that they are an evangelistic method
or strategy. It also is worth recalling our snapshot of neo-monasticism in
chapter 1, where we explained that there are varieties of these communities,
ranging from residential communities like the Simple Way, to dispersed communities like Corrymeela, to communities that mix residential and dispersed
aspects like Iona.

Neo-monastic living serves as a sort of template for how people in the
ECM would *like* to live their lives, even if in actuality they do not. They
see neo-monastic living as the opposite of the Christianity that they define
themselves against: a Christianity in which Christian living is judged by how
often you turn up at church services, how enthusiastically you worship, how
many people you convince to get "saved," whether you have the "correct"
political views on "moral" issues like homosexuality and abortion, and so on.
Bielo conceptualizes new monasticism as "lived religion," marked by "everyday" practices of simplicity and stability. He reports that people in the ECM
relate simplicity to the rejection of consumer capitalism, while the value
of stability is reflected in the decisions of some of Bielo's research participants to move to a particular location and vow never to leave it "irrespective
of their occupational fates, the fates of their families, or the fate of the . . .
community."[48] In many cases, joining a neo-monastic community means setting up house in an economically disadvantaged urban area.[49] Doing this is
as much a *political* as a missional act. By political, we mean that some people
in these communities are committed to living, as far as possible, outside the
structures of consumer capitalism in an attempt to subvert them. They see
this as emulating Jesus, who they conceptualize as a political activist who
worked (nonviolently) outside of the structures of the Roman Empire, ultimately subverting them.

Claiborne seems to embody this ideal. Although people may admire Claiborne, they find it very difficult to live like him. As Bielo observes[50]:

> In his books and public lectures Claiborne references numerous ways
> to be a new monastic: living communally with other Christians, main-
> taining the bare minimum of material possessions, driving a tour bus
> that uses recycled vegetable oil instead of gasoline, making his own
> hand-sewn clothes, growing his own food, transforming "abandoned"
> public spaces into edifying creations like community gardens, and
> "rescuing" discarded items in public dumpsters for community use.
> Claiborne never mandates these practices, but he certainly frames
> them as desirable and attainable for everyone.

This was confirmed for Gerardo in February 2010, when he attended a lecture by Claiborne on the Davidson College campus. The author of bestselling books (including *The Irresistible Revolution* and *Jesus for President*), a popular speaker, and a peace activist, Claiborne is well liked and highly stimulating.[51] For his admirers, as a "white boy" with dreadlock hair dressed in handmade clothing, Claiborne radicalizes a critique of consumerism, corporate greed, and the pursuit of middle-to-upper class status and comfort. Looking at him reminds an older person of the hippie movement of the 1960s and 1970s. He embraces the term "radical" and conveys an impish manner, alternatively silly and sincere, as he challenges people to exit all forms of the military-industrial complex to devote oneself to a prayer-filled, peace-pursuing, and sustainable form of life. Although much of his own community is consciously Christian, the Simple Way attracts anarchist-oriented nonbelievers who find resonance with a range of issues from rejecting easy suburbanism to opposing government-sponsored injustice. The crowd gathered for the lecture was full of anticipation, and the excitement continued over the next hour. Conversations with students revealed how inspired they were by a person who appeared to reject everything they themselves are supposed to desire after they graduate.

Among these elite college students, Claiborne was accepted as a prophet to hear more than as a model to follow. But this does not lessen his influence among them, and may even accentuate it, since it removes the burden to take on what may be considered an extreme lifestyle ("I don't think I can do what Shane does," said one student) and allows them to use Claiborne as a magnifying lens for examining alternative, left-leaning, socially conscious, Christian approaches to living. Students said they were not ultimately motivated to leave college and "join a commune." Rather, they agreed with the values that Claiborne represents and were challenged to find ways to incorporate them in their choices of a major, their considerations of career paths, and their thoughts on constructing a lifestyle apart from the imposed structures from home and school. One student recalled that Claiborne had taken stacks of quarters and threw them on Wall Street to demonstrate his rejection of capitalistic structures. "You gotta respect that," the student said.

The practices advocated by Claiborne and other neo-monastics can be understood as political action, because they deliberately seek to go against the grain of how middle-class Americans are expected to live. Kathy Escobar, co-pastor of the Refuge in Denver, puts it this way in *Letters to a Future Church*:

> You have to dismantle systems that perpetuate inequality, money, power and control. You have to stop hanging with people who are just like you. You have to give up making sure you're the "us" and others not like you are the "them." You have to lay down your idols of comfort and worldly success.[52]

Despite their attempts to live outside the capitalist system, Bielo admits that his participants realize that they are still very much living within that system. The effects of their efforts seem very limited, and the numbers of those living in the most structured neo-monastic communities remain small. In addition, the early idealism of communal life can often give way to frustration as relationships become strained and people realize that changing the world—and, indeed, changing themselves—is a slow and difficult process.

Finally, some have noted that neo-monastic communities are dominated by middle-class whites, and that this can indicate a kind of colonialism by stealth, rather than an idealistic missional or a political impulse. Bielo writes, "As Emerging Evangelicals seek to 'have missional hearts' they construct an imagined missionized Other, the details of which are used to create institutions for fostering evangelistic efforts."[53] Kelly Bean, one of the founders of Urban Abbey in Portland, Oregon, writes of her awareness of her group as a middle-class white haven.[54] Casting herself as "the dreamer," she writes in a stylized "once upon a time" format, with passages such as:

> Despite the denominational and theological hybridity, there was no denying it: in this ethnically diverse neighborhood the Abbeyites were all white, white as could be. The teenaged son of the dreamer attended a multicultural high school where as a white boy he was an ethnic minority. He enjoyed challenging the Abbeyites, reminding them that their stated values and ideals were somewhat disconnected from this reality.
>
> Following the advice of the wise Dr. John Perkins, the dreamer began to attend neighborhood gatherings and to learn from longtime

neighbors. Her dear friend Donna helped by sharing her own experiences and perspective as a black woman in the predominantly white Pacific Northwest. One relationship at a time, one story after another, is how the transformation takes place. The little abbey was open to be taught.[55]

For many in the ECM, the Simple Way vision of living with the disadvantaged in the "abandoned places of the empire" is a compelling one that gets to the very heart of what Jesus's ministry on earth was like.[56] This can be seen among Emerging Christians who are not part of neo-monastic communities, but who try and make social justice causes central to what their congregations are about. Again, the focus on social justice is contrasted to their previous churches. As Brooke said in a focus group discussion, one thing that has changed for her is

> the way I relate to caring about other people. In the church where I grew up it was very much, "The rapture is coming; these are the things that are going to happen before the rapture comes, the world basically has to go to hell in a handbasket before it can come, so we don't really want to"—nobody would say this—"we don't really want to stop it. Things have to get worse before good stuff can come so we're just going to let it get worse."

This provoked knowing laughter, after which Brooke said:

> They talked about getting people saved, but they never really talked about helping people improve their lives now . . . I've really appreciated all the things that [our church] does with World Relief and international justice ministries and all the stuff with getting out Christmas boxes every year, and adopting a local shelter for teenage girls, and the angel tree for the mission kids, and a thousand other service projects, like making scarves, and just all sorts of things that come up like that. I really appreciate that [this church] does care about people's lives *now*. I've seen in my own life that I've tried to do more of the same.

Joseph added that the congregation prompted him to think about these issues for the first time:

> When I moved here I saw people are living on the streets and asking me for money . . . It was the first time I had been confronted with poverty. Hearing it talked about at [our church] was the first time that

I had actually heard a church talk about it. It's really not something that's discussed a whole lot in a lot of Protestant circles.

The discussion continued with one woman joking, "Sorry you're starving, but as long as you say this prayer everything will be all right." This again prompted laughter and murmurs of agreement.

Perhaps more than other expressions of the ECM, neo-monasticism deconstructs dominant evangelical conceptions of Christian living through its physical location outside the boundaries of institutional churches and its political position outside conventional political structures. Even emerging congregations that are not full-fledged neo-monastic communities strive to live out these ideals, at least in part.

## Temporary Autonomous Zones

If neo-monastic communities can be understood as inherently political structures, in that they attempt to enable people to live outside or on the fringes of what they see as an unjust capitalist system, so too can Kester Brewin's Temporary Autonomous Zones (TAZs). Brewin, a popular author in the ECM in the United Kingdom, has borrowed the TAZ concept from anarchist Hakim Bey, who got his idea from the "pirate utopias" of the eighteenth century. These consisted of "remote hideouts" and "illegal trading stations" outside the reach of the state: "whole mini societies living consciously outside the law and determined to keep it up."[57] There's an underlying assumption here that the "State" (and in Brewin's case, also the "Church") can't be trusted to exercise power in a way that is just and life-giving. Therefore it is necessary to operate outside of those power structures. In his book *Other: Loving Self, God and Neighbour in a World of Fractures,* Brewin follows Bey's description of TAZ as "like an uprising which does not engage directly with the State, a guerrilla operation which liberates an area (of land, of time, of imagination) and then dissolves itself to re-form elsewhere/elsewhen, before the State can crush it."[58] In *Other,* an example Brewin gives of how TAZs might work in practice is the United Kingdom's Greenbelt Festival, which he characterizes a "liberated zone" where ordinary life is suspended. He also sees Ikon embodying key characteristics of "church as TAZ." Citing conversations with Peter Rollins, Brewin writes:

> Given the chance to have had a bespoke building and facilities, it may
> be that they would have taken it, but retrospectively [Rollins] is very
> glad that they have never had the chance to do so. Now the fact that
> they remain "homeless" and transient—they have used a number of
> different bars for their gatherings over the years—is central to their

ideology. This is a radically different model to that of the mega-church, which wants to create "facts on the ground" with imposing physical structures and impressive facilities. Church as TAZ then is taking the model of the tabernacle rather than the temple: a temporary, portable structure that claims whatever ground it covers as holy.[59]

Rollins's concept of "suspended space" is similar to TAZ.[60] Rollins uses this idea to explain how Ikon events work, arguing that they create spaces in which people can set aside their religious, political, ethnic, and other identities and encounter the other in a more authentic way. The reasons for creating such spaces seem to be, amongst other possibilities, encouraging people to set aside oppositional political identities, promoting inclusivity, building relationships among people who are different, and prompting people to take responsibility for how they live in the real world—a point Rollins expands on more fully in *Insurrection* when he urges people not to force their pastors to "believe" on their behalf.[61] Katharine Sarah Moody is one who agrees that this approach may be politically transformative. For her, emerging churches can contribute to the suspension of identity politics outside the boundaries of congregations or collectives. This stands in contrast to much scholarship on religion, which almost reduces religion to identity and focuses on its divisive or violent expressions.[62]

While Brewin's examples of TAZ in *Other* were church focused, in *Mutiny! Why We Love Pirates and How They Can Save Us,* he expands the discussion to include TAZ-like spaces in work, leisure, the media, our desires, and our beliefs.[63] He argues that pirates are masterful at creating TAZs, and that this is also what people should be doing in their everyday lives. *Mutiny* does not fit comfortably within the usual ECM genres of popular theology, biographical confessions, or mission studies. Rather, it could be considered a self-consciously radical manual for *living differently,* with suggestions for how to do this conveyed via a mish-mash of stories, analysis, and reflections, including a history of seafaring pirates, meditations on modern piracy ranging from Somali pirates to the pirates of the music industry, psychoanalytical interpretations of Peter Pan and Odysseus, and an identification of Christ as a pirate. In the sections on the history of seafaring pirates, Brewin argues that these men, and a few women, had seen and experienced the injustices of an imperial trading system in which a few became rich based on the toil of the many. Pirates were those who had the courage to reject that system and create their own alternative way of life, marked by a relatively egalitarian "pirate code."[64] He claims that pirates were (and, in the case especially of the first contemporary Somali pirates, still are) relatively powerless people who lack the resources to change unjust systems through gradual compromise (unlike William Wilberforce, who worked for the abolition of the slave trade through the British parliamentary system). Pirates therefore have little to lose by ignoring the system, operating outside it, and creating fleeting spaces of liberation.[65]

Brewin identifies the modern-day fascination with pirates, exemplified in the enthusiasm to dress children up and let them play pirates, as a longing that we too can break free from the systems and institutions that imprison us. He argues that if Christians learn to model that behavior in their own context, they can contribute, at least in a small way, to challenging, and if they are fortunate changing, the institutions that he believes damage so many people. He claims that people can create TAZs in various areas of their lives, even while being conventionally employed. Brewin writes:

> [Playing pirate] . . . does not necessarily mean a rejection of work, or a rejection of positive economic activity, and nor does it mean advocating a communist alternative. Playing pirate to our capitalist economy does not require us to give up our jobs and live in hippy-style self-sufficient farming communes (though some might want to) . . . It means . . . trying to return to a system where work is *craft*, where our labour means something and is rewarded as such, even if those rewards are more modest than we might have grabbed in big business.[66]

In this spirit, Brewin explains that this is why he did not seek a publisher for *Mutiny*, as he had his previous books, choosing rather to "turn to self publishing" so that he could "place a 'stinted copyright' on the text, which will be released into the public domain after a certain time, when I've gained a little private compensation for the time and resources I've put into this."[67] There are parallels between the messages in *Mutiny* and Rollins's similarly titled *Insurrection*, which imply that Christians should be enacting a kind of everyday (nonviolent) rebellion against oppressive structures of churches, governments, and economics. For them, that's how to follow Jesus in the real world.

But Jonny Baker, another popular voice in the ECM in the United Kingdom, writes almost despairingly of Brewin's enthusiasm for TAZs, saying that it is naive, individualistic, and elitist:

> Ironically I fear the world Kester describes works best for the postmodern flâneur (or pirate or heretic or trickster or tactician or artist of the invisible) who has resources and a confidence about their person to tactically navigate the liquid world, but in the way that they choose. And here's the rub: with who they choose (i.e. where's the other now?). They like to avoid fixation, keep their options open as the carnival goes by. In other words it's a world with me at the centre—individualism by another name. . . .

But actually research suggests that the numbers doing anything in
the way of activism a la TAZ are far less than even those in political
parties—really where does it lead in effecting real transformation of
an unjust society? Probably nowhere near where committed engagement does.

Indeed, there is little evidence that Emerging Christians are changing the
world in the direction that they would like to see through the small-scale actions envisioned by TAZs and suspended spaces. Similar to the critique of
neo-monasticism, TAZs seem to be the idealistic playgrounds of the middle
classes. Perhaps it is easier for the middle-class Christians who dominate the
ECM to spurn conventional employment, because they tend not to be forced
into the low-end, minimum wage jobs of the lower classes to make ends meet.
As one man said, "We may try to shed bourgeois ideology, but we can't ever
really lose it."

## Socially Conscious Career Choices

Most people involved in the ECM do not choose to live in neo-monastic communities, but many strive to live out their faith through their career choices.
The ECM appears to be disproportionately middle class and highly educated.[68] While our survey data does not include income levels, 40% of ECM
participants have a college degree, and an additional 36% report some postcollege education (12.3%) and graduate degrees (23.2%), a group which could
be expected to secure well-paid jobs and to participate fully in Western consumerist culture. But our informants and those in other studies of the ECM
explained that they had chosen careers that located them in the community
and voluntary sector, and in some cases involved an intentional choice to work
with the economically disadvantaged. In racially charged American urban
areas, or Northern Ireland divided along sectarian lines, some chose to work
for organizations focused on reconciliation. Wollschleger emphasized this in
his research on the Church of the Apostles, noting that many in the congregation "work in or are studying for work in human and social services."[69] We do
not want to give the impression that every participant or sympathizer with the
ECM has chosen these career paths. Nor is choosing a helping profession in
which one deliberately shuns making more money in another career unique to
the ECM. Christopher Einolf's study also demonstrated that "prosocial" evangelical and liberal Protestants often chose "helping" careers because of their
faith.[70] This resonates with Cherise, who said that her previous experience
in a megachurch made her feel like her work life had become disconnected
from her spiritual life. But that has changed now, she said: "I care for people.

I talk about my spiritual life and I talk about God and bring that into my work. It's not separated." Similarly, another woman said, "[My congregation] has changed my thinking about Christ and who he was and how that affects my life, way more than the 'Here's the three ways of success for your life' [type of sermons]."

Ben described a dramatic change in the way that he approached his career. He said, "I look back at who I used to be, and I'm not even the same person. Before I started going [here] my goal in life was to get very rich. So I went to business school, I read all the books, and now money is just this thing I've got to learn how to use and put up with. It's not the center of my life anymore." Meredith, who was interviewed in 2004, was at that time working for a community-based reconciliation group in Belfast. She linked her career with her faith, crediting Zero28 with helping her "try to figure out how to be Christ-like in this society." She acknowledged that she had chosen a difficult and low-paying career, in which results were slow to come and thin on the ground. She said:

> I don't have grand visions that [my work] is gonna transform North-
> ern Ireland because I've been in this game long enough to know that
> you're lucky if you can effect change with a small handful of people . . .
> This project I work in here, for example: I slave away, and work hours
> and hours and hours, but I know I'm only influencing ten streets. But
> somebody else is working up there on those ten streets. I believe in
> these small dynamic projects in communities.

Others, like Heather, explained how their emerging congregations had helped them think about their career in a new way—their secular employment now became sacred work. She linked this realization to her own well-being: "I also feel that my 9 to 5 job is working for God as well. That's what I've learned here . . . I've just become a better person from this place. I'm just happier, and I certainly have depressive days. But . . . I'm more peaceful. And I'm proud."

We do not know of any research that has systematically investigated Emerging Christians' career choices. But almost all of our respondents said that they wanted their work to change the world for the better and despaired of the undesirable work habits and options bred by Western consumerism. While choosing these careers may involve some sacrifice of financial gain, it should still be recognized that such career choices are in many ways a luxury of the middle class and highly educated. Many in the ECM could be identified with the "creative class," a highly educated, independent, and entrepreneurial class that has options that are almost always not open to the poor or marginalized.[71] But because the vast majority of people who identify with the ECM are not joining inner city, neo-monastic communities, how they choose to express their Christianity through their work in the real world is a major aspect of their religious orientation.

## Authentic, Holistic Lives

For Emerging Christians, following a political Jesus is central to their religious orientation, allowing them to feel that their faith is authentic and holistic. Frank, like many Emerging Christians, said, "It's made me more of a holistic person." Participating in their emerging congregations means that they no longer have to falsely conform to approaches to evangelism and Christian living that they now regard as inauthentic, compartmentalized (maintaining a sacred-secular divide), and damaging to their faith. As one woman said, "I am the daughter of quite a well-known Christian leader, so I've grown up in the Christian world and grown up as so-and-so's daughter. So I've seen a lot of the fickleness and superficiality of the Christian world." By way of contrast, in a focus group conversation Shauna said, "My experience here has been that people and the church are people who want to be real and who are about transformation and not just pretending." She sees this as prompting her to live a better Christian life; in short, to *love* better: "I want to be affected to a point where I love the world in a way that's true, and not this false thing." Blake said that the experience of his congregation had helped him answer questions he had in his previous church: "Why [did the church] seem to do so many things that I didn't really think Jesus would be interested in doing? And why weren't they prioritizing some of the things that he did very consistently? I know it's campy to say what would Jesus do, but it's kind of along those lines." He continued, "My wife and I always called it 'the Christian Country Club.' They establish their group, their 'club,' their things, their rules, which were all not really spoken, and everyone was really comfortable with all that, but we never were."

Emerging Christians contrast their experience to the "Christian Country Club" expression of faith, thus linking their religious orientation with the small "p" political action described in this chapter. As another woman said, "Faith—you know in the Hebrew sense—is action. It's how we act that out in our community." The idea of *authentic faith as action,* and of the location of that faith *outside the walls of the church and in the community,* contributes to an overall sense of holism among Emerging Christians. Indeed, many self-consciously strive to live holistically, seeing this as integral to nurturing their own religious journeys. As a woman with experience in several churches said, "This is the first church I've gone to where they treat you as a whole person. There isn't this spiritual side of you, and this human side of you, and this work side of you, and this mom side of you. It's all one thing." Or as Lilly said, "I really love what [our leader] says all the time about having people experience God intellectually, emotionally, relationally, and aesthetically." Similarly, Dylan related how his congregation "helped me realize things in a more holistic way. It's kind of hard to explain, but that's what's been good for me." In yet another congregation, a man said, "What's new to me is this holistic piece. You're living on earth. Respect the earth . . . I'm a part of this thing, this ball going around the sun, and I should take care of it, it is a gift, and that influences your theology and how you live and everything." Dakota summed it up this way: "It's like life, more so than just church. This is just what you do."

## Following Jesus in the Real World

Rob Bell's *Love Wins* is among the most controversial books published by a figure associated with the ECM. Much of the debate about the book has centered on the question of whether Bell is a "universalist"—someone who believes that everyone will get into heaven in the end.[72] But setting aside that question, an important theme of the book is that some versions of Christianity are preventing people from living like Christians in the real world and enjoying the fullness of life that God intends for them. Bell writes:

> So when the gospel is diminished to a question of whether or not a person will "get into heaven," that reduces the good news to a ticket, a way to get past the bouncer and into the club.
>
> The good news is better than that.
>
> That is why Christians who talk the most about going to heaven while everybody else goes to hell don't throw very good parties.
>
> When the gospel is understood primarily in terms of entrance rather than joyous participation, it can actually serve to cut people off from the explosive, liberating experience of the God who is an endless giving circle of joy and creativity. . . .
>
> Jesus calls disciples to keep entering into this shared life of peace and joy as it transforms our hearts, until it's the most natural way to live that we can imagine. Until it's second nature. Until we naturally embody and practice the kind of attitudes and actions that will go on in the age to come. A discussion about how to "just get into heaven" has no place in the life of a disciple of Jesus, because it's missing the point of it all.[73]

Bell is expressing the commonly held view within the ECM that Christianity is more about what you do than it is about what you believe.

In this chapter, we have explored the ECM's emphasis on "orthopraxy," or living in the "right" way. Emerging Christians agree that their previous experiences with conventional church institutions did not adequately help them live authentically or holistically. They may disagree on the extent that the purpose of their lives is to be "missional" or "political" or both. But following the example of Jesus as they understand it, they agree that faith is inherently political in a way that favors the poor and marginalized. To that end, they choose various paths to "follow Jesus in the real world," including conventional political engagement, forming neo-monastic communities, creating TAZs, and choosing careers that enable them to work for social justice. This means that previously important church commitments, such as attending long prayer meetings, participating in several worship services on a Sunday, or engaging in street evangelism, are no longer important. What matters for their enactment of their religious identity is their work out in the world, not inside the walls of the church.

This mobilization of their religiously deconstructed and reoriented selves represents a repoliticization of Christianity away from an approach in which Christian organizations form links with political parties or champion particular causes, such as preventing abortion. This repoliticization is an approach in which politics has a small "p" and involves self-consciously working *outside* what Emerging Christians see as corrupt and oppressive political, economic, and, in some cases, ecclesial systems. People point to these distinct political practices when they define themselves over and against other, mainly evangelical, expressions of Christianity and their conservative political agendas. And as the passage from *Love Wins* conveys, Emerging Christians think that their new ways of living are freeing them from previous religious burdens that were too heavy for them to bear, providing them with an avenue not only for helping others and for experiencing community but also for undergoing personal spiritual growth. At the same time, it is difficult to evaluate whether Emerging Christians' attempts to follow Jesus in the real world are actually making a difference in the real world. In some cases, the answer must be yes—at least on a grassroots level, as in the work performed by East Central Ministries in Albuquerque (chapter 1), or for individuals who feel empowered to work outside their congregations in carefully chosen careers or as volunteers for various causes. But it is extraordinarily difficult to "scale-up" such small-scale efforts, and there are no signs that this is a goal of the ECM. Packard has asked:

> One measure of a movement, especially a religious one, might be in asking "If this group disappeared, would anyone outside the group

care . . . or even notice?" With the ECM, I think the answer is a re-
sounding, "No," or at best "Maybe." Although this disappoints the
people I talk(ed) with, they don't deny it. If they're doing a different
kind of church than institutional church, then they feel like they need
to be doing different kinds of service as well, but at the end of the day,
just don't.[74]

We see Emerging Christians' service through neo-monastic communities as
a different kind of service than that performed by the institutional church.
But we acknowledge that neo-monastics do not make up the majority of the
ECM. We also think that it is misleading to try and gauge the "effectiveness"
of the ECM's activism by evaluating what its congregations do. Because so
many Emerging Christians eschew the sacred-secular divide, this means that
they just might not see their congregation or religious community as the most
promising site for working for social or political transformation. At the same
time, like Packard, we sense that Emerging Christians' lives in the real world
do not always live up to their ideals—but in this, the ECM is like many other
social movements.

Embracing more amorphous social concerns that cannot be captured in
programmed ministry initiatives and deeply associating with others outside
their congregations are important for Emerging Christians. These activities
and concerns provide multiple, necessary opportunities for experimenting and
implementing a newly individuated religious self. These deconstructed practices and attitudes are wrought in contention with the excessively "narrow"
conventional Christian approaches from their past. Yet Emerging Christians
believe they are more fitting, more substantive, and more satisfying to whatever must be "true" to a genuine representation of Christianity.

# Understanding Emerging Christianity

Our church is an open space where individuals get to work out
whatever they need. Individuals are coming together.
—Samuel, *describing his emerging congregation*

A lot of writing exists about the Emerging Church Movement (ECM)—
mostly a mixture of suppositions, speculations, and various spokespeople representing their visions of it. But sociologists of religion have been reluctant to
pay much attention to these network-dependent, loosely affiliated, and largely
marginalized Christians. Many academics assume the ECM is a fad, a marginal
movement that will stay on the margins or simply fade away. Some observers
characterize it merely as a reform movement within evangelicalism, a "hipster"
Christianity that masks a conservative, orthodox evangelicalism with coffee,
candles, and horn-rimmed glasses.[1] Still others—perhaps those who have read
Brian McLaren, Rob Bell, Tony Jones, or Peter Rollins—claim it is a rehashed
Liberal Protestantism. Still others argue that it appeals to a niche market of
disaffected Christian consumers, those who belong to a certain demographic:
primarily young, highly educated, middle class, and white. Recently, there
have been statements from within the ECM that the emerging church is dead.
In contrast to these claims, we see the ECM as a distinct response to the wider
social, political, economic, and religious forces that have shaped modernity.
Emerging Christians think they have found a path to religious vitality. Their
deconstructed faith is a source of renewal, albeit with a shaky and uncertain
base that reflects the difficulty of building a religious orientation on the same
pillars that one seeks to topple.

We bring our own conceptual lenses to bear on an ambitious task: How do
we frame the workings of a diffuse religious orientation against the backdrop
of the changed society that makes it possible? Gathering together all our interviews and observations as well as a broad reading of books, blogs, and Twitter feeds, we find that the ECM is best understood as an intriguing reshaping
of religious imperatives and the efforts to put them into practice. The ECM

both reacts *against* modernity and simultaneously *draws on* modern Western conceptions of the self and community to produce a form of religiosity that is well suited to our era. In this the ECM can be compared to Renewalist (Pentecostal and charismatic) Christianity, an expression of faith that also reacts against and draws on modernity in shaping a distinctive religious self.[2] Like the ECM, Renewalist Christianity has a direct relationship with evangelicalism. But unlike the ECM, Renewalist Christianity shares with evangelicalism an emphasis on a literalist or inspired view of the Bible and the need to be "born again." The ECM is not interested in retrenching evangelical commitments. Its intent is far more disruptive.

We describe the religious orientation of the ECM as generally *deconstructive*; however, the process of deconstruction should be defined in a sociological rather than a philosophical sense. Misunderstandings of the ECM are rampant. For example, attending an ECM conference in 2013, Barton Gingerich posted a sharp critique on Twitter (@bjgingerich) saying, "'Emergence Christians': pretty sure that means dysfunctional Protestants that read too much Derrida." Besides dismissive comments coming from conservative voices, deconstruction is used loosely even within the ECM. In a blog post, Blake Huggins writes, "Deconstruction becomes a type of easy shorthand for systematically dismantling the components of one's faith or theology, throwing out those pieces that don't make sense and then putting it all together again."[3] For Huggins, ECM deconstruction is not a stop on the journey toward reconstruction; he desires "a Christianity constantly and perpetually infected by deconstruction." The deconstruction of faith "demands constant exploration and re-imagination, not calcified reconstruction . . . deconstruction cannot be abandoned—because this abyss, this wound of divine desire is not something to be overcome and subsequently reconstructed but something the aftermath of which we are constantly wrestling." Huggins's post is theologically saturated by mysticism and negative theology, yet, sociologically speaking, what he calls for is an open-ended, never-finished faith in which Christians see themselves as on a perpetual spiritual quest.[4]

Translated from theological language to sociological practice, the ECM is a case of *collective institutional entrepreneurship* that is forging a religious orientation suited to the society in which we live. Emerging Christians engage in micropolitics against pressures toward conformity from forms of Christianity they perceive to be false and oppressive. As *religious institutional entrepreneurs*, Emerging Christians participate in *pluralist congregations* in which liturgical and devotional practices are deliberately open, inclusive, and drawn from various traditions, which allow people to strategically select which religious practices work best for them. The ECM therefore fosters corporate settings for the enactment of a *strategic religiosity* that allows Emerging Christians to seek out and legitimate a broad spectrum in forms of religiosity while other familiar, often widespread, and often more conventional forms are rendered inadequate. The ECM accommodates *multiple paths* of spirituality accessible through diverse responses to congregational activities. The practices of emerging congregations help people accommodate apparently contradictory priorities: exercising individual religious autonomy while participating in a collective congregational life. Rather than being strictly individualistic, their religious practices are *individuated* while encouraging a consciousness of corporate responsibility. Moreover, congregational participation is not the sole concern for Emerging Christians; their activities and priorities extend holistically to more expansive social, ethical, and spiritual concerns that inhere to their everyday lives.

Overall, Emerging Christianity is a religious orientation centered on individualization. *Religious individualization indicates how individuals develop religious identities from a range of sources, negotiating the imperatives of various religious institutions and taking ownership of their own convictions—however uncertain, ambiguous, and seemingly antireligious those convictions may be.* The religious individualization of Emerging Christians is not a self-contained endeavor. Larger social changes prompt the need for individualization, and societal institutions provide potential resources for it. Indeed, many social scientists believe that all modern religious forms must effectively individualize if they are to endure. In their seminal work, *The Spiritual Revolution: Why Religion Is Giving Way to Spirituality,* Paul Heelas and Linda Woodhead argued that forms of religion that could not effectively adapt to the individualized "subjectivization" of modernity would continue to decline, while those which emphasized the autonomy of the self within a supportive community would thrive.[5] They argued that conventional Christian congregations do not go far enough in nurturing people's individualized spiritual quests. For us, this is precisely what the congregations of the ECM are doing. Similarly, the charismatic Vineyard congregations that are the focus of Tanya Luhrmann's *When God Talks Back* help people cultivate an individualized, yet communally expressed, spirituality in which prayer and worship form a bedrock for people's *individual* experiences of God.[6]

Bryan Turner in *Religion and Modern Society* also highlights religious individuation as a condition of postsecular society.[7] For Turner, we live in "faithfull" societies because religion represents (among other things) a key dynamic for the cultivation of personal identity in a world increasingly oriented toward expressive individualism. Religious individuals are motivated, energized, and fit the modern imperative of becoming an "individual." They engage the mechanisms of liberal democracy to advocate for their values and priorities, thereby giving religion a newly explicit public role to affirm their individualism. In the face of increased religious competition, adherents sense the need to justify their preferences for particularistic views. Revising Weber's *Protestant Thesis*, Turner asserts that religion is unavoidably caught up in the commercialization of everyday life. Religious selves are upheld through outlets that enthrall and entertain. The aesthetics of religion come to matter even more as a point of attraction and connection. Piety becomes a creative amalgam of habits and attitudes that form a new habitus in disposition and tastes in relation to a pluralist world that discourages religious authority, amplifies individual consumption, and keeps people engaged in dominant economic structures. In consequence, religion emerges as today's richest vehicle for individualism, one that accommodates increased subjectivity and provides coping mechanisms for incessant demands for self-help. Since lifestyles and their associated cultural institutions become a necessary part of religious life, there is an intriguing parallel between secular and religious consumerism driven by the nation-state's craving for economic prosperity.

Individuals' reflexivity, agency, and capacity to choose, and the historical contingency of religious institutions and other "sacred forms," have been important also in the development of the "sociology of the sacred," associated with Jeffrey C. Alexander,[8] as well as Gordon Lynch.[9] The sociology of the sacred adds a further dimension of complexity to our analysis by locating "sacred forms" in "different kinds of social structure—for example, the nation state, the diasporic community, the transnational organization or movement, or other kinds of subcultural structure."[10] Crucially, *"modern society is characterized by the emergence of multiple sacred forms* in the wake of the fragmentation of more inclusive sacred canopies."[11] The sociology of the sacred not only alerts us to competing (institutional) religious options for individuals, it explores how individuals and communities find sacred meanings in causes such as gender, human rights, the care of children, nature, and the neoliberal marketplace.[12]

Sociologist Ulrich Beck in *A God of One's Own* presents a comprehensive approach that encompasses globalization, individualization, and religious vitality. For too long religion took on too many burdens, accepting responsibility for societal tasks it could not complete. Beck goes so far to say that secularization is "a gift of God," a necessary corrective for recovering the essential goals of religion. For Beck, "religion is forced to be *religion and nothing else.*"[13] In short, "The enforced secularization of religion has paved the way for the revitalization of religiosity and spirituality in the twenty-first century."[14] The "spiritual revolution," "postsecularity," the "sociology of the sacred," and a "God of one's own" are all bold revisions of the theory of secularization that associates the rise of individualization with scientific rationality, the weakening of religious institutions, and the exodus of belief from citizens of modern nation-states.

In this chapter, we briefly outline why we do not see Emerging Christians as evangelicals in disguise, Liberal Protestants, religious consumers, or simply "dead." We then suggest how Emerging Christians' orientations and practices situate them so well in the modern (though Emerging Christians would prefer to call it postmodern) landscape. The ECM was developed and continues to persist because the orientations and practices of the ECM resonate with the (modern) emphasis on the self. Its practices of flat leadership, communication, and dissemination of ideas echo the experience of networking that modern individuals already experience in the secular realms of work and leisure. Most importantly, emerging congregations provide settings where pluralism is embraced and where the otherwise isolated self can find meaning and fulfillment through others. The ECM not only provides opportunity for enacting their individualized religiosity but also for entering into caring relationships and acting out of mutual concern, what we characterize as *cooperative egoism. Cooperative egoism involves the management and assertion of one's individuated self yet simultaneously involves connection, empathy, and love for others.* The cooperative egoism of Emerging Christians compliments their processes of religious individuation. In short, the ECM offers collective religious structures that legitimate Emerging Christians' individuated orientations.

## Persistent Questions Regarding the Emerging Church Movement

To counter dominant perceptions of the ECM, we first discuss the most common conclusions regarding the ECM, offering our understanding of why each one is insufficient to capture the greater nuances and complexities of the movement.

### Evangelicals in Disguise?

In chapter 1, we explored how the ECM developed out of a cohort of evangelical church ministry workers who sought to bridge the gap between a closed, institutionalized church world and the broader dynamics of media, politics, pop culture, and technology. But the activity of these youth pastors and lay leaders became a much broader attempt to break free of established forms of the congregations they knew. The ECM quickly moved beyond changing congregational practices to critiquing the core tenets and assumptions of evangelicalism, such as the inerrancy of the Bible (the belief that the Bible is *literally* true—a belief held by some, not all, evangelicals), the necessity of a born again conversion experience, the adherence to conservative political agendas, and the lack of focus on social justice. Next, Emerging Christians began to refine their own theologies—often in direct opposition to conservative evangelical and/or neo-Calvinist perspectives, as explored in chapters 4, 5, and 6.

Conferences, websites, blog posts, Twitter feeds, and especially the writings of leaders like Rob Bell, Brian McLaren, Peter Rollins, and Tony Jones offered alternative interpretations of standard evangelical readings of the Bible, positioned doubt as an inevitable and even healthy aspect of faith, and contradicted evangelical assumptions about the nature of truth and the nature of God (chapter 4). Emerging Christians found each other both in face-to-face settings and online, creating affinities and alliances that crossed (and sometimes violated) conventional hierarchies. Emerging Christians also advocated a small "p" political agenda in which social justice issues were foregrounded and increasingly began to take up LGBTQ rights as an issue in the big "P" political sphere (chapter 6).

An increasingly sharp differentiation between evangelicalism and the ECM was perhaps to be expected. As we have shown throughout this book, Emerging Christians almost constantly identify problems within evangelicalism and attempt to "normalize problematizations."[15] Problems fuel arguments for supporting innovative practices such that "reforms benefit from problems."[16] The acknowledgment and even exaggeration of problematic situations promotes experimentation in new frames for individual action and corporate organization.[17] Emerging Christians problematize established logics and practices by asserting their negative impacts, categorizing them as unethical, undesirable, or inappropriate, and calling for change. Previously taken-for-granted conclusions about Christianity (like positions on gay rights) become rich points of contrast to draw out a new orientation of appropriate faith. Ultimately, the work of problematization provokes defensive work from those invested in conventional Christianity, as it exists, thus accounting for the overwhelming criticism of the ECM. As Steve Maguire and Cynthia Hardy write, "A range of new actors produce texts that support and promote problematizations; existing actors begin to produce counter texts; and the number of both problematizing texts and counter texts increases."[18] Further translation and reinterpretation of new discourses create both variety and contradictions, which make the emerging institutional forms both less coherent and less recognizable to their origins.

Indeed, the ECM has moved so far from the central convictions of evangelicals, they have become anathema—dangerous heretics to be avoided. As conservative pastors, churches, and national organizations became more aware of the ECM, they organized responses condemning it. One of the more striking reactions came from delegates at the 68th Annual Convention of the

American Council of Christian Churches, meeting in Toronto, Canada, in 2009 who resolved together "to reject and repudiate the Emerging Church movement as heretical." In one of several resolutions passed that year, the group claimed its "adherence to the Word of God" and pledged to define "the Bible as the only guide for all matters of faith and practice." They named Brian McLaren, Rob Bell, and Erwin McManus as leaders of the movement and promoters of "errors." In rejecting the ECM, they resolved to "do all within our power to expose the unbiblical and deceptive concepts of the Emerging Church movement, to warn of its dangers, and to call all mankind to return to Scripture alone as our sole source of knowledge regarding all that is spiritual." As an outgrowth of such conservative reactions, our respondents shared stories of domestic missionaries showing up in ECM churches with the goal of correcting heresies and drawing back the wayward. Emerging Christians from evangelical backgrounds eventually removed themselves from the category of evangelical altogether.

## Liberal Protestants?

While some may realize that Emerging Christians are not evangelicals in disguise, they may nevertheless go on to characterize them as Liberal Protestants. In 2011, Rodney Neill posted a comment on Gladys's blog, asking, "I wonder if those who might be sympathetic to the emerging church in Northern Ireland are in essence part of the liberal progressive tradition within Christianity and thus have considerable doctrinal differences with their evangelical counterparts?"[19] Neill then posted an eight-point description of progressive Christianity from the Progressive Christian Network (PCN) website, which included a spirituality based on the humanity of Jesus, a willingness to acknowledge multiple paths to God, an open table for communion, a conviction that our treatment of others is the best testament to Christian beliefs, a prioritizing of questions over absolute certainty, a striving for peace and justice that includes both humans and the environment, a call to renounce privileges in the service of others, and a welcoming community which invites all:

> To participate in our community and worship life without insisting that they become like us in order to be acceptable, including, but not limited to: believers and agnostics, conventional Christians and questioning skeptics, women and men, those of all sexual orientations and gender identities, those of all races and cultures, those of all classes and abilities, and those who hope for a better world and those who have lost hope, without imposing on them the necessity of becoming like us.[20]

At first glance, there seems little to distinguish "progressive Christians" from Emerging Christians—indeed, most Emerging Christians would agree with the points listed. But what most distinguishes Emerging Christians from Liberal Protestants is Emerging Christians' much more radical individualism (a radical individualism they share with Renewalist Christians). Heelas and Woodhead noted a striking *lack* of individualism among congregants in the Liberal Protestant churches in their study. They observed: "The effect of their strongly moralistic emphasis on caring for others, and putting God and neighbour before self is, however, to render these the *least* subjectivized of all the congregational types. Instead of focusing on individual experiences, needs, desires, moods, bodily and emotional sensations, they direct their members' attention not inwards to themselves, but outwards towards God and fellow humans in need of care."[21]

The ECM offers a far more individualized, subjective religious experience than Liberal Protestant churches, which tend to place the focus of religion *primarily* outside the self and on others. Moreover, while it may be easy to equate any move away from the strictures of conservatism as an indication of becoming liberal, this labeling misrepresents both liberalism and the ECM. Liberalism maintains an acceptance of the transcendent realm while simultaneously urging sacrificial care for others and for the earth. In contrast, the ECM sidesteps such confidence in a transcendent realm in its nascent development of "A/Theism."[22] Katharine Sarah Moody describes A/Theism as "organized around a motif of deconstruction, asserting that the Christian tradition is itself 'auto-deconstructive,' meaning a faith that attempts to cut across the boundaries between atheist and theist, and between the secular and the religious, disturbing these and other dualisms."[23] Similarly, Peter Rollins has written on "Incarnational A/Theism," by which he is referring "not to an intellectual disavowal of God, but to the *felt experience of God's absence*; an experience that must be distinguished from the idea of a mere absence of experience. To understand the difference take a moment to think about the difference between the absence that exists before you meet someone you later come to love and the absence you experience once they are gone."[24] As such, the A/Theism of the ECM is theologically distinct from mainstream Liberal Protestantism. In particular there is more room for people to embrace uncertainty and brokenness.[25] This approach is also associated with the work of John D. Caputo and Slavoj Žižek, philosophers who Rollins draws on extensively.[26] In its failure to provide believers a consistent vision of overarching transcendence, the ECM's approach to religion actively denigrates rather than buttresses what many see as the comforts of Liberal Protestantism's Golden Rule Christianity.[27]

Further, Emerging Christians deny that they are Liberal Protestants almost as strenuously as they deny they are evangelicals. This is not just because the term "liberal" carries negative connotations, especially in the United States. Rather the disassociation with liberalism stems from philosophical or theological conviction. Some, like Rollins, identify themselves with radical theology, contrasting it deliberately to liberal theology. In 2013, Gladys participated in an online "Radical Theology Summer Reading Group" with Rollins and Tripp Fuller through the Mission Solutions website. One of the first readings was by John Macquarrie and titled, "Liberal and Radical Theologies: An Historical Comparison." In drawing out what distinguishes radical theology from liberal theology, Macquarrie argues that radical theology takes as its point of departure "the death of God," that radical theology is a theology of "revolution" while liberal theology is a theology of "evolution," and that "radical theology seeks the overthrow and transformation not only of traditional religious values but the values of the prevailing culture as well."[28] Macquarrie lists conflicts between the two theological traditions in detail:

> Liberal theology is oriented to the present, radical theology (as eschatological) to the future; liberal theology seeks to relate positively to the prevailing culture, radical theology denies it as the present age which must perish so that the new can be born; liberal theology is tolerant to the point of indifferentism, it is ecumenical and well disposed even to non-Christian religions, while radical theology has the intolerance (not necessarily a persecuting one) of an urgent conviction and tends to operate through the self-conscious sect or pressure group; liberal theology, though not indifferent to the ethical, sets itself above all the goal of intellectual honesty and employs categories drawn from science and philosophy, while radical theology is mainly practical and uses political categories. Perhaps the fundamental point is that liberal theology is embarrassed by apocalyptic, which must therefore be either eliminated or demythologized, while for radical theology such ideas as the end of the age and the resurrection of the dead are of the very essence of Christianity.[29]

Doubtless, there are Emerging Christians who would identify with some aspects of both liberal and radical theologies, and Rollins's "pyrotheology" goes further than most in pushing toward the radical. But the anti-institutionalism of the ECM that we have described throughout this book resonates much more with radical theology's imperative to transform religion and the wider world. In contrast, it seems Liberal Protestants would rather create slightly reformed institutions that still fit within current religious and political orders.

## Religious Consumers?

Josh Packard claims that Emerging Christians are a certain "type" of person, those who are also likely to be "anti-institutional" in other parts of their lives, shunning Walmart and Starbucks in favor of local boutiques and farmers' markets.[30] This type of person strongly resists what they see as consumerist religion; as Nadia Bolz-Weber writes, "We had started HFASS [House for All Sinners and Saints] out of a disdain for consumer culture in religion."[31] This type of person is also disproportionately young, white, middle class, and well educated; and often possesses resources of time, energy, and money dependent on a particular stage of life (single or recently married with no children). Drawing on the work of Ann Swidler, he argues that maintaining a resistant organization requires Emerging Christians to lead "permanently unsettled lives" as they keep up a relentless schedule of questioning and conversation about their faith. Only a minority of people, it is implied, are able to keep this up over time. Packard's description indicates that Emerging Christians could be seen as tapping into the relatively "niche" market provided by emerging congregations. Packard does not conceive of a niche as limited in terms of persistence, nor does he necessarily equate occupying a niche with religious consumerism. Rather he emphasizes that the appeal of the ECM is concentrated in a demographic that can be quite clearly defined.

Our survey data of eight emerging congregations (albeit drawn only from the United States) generally affirms Packard's demographic picture; nevertheless, it is necessary to note that merely listing brief characteristics like "well-educated," "young," "single," and "white" obscures the number of Emerging Christians who fail to fit into these categories. Our data show that ECM participants are indeed highly educated: 40% had bachelors or vocational education, 12.3% had some level of graduate education, and an additional 23% had completed a master's or doctoral degree. However, contrary to expectations, about a quarter of ECM participants are "middle aged" (36 to 55 years old), and 44% are married or cohabiting. Roughly one-third have minor children. Moreover, despite the supposed "maleness" of the ECM, our data indicate slightly more (54.5%) female than male involvement in emerging congregations. Finally, while 93% of our respondents are white, comparative analysis of our survey data reveals that Emerging Christians are *significantly more* racially diverse than participants in other religious categories (evangelical, Catholic, mainline, and "nones") who are located in the same region.[32]

House for All Sinners and Saints offers an interesting example of what may happen when an emerging congregation breaks out of a niche and begins attracting a more middle-aged, suburban demographic, as happened when the *Denver Post* profiled the congregation. In *Cranky, Beautiful Faith,* Bolz-Weber

recounts how she was initially horrified by this invasion of soccer moms, lamenting, "My precious little indie boutique of a church was being treated like a
7-Eleven, and I was terrified that the edgy, marginalized people whom we had
always attracted would now come and see a bunch of people who looked like
their parents and think, 'This isn't for me.'"[33] Bolz-Weber describes how she
and the church finally embraced this new form of diversity, concluding:

> You can look around at the 120 or so people gathered on any given
> Sunday and think *I am unclear what all these people have in common.*
> Out of one corner of your eye there's a homeless guy serving commu-
> nion to a corporate lawyer and out of the other corner is a teenage girl
> with pink hair holding the baby of a suburban soccer mom. And there
> I was a year ago fearing that the weirdness of our church was going to
> be diluted.[34]

So, while our data show congregations with predominantly young, single,
childless, and well-educated members, the full scope of the data indicates a
much greater range of demographic categories involved in the ECM. Especially when examined in light of the qualitative data, we would not focus
on a singular niche of members who are thereby attracted to the "culture" of
emerging congregations. Rather, we would instead emphasize that the structure of emerging congregations discourages participation by certain people.
For example, the hybridization of liturgical practices, the spontaneous and
discursive nature of gatherings, the use of nontraditional times and spaces for
services, the absence of children's programming, and the haphazard nature of
organizational processes pose challenges for parents with children, for mature
men and women embedded in extended family activities and networks that
require planning and coordination, and for older adults who are satisfied with
existing forms of religiosity.

Even more, the supposed cultural characteristics of Emerging Christians
as "anti-institutionalists" who shun the dominant culture may be oversimpli-
fied. We hesitate to assign a narrowly defined, monolithic attitude to Emerging
Christians. And while we do not dispute that the ECM is on the margins of
contemporary Christianity, we think that its potential appeal is much greater
than is currently supposed. Indeed, as we argue in this chapter, the ECM reflects immersion in mainstream aspects of modern society much more so than
other expressions of Christianity. Ironically, it is these mainstream aspects of
the ECM that have led to more critical assessments of the ECM as consumer
religion, shaped by and for its market. An entire book in the Fresh Expressions' *Ancient Faith Future Mission* series is framed around responding to this
critique, as articulated by Church of England Archbishop Rowan Williams:

"One of the sharpest criticisms of . . . fresh expressions . . . is that it accepts without challenge a private and apolitical perspective that simply colludes with the general culture of consumer choice and the search for what makes me feel better rather than what is true."[35] Many of the chapters in this collection are written by activists and provide counter-examples of congregations serving others outside of their immediate group.[36]

Similarly, in a blog post titled "Neoliberal Church?," Stephen Keating writes:

> I've followed Peter Rollins' work for a couple years now and this weekend I had an epiphany: Are "transformation art collectives," as he calls his communities (read: churches in a pub), really just a new kind of church for a new kind of capitalism? . . . Under the regime that we have entered and are currently living in, which, following Mauricio Lazzarato, I will call a debt economy, we now embody a new form of subjectivity . . . Institutions in the debt economy discipline subjects into a new form of subjectivity. We must build our personal brand and bring every aspect of our lives into the realm of exchange. Perpetually in debt, we are all required to deepen the "self," because it is towards this biometrically reduced self that our debts are targeted. We must take responsibility for our selves, always fostering our creativity and injecting more and more energy into the institutions within which we participate. Employers monitor Facebook to see how employees are representing The Brand. Hobbies are no longer for fun, but must lead to a Kickstarter or an Etsy store. Where do Rollins' collectives, or more generally emerging churches, fit into this trajectory? . . . Members of these groups are expected to contribute their creativity. New versions of old liturgies and scriptural texts must continually be produced. New brands are built and carefully maintained. The self must be deepened in the drive to "be more human." Neoliberalism has been with us for around 30 years now. I hate to make a pure base/superstructure argument, but is "the church" finally catching up to the debt economy?[37]

Keating argues that the ECM is not a niche but rather falls head-first into wider neoliberal structures. In a comment on Keating's post, Rollins unsurprisingly resisted being characterized as "an (unconscious) instrument of neoliberalism" and lumped into the consumer or "debt" economy. Taking care to distinguish his written work from the activities of Ikon, Rollins commented, "While I might be open to critique for being an armchair theorist fully immersed in, and perpetuating a neoliberal ideology I would ask anyone to spend a week with those involved in Ikon Belfast and come to the same conclusion about them in either their beliefs or practices." In chapter 6, we discussed how Emerging Christians understood themselves as trapped within capitalist frameworks. Some self-consciously try to subvert capitalism by living "outside the system" in neo-monastic communities, or creating Temporary Autonomous Zones (TAZs) and "suspended spaces" that can contribute to transformation in social, economic, or political life. Of course, the effectiveness of these strategies remains relatively untested. We see Emerging Christians as embedded agents in this framework, whose projects to transform their worlds will inevitably meet with varying degrees of effectiveness (however that may be measured).[38]

Our findings suggest that the ECM is not a narrow niche characterized by a tidy set of variables or strict cultural homogeneity. As a contrast to the niche concept, the literature on organizational change alerts us to the possibility that a new industry category does not necessarily produce a single coherent identity (what is termed "identity convergence"). Rather, organizational entrepreneurs learn new ways of doing things, experiment, and develop organizational identities that give their organizations a degree of distinctiveness.[39] The result is a process of form emergence that yields several distinct clusters of identity within the same nominal category and appeals to those with various characteristics. We try to capture this dynamic with our characterization of Emerging Christians as sharing a religious orientation, rather than a single, fixed religious identity. As the ECM strives to revise its relationship to mainstream Christianities, their pluralist congregations allow for multiplicity in the backgrounds and religious orientations of their constituents.

## The Emerging Church is Dead?

Even if the ECM is distinctive, has the movement run its course? Emerging Christians have posted various blogs claiming "the emerging church is dead."[40] But some insiders understand the "RIP ECM" discussion not as an indication of its weakness but rather as its growing maturation away from merely reactionary stances. Brian McLaren insists that the movement is "stronger than ever," and explains, "Evangelical/Charismatic gatekeepers have successfully driven the emergent conversation underground." McLaren continues, "My sense is that more and more of us who are deeply involved with emergence Christianity are simply talking about God, Jesus, the Bible, mission, faith, spirituality, and life . . . and doing so from a new and fresh perspective, but not using the 'e' word so much. Sometimes it's the word 'missional' that works, sometimes it's 'progressive,' sometimes it's 'new kind of'—it goes under lots of labels."[41]

Alongside advocates of the ECM like McLaren, we observe that the general phenomenon of Emergence Christianity across the spectrum of Christian communities (Catholic, Orthodox, Protestant) is not only viable but shows some signs of spreading. Scholars of religion (nearly all of whom are distant outsiders to the movement) lack exposure to the ECM and are unaware of the growing flow of adherents to it and even less aware of people who remain in conventional congregations but who are influenced by reading books and blogs by Emerging Christians. Those attending a 2010 session of the Association for the Sociology of Religion questioned if there was anything genuinely "new" to this movement and wondered about dedicating scholarly attention to it. Yet, the many local and national conferences attracting longtime allies as well as first time religiously curious are a sign of strength that is often ignored. This challenges us as researchers to be more careful about specifying what we are observing and to be more explicit about pointing to locations besides church services as sites where people are finding Emerging Christianity for themselves.

Organizations in environments that are rich in alternative models (like contemporary Christianity) are less likely to conform to their peers because they have access to more diverse identity templates and the work of identity differentiation itself has legitimacy. Congregations in such environments may be freer to deviate from external identity constraints and create innovative designs.[42] Multiple standards may arise. These diverse standards, observed as distinct identity clusters, can eventually crystallize into competing institutional logics or can coexist peacefully as alternative modes of organizing.[43] This type of environment is fertile ground for the ECM. As such, the relatively haphazard and uncoordinated efforts of Emerging Christians mean that "outcomes, being dependent on the actions and reactions of multiple actors, [are] by definition uncertain."[44] And one outcome that is uncertain is whether Emerging Christians will recognize themselves, or ultimately define themselves as, "Emerging Christians"—an uncertainty reflected in the "RIP ECM" debate. While the possibility for more regularized multiple religious identities to coalesce out of the ECM is viable, it is not expected any time soon.

To summarize—rather than declaring its death, we see the ECM as moving beyond specific groups, congregations, and collectives that explicitly take on the moniker of "emerging" or "emergent." The ECM is not dying but persistent. Many who do not take on the label still participate in the movement through their questioning of established orthodoxy and active negotiation of conventional practices. The analytical approach required here is to move from *specific organizations* to an investigation of a *broader movement* that manifests in various religious arenas—a movement characterized by a set of features we describe in this chapter.

## Persistent Characteristics of the Emerging Church Movement

Throughout this book, we have emphasized that the ECM, more so than many other expressions of contemporary Christianity, caters to the *individual*. It creates spaces where people can strategically exercise their freedom and autonomy to embark on individualized religious imperatives. Like Renewalist Christianity, the ECM is what Heelas and Woodhead would categorize as an "experiential" form of Christianity, well suited to appeal to modern, reflexive, subjective individuals. What we see in the ECM also affirms Beck's broader conclusions in *A God of One's Own*. Beck's goal in that book is to profile "the individualization of religion in its relation to the religious revival of the beginning of the twenty-first century."[45]

By tying the development of the ECM to the broader changes in global society as described by these and other scholars, we find there is a viable sociological basis for the principles that guide the ECM to become more widespread. This could occur either through the development of new congregations or through inspiring change within the congregations of traditional denominations. Some combination of these options is currently underway transnationally, with Archbishop Rowan Williams describing the ongoing results of this in the United Kingdom as a "mixed economy" of "fresh expressions and 'inherited' forms of church existing alongside each other, within the same denomination, in relationships of mutual respect and support."[46]

By whatever name or names it comes to be known, we think the structures and practices of the ECM will persist, perhaps even thrive, in the modern religious landscape. We base this conclusion on our observation that the ECM manifests a distinctive religious orientation that reflects and resonates with key modern developments and values focused on the dynamics of individuation. We suggest the following conceptualizations as theoretical groundwork for understanding the integration of the fierce egoism of Emerging Christians with the immersive relationships characteristic of their pluralistic congregations.

## The Emerging Church Movement is a Transnational Network

The ECM is a relatively coherent transnational phenomenon in part because Emerging Christians have developed strong relational networks both on and offline. Lacking the traditional structures of denominations, Emerging Christians turn to their networks to share information, gather ideas, and participate in the conversation (chapter 4). Most often as *individuals* logging on to their computers or attending conferences, Emerging Christians choose what networks they will participate in through the blogs they visit, the social media that they use, and the people they choose to meet. In this, Emerging Christians' practices resonate with Beck's observation that "the religious practices associated with 'a God of one's own' presupposes the possibility of *choosing* a form of community or anticipate it as a future option; such practices function transnationally in networks and organizations appropriate for the purpose."[47]

When Emerging Christians make connections to a broader network of similar minded people, they find reassurance that they are not alone in their orientation. Yet, more than simply alleviating loneliness, their manner of engaging these networks is "normal" given that they are modern individuals who regularly practice networking with others for a variety of other purposes. In their immersion in networks, Emerging Christians comfortably inhabit the world described by Manuel Castells in his discussion of the network society.[48] In the network society, information is exchanged primarily in electronic networks through "flows" that resist regulation by nation-states and hierarchical institutions. Castells describes a "space of flows," hubs where networks crisscross and where power is found. Opportunities in the network society include a large-scale democratization of the ability to share and access information so that more people have (varying degrees of) power. In his later work on "networked social movements," Castells stresses the liberating power of networks through studies of the Occupy movement and the Arab Spring.[49] He claims that effective networked social movements must be "multimodal," existing online through social media and offline in real time. Further, the Internet and networked social movements *"share a specific culture, the culture of autonomy, the fundamental cultural matrix of contemporary societies."*[50]

As such, the network society simultaneously accentuates individual autonomy and personal interaction—characteristics that correspond to our observed religious individuation and cooperative egoism among Emerging Christians. For Castells, the culture of autonomy was boosted in the early twenty-first century, when Internet usage shifted "from individual and corporate interaction . . . (the use of email, for instance), to the autonomous construction of social networks controlled and guided by their users."[51] Now, Castells argues, the most important Internet activity happens on social networking sites. In addition, Castells emphasizes that the Occupy movement and the Arab Spring were deliberately leaderless, both on and offline, and strove for maximum participation. Castells writes that the Internet

> creates the conditions for a form of shared practice that allows a leaderless movement to survive, deliberate, coordinate and expand. It protects the movement against the repression of their liberated physical spaces by maintaining communication among the people within the

movement and with society at large in the long march of social change that is required to overcome institutionalized domination.[52]

Emerging Christians are active participants in the network society; the structures of which provide an almost ideal environment for a religious movement that seeks to heighten individualism and autonomy alongside experiences of conversation and community. The ECM's practices of flat leadership, communication, and dissemination of ideas echo the experience of networking in which modern individuals already partake in the realms of work and leisure.

In her study of religion and the Internet, Campbell examines the online practices of a variety of Christian communities, without focusing on the ECM.[53] But the practices she describes have been taken up most enthusiastically by both Emerging Christians and evangelicals.[54] Drawing on Castells, she explains the development of "networked religion," which she defines as

> religion informed by the technological structures and characteristics of the internet such as flattening of traditional hierarchies, encouraging instantaneous communication and response, and widening access to sacred or once-private information. The nature of computer-networked society means conventional forms of connection, hierarchy, and identity management must adapt or be reconfigured as they are transported online.[55]

For Campbell, networked religion has five traits: networked community, storied identity, shifting authority, convergent practice, and multisite reality. Each trait she describes resonates with the practices of Emerging Christians described throughout *The Deconstructed Church*, practices that facilitate their efforts to uphold individual choice and autonomy with relationship building. From our observations of online interactions, we found Emerging Christians utilizing some aspects of networked religion—such as shifting authority—more so than Renewalists or evangelicals. Elizabeth Drescher, whose analysis of the web presence of an evangelical church emphasizes the efforts of its leadership to keep people on message rather than to use online resources to flatten authority structures, confirms this.[56] But religious actors are not unique in adapting to the network society. Rather, the traits and trends Campbell identifies are also "investigated within internet studies as markers of the impact of the internet on the social sphere."[57]

Recognizing the networked structure of the ECM allows us to embrace a more comprehensive model of religious institutional entrepreneurship, combining concepts from social movement and diffusion theories of social change.[58] In addition, while we know of no comparative scholarly studies of the ways Emerging Christians, Renewalists, and evangelicals use the Internet and social media, it appears that tapping into online networks may be the one area in which the ECM is ahead of these two other prominent expressions of individualized, modern Christianity. Certainly the ECM's lack of conventional structures of communication—such as denominational agencies and seminaries—means that Emerging Christians almost exclusively use their transnational networks (on and offline, formal and informal) for communication. Packard and Sanders even define the ECM in terms of a network: "The Emerging Church, as it exists today, is a series of grassroots groups connected via the web in a global network."[59]

In short, the networked practices of religious actors in the ECM reflect and reinforce an important characteristic of the world around them. With their enthusiastic and self-conscious use of Internet, social media, and offline practices focused on community and relationships (the multimodal or multisite aspects emphasized by Castells and Campbell), Emerging Christians take advantage of opportunities for religious affinity, affirmation, and solidarity characteristic of the network society. The transnational network of the ECM fuels and enables a particular form of religious individualization, one that is enacted in congregations—which are often discovered through Internet searches—that model and encourage practices for each other online.

## The Emerging Church Movement is Centered on Religious Individualization

The dynamics of the ECM occur within a modern Western cultural framework, one that builds on the development of the secularization of Western Christendom. One viable option for the modern religious person is to enter a closed religious system, a form of unbending fundamentalism that "denies the reality of religious plurality, repudiates modernity, denies individualization and . . . takes refuge in dogmas of faith that are incompatible with individualized experiences and ambivalent feelings."[60] However, such an option faces challenges in a society characterized by a density of diverse encounters—especially a networked society as described above. Religious groups who seek to "individualize" religion on the basis of maintaining separation of their members from the ever-present proximity of diversity in globalized society appear doomed to fail.[61] In contrast to a closed and conforming religiosity, Emerging Christians are characterized by a distinctive approach to religious individualization.

The demand for individualization originates in changed social structures that affect every area of life, including religion. The lack of a single, primary foothold for personal identity stimulates the peculiarly reflective nature of modern individuals. Beck writes, "[Individuals] are forced to learn how to create a biographical narrative of their own and continuously to revise their definition of themselves. In the process they have to create abstract principles with which to justify their decisions."[62] People are constantly forced to reflect and rationalize their lives in a quest for meaningful coherence of the self. Together, these make the modern self peculiarly individuated such that freedom and autonomy are especially important.[63] Beck stresses that individualism is not simply a value; it is a socially structured and morally enforced "*institutionalized individualization*."[64] Alongside theorists Zygmunt Bauman and Anthony Giddens, Beck maintains that individualization does not arise from conscious choice but is rooted in "the long history of modern institutions."[65] Modern individuals are putting themselves together and becoming "ingenious tinkerers and do-it-yourself creators of their own increasingly unviable identities."[66] The modern self is burdened with becoming an individual.[67] As the philosopher Terry Eagleton asserts, individuation "is something that we do, as we come to negotiate a unique identity for ourselves . . . It is a project we have to accomplish."[68]

The imperative for individualization does not therefore indicate the waning of structures but rather the reorientation of structures such that new forms of agency are created. The consequence for religion is not abstract syncretism; rather, believers from different backgrounds discover new religious freedoms, change their old religious worldviews, and develop religious identities from a range of sources.[69] For Lynch, this "fragmentation of the modern sacred . . . does not mean that society is simply . . . formed around competing sacred forms, but that social life is negotiated through the complex fields of gravitational pull simultaneously exerted by different sacred forms. The individual human subject in late modernity therefore rarely lives in relation to a single sacred form, but rather in relation to multiple forms in contingent and complex ways."[70] Individuals must simultaneously negotiate various religious institutions and sacred forms in their everyday lives. As such, Beck writes that the "struggle for a 'life of one's own' [involves] spiritual odysseys in search of a 'God of one's own.'"[71] Individual efforts to craft spirituality create conflicts with "the clerical guardians of the truths of institutionalized national churches."[72] Beck adds, "What is astounding is that people who feel free to take these liberties continue to call themselves 'Christians.'"[73]

Like the modern religious selves described by Beck, Turner, Alexander, Lynch, and Heelas and Woodhead, Emerging Christians are modern individuals who must cope with the demands of juggling multiple identities and participating in multiple social structures simultaneously. They strive to achieve authenticity and holism in all areas of their lives. Religion becomes a resource for individualization. As Beck writes: "*Go and pray to the God of your own choosing!* Religion is based on the decision of the individual to believe and thus ultimately on the assumption that the individual is free."[74] The ECM is one of many individualized faith movements.

Drawing on Robert Bellah and his colleagues, we might say that "Sheilaism" is now a global, transreligious phenomenon.[75] It is not so much that the world today encourages egoistic individualism, but rather that people are caught within structures that force individualization. In short, the mechanisms that account for the ECM—in particular religious individualization as a product and process of modernity—are inescapable. At the same time, the ECM is not merely individualistic but inherently corporate, reflected in its emphasis on conversations, relationships, and networks described in previous chapters.

## The Emerging Church Movement Supports a "Legitimate" Religious Self

The modern self is faced with an array of competing secular and religious structures through which to enact its beliefs and practices. Actors stand on the sense that their beliefs and behaviors are right, good, and true; in other words, that they are *legitimated*. All principled action—even when it seems rooted in individual conviction—takes its force from being legitimated. And the legitimation of beliefs and behaviors do not come from within individuals, they come from organized groups. As Meyer and Jepperson argue, "Structured social organizations arise to pursue with great legitimacy, validated individual and collective purposes and responsibilities."[76] For Beck, religious individualization "means raising the question of the *legitimacy* of faith."[77]

Emerging Christians are anxious that their religious selves are legitimated and affirmed. We see within the ECM continual efforts to legitimate their "kind" of Christianity in both the secular and religious realms. One woman implicitly recognized her need for legitimation when in an ECM gathering she looked at the group and said, "We think we're crazy, but it shouldn't feel crazy. I feel less crazy the more I meet people like you."

Legitimacy—even of seemingly private religious convictions—is a social process.[78] One example of the quest for legitimation among Emerging Christians is found in the film *Blue Like Jazz*, based on the *New York Times* best-selling memoir by Donald Miller, which premiered nationwide in April 2012. When the book *Blue Like Jazz* appeared in 2003,[79] it was banned from many conservative Christian bookstores. Not only did it shun a strait-laced image of the faith, it also avoided strident remarks on the evils of the world, refused to idealize conversion or discipleship, and conveyed stories that were far from the sentimental Sunday school portraits that would have won over the family-friendly crowd. Conservative Christians concluded the book did not represent orthodox Christian theology and espoused a liberal political agenda. Six years later, when the film arrived—featuring a trailer with a voiceover that says, "I'm ashamed of Jesus"—discussion emerged on whether *Blue Like Jazz* is a Christian film.

True to the spirit of the book, which was subtitled, "Nonreligious Thoughts on Christian Spirituality," the film includes swear words, drinking, a lesbian character, and is open about the hypocrisy found in Christian churches. Miller's public struggle with faith makes any film based on the book a type of Christian film. More specifically, this film, featuring an evangelical as the hero, is a new type of "anti-Christianity" Christian film. There was no surprise that the film drew critics from the self-proclaimed Christian realm. It addresses spiritual struggles in a forthright manner, one that is attuned to the complicated, cosmopolitan, and fiercely egoistic society we live in today. As Paul O'Donnell writes, the film allows for more nuance in understanding evangelicalism, one that is in conversation with forms of secularism and eschews any tone of moral superiority.[80] But for some conservative evangelicals, this is not a legitimate portrayal of Christianity. Indeed, Rebecca Cusey wrote that there is a virtual "Christian fatwa" against the film.[81] However filmmakers like Miller are seeking a different type of status: legitimation and acceptance by mainstream audiences for a new type of Christianity. *Blue Like Jazz* portrays a Christianity that is very different from the impressions and stereotypes of Christianity held by many unchurched or dechurched people. In its presentation of a more complex, humble, and socially conscious Christianity, *Blue Like Jazz* tries to establish Christianity as a legitimate identity in a modern, secular West.

Emerging Christians also seek legitimacy by portraying their faith as "reasonable."[82] They contrast their perspectives to those of "anti-science" evangelicals, who believe in six-day creationism, reject evolution, and deny that people can be born with a homosexual orientation. Emerging Christians are in dialogue with general developments in science, philosophy, and technology; and the lack of keeping up with one or more of these aspects of society is inherent to their critique of conventional churches. Indeed, a significant portion of Bell's *What We Talk About When We Talk About God* is given over to consideration of scientific developments, including galactic dispersal, singularity, and subatomic physics.[83] While Bell presents the scientific information poetically in an effort to encourage readers to "open" their minds, he also wants to move them beyond "either or discussions" about "God or science."[84] Emerging Christians are aware that because naturalistic, scientific outlooks define what it means to be "rational" and "progressive," new definitions of reasonable, responsible persons have emerged. Reasonable, responsible people (mature, clear thinking, level headed) are those that take scientific knowledge into account when determining their beliefs and their behaviors. So, through their embrace of insights from science and learned professions (psychology, philosophy, sociology, etc.), science comes to legitimate and expand religious concerns and is used as a resource to establish Emerging Christians as legitimate, rational actors in a secular society.

For some Emerging Christians, the quest for a reasonable, responsible religion has gained urgency in light of the critiques of religion by New Atheists like Richard Dawkins. An intriguing response to New Atheism was the "Rescuing Darwin" project implemented by Theos, the "public theology think tank" based in the United Kingdom. Theos is not an emerging congregation, but in his study of the British and Foreign Bible Society (of which Theos is part), Matthew Engelke notes that the assumptions of Emerging Christianity inform Bible Society staff (see chapter 1). Emerging Christianity's quest for a reasonable religion certainly informed the logic behind "Rescuing Darwin." Conceived to coincide with the 200th anniversary of Charles Darwin's birth and the publication of the 150th anniversary edition of *The Origins of the Species* in 2009, the project included a flagship report and events throughout the year. In contrast to the fundamentalists caricatured by New Atheists, and the creationist, antiscience perspective championed by some conservative Christians, Theos wanted to portray Christianity as a reasonable religion whose adherents were open to the insights of scientific inquiry. They saw themselves as Christians and theistic evolutionists, so they enlisted Darwin himself as their ally. As Engelke writes: "The Theos team wanted to present Darwin as a reasonable man in the sense that he knew the limits of his own expertise (in science) and did not seek to extend it into another domain of life (religion)."[85] Further, Engelke claims, "by 'Rescuing Darwin,' the Theos team reckoned they could get much closer to their goal of modeling a *reasonable religion*."[86] Underlining their desire to gain legitimacy among the secular public, Engelke emphasizes that "they were *never* troubled or challenged, intellectually or otherwise, by the arguments from design or the presence of creationists. But there was something about the way in which the New Atheists were claiming the mantle of reason that presented a threat to the very project of public theology to which they were devoting themselves."[87]

Although not all Emerging Christians would identify with the term public theology or approve of Theos' approach, most are deeply concerned that the "unreasonable" religion from which they see themselves as escaping—or which they see New Atheists attacking—is what seems to count *as religion* in the public consciousness. That said, Emerging Christians do not seek legitimation *primarily* from secular sources; in fact, their most strenuous efforts for legitimation exist within a larger field of religious structures, including mainstream, conventional, evangelical, mainline, megachurches, etc.[88] Individual congregations may vary in liturgy, authority structures, and membership characteristics, yet there seems to be an overall sense of what mainstream

Christianity consists of in the West, one that is characterized by "institutional logics": familiar sets of beliefs and practices. Institutional logics are the organizing principles that inform field participants how they are to behave.[89]

In short, Emerging Christians need to be legitimized by some portion of already established Christian structures in order to grow and persist. To do so, they continually negotiate the institutional logics already embedded within Christianity. Logics may be cryptic and "code-like" but they serve to prescribe and proscribe behaviors.[90] These are orientations and frameworks, shared conceptions that help give social actors "nods" of agreement to one another.[91] Congregations are organizations that adopt institutional logics according to schemas, scripts, or recipes, yet adapt them to their own context.[92] Even more, institutional logics indicate a proper sense of self. As Jaco Lok writes, "Institutional logics not only direct what social actors want (interests) and how they are to proceed (guidelines for action), but also who or what they are (identity)."[93] Emerging Christians strive for legitimation through drawing on Christianity's existing institutional logics (categories, schema, and practices), while also drawing on available discourses to make the change meaningful to other actors, enlist allies, and build coalitions (chapter 4).[94]

Legitimation is a critical task faced by all institutional entrepreneurs, and the effort expended in the religious realm is particularly threatening to established structures who perceive in this process that which is sacred being profaned. Describing internal inconsistencies, the impurity or lack of cogency in established structures, or pointing out diversity of thoughts and practices are all counter to the naive belief in a good, right, monolithic tradition to which all conform. We should not be surprised to see that the ECM's quest for religious legitimation has prompted a push back from some sectors of Christianity. In contrast, the cumulative efforts of every Emerging Christian's quest to construct a reasonable, legitimate religious self results in a malleable religious orientation that fits with being a reasonable citizen in the modern West.

## The Emerging Church Movement Builds on a Sacralized Self

Religious individualization is clearly part of a larger shift in the sources of authority in the modern world, a shift that increased the agency of individuals. As the world became increasingly explained by science, the deus ex machina of explanation of unknown natural processes by the operation of a god became less viable. The scientific method provided regular patterns and established laws of nature. God became distant and the natural world disenchanted.[95] Human beings became increasingly able to intervene in natural processes, lessening dependence on a god or gods. The ability to manipulate nature and harness the natural environment increased the agency of individuals, making humans the only viable actors in the world.[96] The individual self seemed able to take on sacred activities that might have once been assumed the preserve of God. Meyer and Jepperson describe this as an ontology that is "increasingly simplified and abstract over time, consolidated in a high god who is rendered eternal, lawful, and relatively non-invasive in both nature and society—and thus not what moderns would consider much of an actor."[97]

In such a context, the church and other religious institutions are less likely to be seen as sacred structures for controlling outcomes. The sacralization of the individual takes away from the agentic powers of religious institutions. And as religious institutions lose their status as the centers of religious action, sources of action become more distributed. More specifically, when an institution is no longer sacred yet the principles that are intended to guide such institutions remain sacred, more charismatic power is available to individuals. The individual does not replace God; rather, godlike initiative and sustaining broadly encompassing ideals for all humanity become the burden of individuals. Meyer and Jepperson talk about this as the devolution of agency: "godly authority and powers devolve into social organization, but find different institutionalization."[98] For them, "'Man' as actor—individuals, organizations, states—carries almost the entire responsibility for the *now-sacralized human project*, with gods, other spiritual forces, ancestors, or an animated nature drained of agency."[99]

When individuals are empowered for religious actions once attributed to institutions, religious structures are seen as disposable. As Beck puts it, "The sacredness of religion was transferred to the sacredness of the individual."[100] It is the transcendent project—not organizations or structures—that is held sacred, and if institutions are viewed as failing to achieve those projects, then they are declared to be mundane (or profaned, as in corrupted and hypocritical). Meyer and Jepperson summarize it this way: "The status of the individual as responsible creator and carrier of purpose and the moral law is greatly enhanced [and] individuals attain sacral standing."[101] Emile Durkheim classically argued that sacredness becomes a quality of the modern individual, saying, "All the evidence points to the conclusion that *the only possible candidate is precisely this religion of humanity* whose rational expression is the individualist morality."[102] Later, the theologian Dietrich Bonheoffer described this as a major challenge for Christianity and it gave rise to his ambiguous remarks on the need for a "religionless Christianity."

Several social theorists trace the source of this emphasis on the individual to Christianity itself. In contrast to theologians who emphasize

Christianity as primarily communitarian, Beck writes, "Individualization is, as we have noted, an original Christian invention. From the very outset, Christianity addressed its gospel to the individual—beyond all questions of status, class, ethnicity, and nation—and in that respect it is more modern than many of its opponents."[103] Similarly, social theorist Hans Joas also links the modern "sacralization of the person" to Christianity.[104] He quotes Durkheim who wrote, "Christianity expressed in an inward faith, in the personal conviction of the individual, the essential condition of godliness . . . The very center of the moral life was thus transferred from outside to within and the individual was set up as the sovereign judge of his own conduct having no other accounts to render than those to himself and to his God."[105] For Joas, "We cannot overstate the significance of Christianity as a cultural prerequisite for the emergence of modern individualism."[106] But it is important to emphasize that the individualized self is not inevitably narcissistic or egoistic. For Joas (as it is with every other theorist discussed throughout this chapter), the individual is inherently social, and this produces "a specific type of social life of which the personhood of every individual is constitutive."[107]

It is not a pure egoism but a *moral individualism*. It remains connected to sympathy for human misery and notions of the rights and dignity of human beings. The ECM's concern with the world "down here" rather than heaven "up there" is therefore consistent with the greatly reduced agency of God in the modern world and the consequent emphasis on the self. The activity of God is seen as involving the work of people; that is, God works through people. The individual is continually validated as the source and repository of sacred principles and is the locus of action for achieving ideals. Individuals have both more functions and more responsibilities—especially as "they are now agents of higher principles, and hence highly legitimated in ways unique to modern Western culture."[108] The ECM in all of its manifestations encourages and nurtures this modern, sacralized self.

The primacy of the sacralized self can be illustrated through Kester Brewin's *After Magic*, which explores the worlds of comic book heroes and literature, including Macbeth, Harry Potter, and Batman.[109] Seeing "sacred" significance in these "profane" sources, Brewin asserts that heroes' attempts to exercise "super" power over nature are archetypal, appearing so frequently in culture that they should not be ignored. These stories teach us that it is only when heroes renounce magic that they become fully human or learn to love. For Brewin, Jesus's refusal to accept God's magical intervention to save him from death makes him heroic. Further, Brewin identifies the resurrection *not with Jesus's physical resurrection* but with the Christian community. He writes:

> Here is the brilliance of God . . . there *is* . . . no supernatural return of
> the body . . . By breaking up, distributing and ingesting these symbols
> of God's death [in the act of communion/Eucharist], *we* become the
> resurrected body of Christ—we become his "good hands" materially
> at work in the world in which we live.[110]

While it looks like Brewin is denying Jesus's physical resurrection, to focus on
that as "heresy" (as conservative Christian critics are most likely to do) misses
his point. He writes:

> Seeing the descent into inhumane thought and practice that drawing
> on the supernatural seems to inescapably bring, faith "after magic" re-
> fuses to attribute blame for illness either to the grand scheme of God
> or to the work of super-villains (and similarly refuses to praise God for
> the provision of parking spaces.) Instead, it boldly accepts the radical
> responsibility of . . . becoming the resurrected body of Christ, and
> thus living for all that the Son of Man stood for: justice for the poor,
> fair taxation, rights for women, love for the marginalised, great festi-
> vals, shared meals and freedom for the oppressed.[111]

Brewin suggests the "most godly" thing to do in our "toxic religious climate"
is to "live as if god did not exist"—in other words, live without acting like we
believe God is a cosmic magician, always acting on *our* behalf.[112]

For us, the phrase "living as if god did not exist," neatly describes a particular version of the modern development of the sacralized self. A number of
processes linked to modernity—the reliance on science, secularization, and
the rise of commercialization and consumption—have helped shape a context
in which God and his providential interventions have receded from everyday
life. Individuals, rather than God or religious institutions, are now assumed
to have ultimate responsibility to choose how to think and act. Such a version
of the sacralized self contrasts, of course, to the religious selves of Renewalist
Christians, who claim God's interventions in their everyday lives and describe
how God speaks directly to them. While the Emerging and Renewalist versions of the self-God relationship may seem diametrically opposed, there are
in fact similarities in how Emerging and Renewalist Christians place responsibility on the individual to act on behalf of or at the behest of God. Luhrmann's
study of charismatic Christians in Vineyard congregations confirms this; she
describes an exacting process of prayer through which people train themselves
to hear God's voice.[113] While the Renewalist version of the sacralized self could
be regarded as more popular, in terms of numbers, the Emerging version of the
sacralized self is also a viable alternative for Western Christians.

## The Emerging Church Movement Promotes
## Religious Heterogeneity

Emerging Christians, like many prototypically modern individuals, value diversity and pluralism, seeing their tolerance or celebration of diversity as a good in and of itself. Emerging Christians are "outlaw entrepreneurs" reacting against evangelical and mainline congregations because they see them as homogenizing—trying to fit individuals into "boxes" that are too tidy.[114] Working as collective institutional entrepreneurs, Emerging Christians choose to resist this through their heterogeneous, pluralist congregations, as we discussed in chapters 2 and 5. Even though emerging congregations usually fall short of achieving diversity, Emerging Christians conceive of themselves as pluralist religious selves (as seen in chapter 3).

The pluralist ethos characteristic among Emerging Christians is further evidence of what Beck describes as pervasive *cosmopolitanism*: "The erosion of clear boundaries separating the markets, states, civilizations, cultures and not least the lifeworlds of different peoples and religions, as well as the resulting worldwide situation of an involuntary confrontation with alien others."[115] Cosmopolitanism involves welcoming "multiplicity and alterity in one's own life."[116] What we therefore see among Emerging Christians is a *religious cosmopolitanism*. Religious cosmopolitanism lies in "the fact that the recognition of *religious otherness becomes a guiding maxim* in its way of thinking, its actions, and its social existence. Cultural and religious differences are neither hierarchically organized nor dissolved, but accepted for what they are and indeed positively affirmed." Religious cosmopolitanism "perceives religious others as both particular *and* universal, as different *and* equally valid."[117] Emerging Christians generally subscribe to this cosmopolitan outlook.

Pluralist congregations make sense in an environment of increased pluralism in social, economic, and other spheres of life, as well as reflect the diversity and contradictions already present within Christianity—variations that are often deliberately denied or suppressed. Some congregations allow for variety within religious traditions, while others accept people from outside their religious tradition entirely. As such, we see the pluralist congregations of the ECM as a consequence and reflection of "the fragmentation of modernity" characterized by the "new pluralism."[118] Pluralism is associated with the enforced proximity of difference that is ubiquitous in modern society. As Beck writes, "the *pluralization* of the religions has come to replace the linear process of secularization."[119] For Lynch, "the moral and cultural plurality of modern society" exposes the myth of monolithic religions and "makes simple models of ritual increasingly irrelevant for contemporary social analysis and instead demands concepts that allow for plurality, contestation, and failure in social performances of the sacred."[120] For Beck, this results in a situation where individual identities acquire even more importance. He writes, "Universal proximity supplies the contemporary context of all religious belief systems and symbolic systems in which individualization becomes possible and necessary, and even acquires its meaning."[121]

We recognize that even in the context of religious heterogeneity and freedom, modern society produces multiple forms of standardized, scripted agency, even within religious spheres, that depend on personal belief and passionate conviction. Beck notes that such forms of agency may include an individualization in which the individual conforms or becomes "de-individualized."[122] Similarly, part of Emerging Christians' critique of conservative Christianity is that it produces conformity or "strikingly similar agentic structures and dynamics."[123] For them, the broad institutionalized manner in which conservative Christianity supports, channels, and ultimately legitimizes the activity of *faith-full* living follows sets of cultural boundaries. For example, a bumper sticker popular among American evangelicals reads, "The Bible says it, I believe it, that settles it." The sentiment expressed is a seemingly straightforward one: because the Bible is infallible and inspired by God, believers should follow its teachings. Of course, the slogan does not leave room to admit that the Bible may be open for interpretation, so that following it may be more complicated than believers suppose. Indeed, the slogan assumes an easy consensus about what the Bible says, one that denies diversity and contradictions within Christianity. So religious agency is evident among conservative Christians, but the type of life that is acceptable to conservative evangelicals is seen by Emerging Christians as suffocating and constricted. Emerging Christians ultimately see conservative Christianity's establishment of cultural boundaries as homogenizing—denying the diversity and complexity that exists both within the secular and spiritual realms.

Emerging Christians consistently point out that Christianity is a remarkably diverse and contradictory field. Emerging Christians look around and have no difficulty finding multiple Christian traditions. This involves recognition of what Beck names the *"historical impurity of world religions."*[124] A singular, monolithic Christian tradition is a myth. What is left for us are traditions that are considered "official" or "normalized" or simply "accustomed" or perhaps "approved." As such, Christianity is characterized by the simultaneous existence of numerous logics and meaning systems, characterized by multiplicity and heterogeneity, complementing and competing with each other.[125]

We learn from studies of institutional change that change is more likely within fields that are diverse and complex, and actors on the margins or periphery of these fields are most likely to initiate change. Meyer and Rowan point out that "institutional environments are often pluralistic, and societies promulgate sharply inconsistent myths."[126] Jill M. Purdy and Barbara Gray show that multiple and competing logics can coexist.[127] Even in the case where there is one dominant logic, an institutional field can still be "littered with [the] flotsam and jetsam" of alternative logics.[128] That is, alternative logics may represent the legacies of previous change processes.[129] Such fields are characterized by constant struggles between competing logics and, even though a settlement may be reached, other logics remain in the background, to be revived whenever the opportunity arises.[130] The position of Emerging Christians on the margins gives them more freedom (and less to lose) by criticizing existing institutions, while at the same time exposing them to environmental complexity and influences outside the established field. With their self-conscious embrace of pluralism, Emerging Christians feed off the diversity and complexity of everyday life in the modern West, Christianity, and other institutional fields, drawing on various strands as they strategically construct their pluralist religious selves and implement a range of religious practices.

## The Emerging Church Movement is a Religious Fulfillment of Cooperative Egoism

A foundational irony of the ECM is this: To actualize their individualized religious selves, Emerging Christians must be involved in community, in some type of congregational life. No religious self, even a critically oriented religious self, can thrive without a community of others. Emerging Christians value freedom and autonomy, but they also seek affirmation through close relationships with others in their congregation. Even Emerging Christians find that religious selves cannot be legitimatized or sustained apart from communal gatherings. Despite their anti-institutional convictions, Emerging Christians desire to meet together *as Christians,* demonstrating that very, very few people actively pursue a spiritual life apart from participation in religious communities.[131]

As described throughout this book, Emerging Christians are not isolated individualists but rather purposefully pursue their religious faith—however doubtful, however uncertain, and however shaky—in relationship with others. In this, Emerging Christians' religious orientation is in line with Beck when he insists, "Radical individualism does not mean a society of radically egoistic monads."[132] For Beck, such egoism involves welcoming alternative forms of social organization, those that encourage participating "by facilitating people's ability to weave it into their self-chosen lives."[133] Similarly, Alexander emphasizes the importance of forms of civil society that simultaneously affirm individuality and solidarity.[134] Individuals resist involvement in certain societal institutions because they reject their hierarchical structure. In Beck's view, the system of modern society must recognize that if people are going to participate in society-wide institutions, most will do so "as a form of personal exchange that gives them self-fulfillment in return."[135]

Yet the pursuit of self-fulfillment does not mean Emerging Christians fall outside caring, mutual relationships. Individualization is not incompatible with establishing interpersonal structures of mutual care and concern. Beck describes this as a process of the harmonization of "individualism and social morality" and a reconciliation of "free will and individuality."[136] He states, "Those people who are the strongest exponents of egoistic values, who most came out in favor of the importance of career and self-realization, were almost always also people who not only valued communal activities highly, but who spent a great deal of their free time taking care of others."[137] Beck concludes by "typologizing" the phenomenon of valuing both egoism and care for others as "altruistic individualism or cooperative egoism."[138]

We see the strategic religiosity evident in the ECM as exemplary of Beck's cooperative egoism in action. We are not the first to note Emerging Christians' dual emphasis on individualism and community. Packard characterizes Emerging Christians' relationship between individualism and community as like a "gyroscope," a navigational instrument that relies on movement between two opposed forces to propel itself forward.[139] Cooperative egoism also is expressed in the importance Emerging Christians place on being involved in their congregations. As we explored in chapters 2 and 3, almost all the Emerging Christians interviewed for this research indicated their immersion in the relational networks of their pluralist congregations and perceived their congregational activities as consistent with their core values and concerns. This made for what they described as an authentic, holistic Christianity, which nurtured them as individuals but also connected them deeply with others in their congregation and with the world around them.

Further, cooperative egoism is reflected in what Tony Jones describes as "the relational ecclesiology of the emerging church movement."[140] Jones enlists the theology of Jurgen Moltmann to reflect on the social trinity, liberation theology, adult baptism, open communion, the relational understanding of church, and the sense that we have entered a millennium of the Holy Spirit. Moltmann's (and Jones's) relational ecclesiologies link Emerging Christians' commitment to relationships to theological orientations that connect doctrine with other people.[141] The Emerging Christians we talked with seemed to have absorbed a commitment to relational ecclesiology. One man connected his individual responsibility for a relationship with God with involvement in community. He said, "That's actually how I engage God, is in community." Another man said the antithesis was not between "relationships and something else . . . it's not theology or relationship," because he believes his congregation has a "relation-based theology." He said, "There is a theology of relationship here, and by focusing on Christ . . . going through the gospels and watching Jesus relate, we're putting ourselves in relation to something and we're putting ourselves in relation to each other as we're going on this journey." Another woman said, "It's not just coming to church. It's actually forming relationships and great ones." Wyatt said, "I actually ascribe more responsibility to the community for my spiritual life than I had previously."

Some, like Lauren, have changed the whole way they think about Christianity. Her words capture the dynamics of a move from what seemed to be an almost purely individualized faith to one characterized by cooperative egoism:

> I always thought of church as the place where I went to be fed, and I went to get what I could get out of it, especially to help me shape my thinking. Here I've moved to that whole concept of being missional where we're on a mission together. It's helped me to understand that the church is not for my benefit. It's been life changing for me to allow the church experience to not be about me, but to be about God and about others.

We also see cooperative egoism reflected in the emphasis Emerging Christians place on living authentic and holistic lives (terms they used often), inside and outside the walls of a congregational gathering. One woman said, "You don't have to be two people. You can have interests in art and music and things that speak to you, that you identify with, but you can also make it part of your faith." Joel said that from the first day he attended there was "a feeling of 'these people fit me.'" Amber followed up and said, "I felt, like Joel said, that I fit here with these people and this place, and it was just *right*."

Emerging Christians' balancing act between the individual and the communal is not unique to the modern era. Nevertheless, in the ways they link their individual spiritual development to their care for and relationships with others, Emerging Christians embody the qualities of Beck's cooperative egoism. Their deliberately heterogeneous, pluralist congregations provide mechanisms for sustaining this delicate balance, underlining the irony that Emerging Christians believe they cannot authentically become themselves without being in community with others. The structure of their deconstructed emerging congregations is implicit in their strategic effort to accomplish an integrated, fully authentic life.

## The Future of Emerging Christianity

Our findings affirm one of sociologist Ulrich Beck's key assertions regarding religious individualization; namely, the decline of established religious institutions is simultaneously associated with a rise in individual religiosity.[142] Beck argues "that with increasing modernization, religions do not disappear but change their appearance."[143] We agree. The structure of contemporary society pushes the task of religious coherence onto the individual. But the development of a "God of one's own" assumes, and even necessitates, a radicalized religious freedom.[144] Actualizing this imperative requires a site for enactment. The moral imperative to exercise religious freedom is increasingly found in places that allow conversational spaces that sanction this work and ritualized gatherings that allow a pluralism of alternative convictions to coexist—even to co-worship—in the same congregation.

The selective, hybridized practices of pluralist congregations may at first appear to be unexceptional. Emerging Christians are embedded in the wider Christian field, with their beliefs, practices, and institutionalizing structures attempting to change Christianity from within. This makes Emerging Christians "embedded agents."[145] The concept of embedded agency explains how actors embedded in institutional fields come to envision new practices,[146] a process we described in chapter 4 when we characterized Emerging Christians as collective institutional entrepreneurs. Emerging Christians are not so embedded that they lack the motivation to change the system, yet they are not so peripheral to be deprived of all ability to change it.[147] Embeddedness in existing forms of Christianity is a resource for the legitimation of their religious orientation. So while they say they are rebelling against their previous Christian traditions, Emerging Christians are dependent on established structures for actualizing their own deconstructed religious orientation. By definition, institutions are firmly rooted in taken-for-granted rules, norms, and routines that involve formal rule sets;[148] ex ante agreements;[149] less formal shared interaction sequences;[150] and assumptions that organizations and individuals are expected to follow.[151] Institutions govern social behavior such that departures from institutionalized practices activate social controls that make such deviations costly.[152] Institutions are not based on efficiency but on legitimacy and familiarity.[153]

It is precisely the taken-for-granted aspects of Christianity that the ECM attempts to make obvious in order to play and subvert. The ECM's apparent informality in so many settings can be seen as an attempt to create slack in rule-following, and a space for experimentation, thus engaging the tensions of pluralism. Even in a pub, where the drinks appear to allow for a great reduction in sanctity, drinks can actually be familiar objects to hide behind (drinking with friends on a night out) while new normative imperatives flex their way into the scene. One pub church leader writes meeting at the pub "has helped me consider not only the content of my faith—*what* I believe—but even more so, *how* I hold my beliefs and my faith. And I've discovered that at the pub, with fellow believers, atheists, agnostics and believers of other traditions, something magical happens around that table, with half-full pints and honest conversation."[154] It becomes a social space that allows individual convictions yet a cooperative place for expression. He continues:

> My hunch is that our world would be a better place if more people with differences came together to learn from each other, rather than allowing unwarranted assumptions to grow into ignorance, hatred and division. Around this table, instead of building walls, we tear them down. Instead of assuming, we ask, and say, "Teach me." Instead of attacking each other, we buy another round. Instead of "moving on," we become friends.

But if legitimation is to hold, new groups that provide legitimation must remain relatively coherent over time. Groups that legitimate ethical and religious principles must become *organized* if they are to sustain the power required for individual adherents to put profound stakes into their convictions.

While legitimacy is often achieved through isomorphism (conformity to institutionalized preferences), conformity is a threat to organizations like emerging congregations that are concerned with distinctiveness and diversity alongside a reaction to dominant forms.[155] This makes it necessary for Emerging Christians to reinvent congregations as they have known them from past experience. It necessitates their becoming religious institutional entrepreneurs. Their pluralist congregations deconstruct conventional liturgical practices. At the same time, none of the practices within the ECM are radically new. It lies in the nature of legitimation for the people developing new logics, arrangements, and congregations to borrow and hybridize already accepted practices.[156] As organizational theorists Myeong-Gu Seo and W. E. Douglas Creed state, "No institution is created entirely anew; instead, institutions are created and transformed within socially accepted frames or models." Thus, they suggest that an important challenge for institutional entrepreneurs is to embed their change initiatives within frames or models available in the broader field—to achieve legitimation. Their work of legitimation belies the strategic, rather than inherited and reproduced, stance taken in constructing their religiosity.

The Emerging Church Movement will surely shift and current terminology may get lost in the fluxes of change. Nevertheless, our goal has been to describe a type of religious orientation that is not only recognizable across persons and formats transnationally but more importantly, will also become more pervasive in all religious environments. We are not especially concerned if the ECM is growing or sparking change within Christianity—although we see some indications that both of these are taking place. Rather, what is significant about the ECM from a sociological perspective is that the principles with which it operates are pervasive within contemporary religions and substantially grounded in broad social changes captured most concisely in Beck's term "religious individualization." Such a broad assessment cannot be proved decisively using the data available to us. Yet, the phenomenon of religious individualization and its consequences within particular congregational communities accounts for the structures (e.g., pluralist congregations, dialogue-centered spaces, and flatter leadership hierarchies) and practices (e.g., strategic religiosity, faith as conversation, open liturgy, and cooperative egoism) found in the ECM.

As one Emerging Christian told us, his congregation is an "open space where individuals get to work out whatever they need. Individuals are coming together."

In the ways it has responded to modernity, the ECM (and the other expressions of Christianity it may influence) is remarkably well adapted to persist, even thrive, as a viable religious alternative in the West. The patterns of religious individualism, the formation of pluralist congregations, the allowance for multiple forms of legitimate spirituality, and the desire to strategically construct a personal faith that is valid and even strengthened by life lived in the real world will be ubiquitous elements of modern religiosity.

*Appendix*

# RESEARCH METHODOLOGY

In this book, our goal has been to provide a vivid, social scientific analysis of the Emerging Church Movement (ECM), thus promoting a more holistic understanding (rather than a mere caricature) of its religious orientation and practices. We located our understanding of the ECM in the context of broader patterns of the religious streams in which Emerging Christians (knowingly or unknowingly) participate as well as the broader, secular world in which they operate. Rather than impose our understanding and impressions of the movement onto Emerging Christians, we primarily used qualitative research methods to uncover the understandings and practices of leaders and attendees and to bring conceptual order to what we found. By choosing a qualitative approach, we engaged directly with people and sought to understand their "lived experience": how they appropriate, experience, and negotiate Christianity in their lives and communities. While the emphasis of this analysis is on those who regularly participate and provide leadership and organization for emerging congregations, the implications about the formation of religious orientation and the connection between congregational practices in contemporary society are addressed as well. Congregations matter, yet they do not in themselves summarize all religious activity nor are they the only loci of religious action. As the theologian and social observer Harvey Cox wrote, "Religion is larger and more pervasive than churches."[1]

Our conclusions are based on more than a decade of research within the ECM, primarily in the United States and Northern Ireland. Most of our data were collected from ECM participants, gatherings, and conferences from 2010 through 2013 using participant observation, focus groups and in-depth interviews, congregational surveys, observation and interaction using social media, and examination of available textual sources. Numerous conversations at ECM gatherings informed our thinking. Gerardo participated in several ECM congregations and conferences in the United States and the United Kingdom.

In addition, he participated in focus group conversations, closely followed a curated Twitter feed of ECM leaders and participants (and their associated hyperlinks), and read printed and digital writings by a variety of ECM insiders. Gladys's work consisted primarily of in-depth study of the Belfast-based Ikon collective, immersion in online networks (including interaction through posts on her personal blog), visits to other emerging communities in the United States and United Kingdom, and close analysis of the writings of public figures in the movement, whose books and blog posts were treated as primary source texts. In all observations and when reading textual material, we sought to go beyond what was said "officially" by leaders and attendees. We looked at written records (physical and online), observed ongoing interactions, and sought to discover patterns of behavior rather than merely record words and meanings. Our data are supplemented by observation of the movement since its beginnings in the late 1990s, some of which included formal research and some of which included interaction with Emerging Christians in our everyday lives. This might be called "opportunistic ethnography,"[2] which indicates "scholars who have acquired (and then exploited) multiple group membership derived from their own personal interests and backgrounds."[3] Our data and previous exposure to the movement were also supplemented with qualitative and quantitative data collected by Tony Jones for his doctoral dissertation in practical theology at Princeton Theological Seminary.[4] We acknowledge that Jones is not only an insider to the ECM but also a very public and outspoken one. Nevertheless, in reviewing his data we find him appropriately reserved in sharing his own opinions and remarkably open in his questions and manner of soliciting information for his research. Jones's data included participant observation, focus groups, semiformal interviews, and congregational surveys of eight ECM churches. We incorporated use of the full data set as provided by him. Taken together, we drew on a large and varied data set that is both broad and deep.

Throughout our collaboration, we conducted our readings and observations independently and discussed our ongoing experiences and interpretations via e-mail or Skype. Our cross-national collaboration, our social scientific methodologies, and our broad range of data comprise an attempt to overcome bias and blind spots. A picture is constructed that creates a synthetic whole out of the various pieces presented from our observations and the reported experiences of our respondents. When information does not match or is seemingly contradictory, we consider the source and weigh the evidence to obtain the best interpretive sense of what is happening sociologically. Concepts are provided throughout the text in the hope of their utility to future researchers.

# Participant Observation

The backbone of our study was participant observation. We attempted to im-merse ourselves in the worlds of Emerging Christians, both in face-to-face and in online interactions. There is a long tradition of participant observation in the social sciences, which appreciates that "hanging out" with purpose can be the source of rich data.[5] Participant observation requires listening skills and attention to detail, including the ability to focus one's attention on what people say and how they say it, and to note what people do and how they do it.[6] So we worked toward an understanding of the ECM through ongoing interactions with participants on their home ground. This involved an effort to "share first-hand the environment, problems, background, language, rituals, and social relations of a more-or-less bounded and specified group of people."[7]

Participant observation is especially well-suited to allowing researchers to discover how people themselves interpret their own worlds, including their subjective inner experiences.[8] Watching and listening, participant observers identify how people give meaning to their daily, mundane tasks, as well as to the institutions of work and leisure in which they participate. We were inter-ested in microlevel processes, including how people's religious orientations had developed, how they structured the communal life of their congregations, and how they lived in the "real world" outside the walls of their congregations. While their social lives may seem unremarkable and self-evident to partici-pants themselves, social scientists seek to order people's patterns of behavior and then relate them to wider sociological concepts—or develop new concepts based on their observations. As much as possible, this facilitates drawing in-sights from participants themselves, rather than serving to confirm research-ers' prejudices or preconceived notions.

Of course, participant observers are aware that their very presence *as re-searchers* changes the social interactions of the people they are observing. Participants' awareness of the researcher may subtly (or not so subtly) change what they say or do. This makes it especially important for researchers to gain the trust of research participants, so that their interactions are as natural as possible. As such, the relative success of participant observation can depend on researchers' relationships with the observed.

Gerardo participated in five emerging congregations (in California, Minne-sota, and North Carolina as well as Belfast, Northern Ireland) and eight ECM conferences (in Raleigh; Charlotte; Chicago; Los Angeles; Memphis, Green-wich, Connecticut; and Washington, DC; as well as Belfast, Northern Ireland). In these various settings, Gerardo had numerous conversations—both casual and intense—that occurred before, during, and after the many gatherings he attended. Gerardo quickly found ECM conferences and congregations to be immersive experiences—one overnight gathering was jokingly referred to as a "post-Christian slumber party." Most gatherings are not structured to allow unobtrusive observation by sitting in the back, rather the occasions included reflections on topics of the moment, reactions to social and historical events as they were occurring, and sharing of memories and other life experiences. Meals were always encouraged as continuations of gatherings (if the gatherings were not already centered on drinks or meals), such that further conversations happened at restaurants, coffeehouses, and bars—even while walking or driving to these places. There were many one-on-one conversations in all these settings as ECM leaders and participants openly shared their thoughts and experiences. In larger groups, Gerardo most often could hang back to let conversation and interactions happen. On some occasions, Gerardo was largely ignored as a newcomer with few connections to the group; yet after attending several meetings in different cities, Gerardo became a familiar face and developed some friendships alongside many acquaintances. In all cases, informal occasions beyond programmed activities were always available and accessible since ECM participants are quite willing to include strangers in their events and are remarkably open in discussing all manners of issues happening among the people and ministries of their congregations. Except for the public leaders within the ECM, the names of participants were obscured or changed.

This more recent fieldwork was supplemented by Gerardo's experiences of other ECM conferences and interactions with ECM insiders since the 1990s. Gerardo has written about his American evangelical background, describing the insider/outsider dilemma in fieldwork in which one is a member.[9] Although he is not an insider to either the ECM broadly or to an ECM church specifically, as a result of other research as well as his involvement in congregational leadership networks and various speaking engagements, Gerardo has frequently had immersive interactions with ECM leaders and members. For example, he first met Brian McLaren and Doug Pagitt, two leaders who figure prominently in the ECM, as a member of the Council on Ecclesiology meeting at Willow Creek Community Church in 1998. He also attended the first Emerging Village Theological Conversation on the campus of Fuller Theological Seminary in 2001. Involvement on pastoral staff at Mosaic under the leadership of Erwin McManus brought him into frequent contact with the ECM and the growing stream of publications from its leaders.[10] Although McManus was initially considered to be a leader within the ECM, both he and ECM insiders reject that affiliation, and he has stated positions that are contrary to other leaders in the movement.[11] Other occasions, like speaking as the Earl Lecturer at the Pacific School of Religion or attending conferences in the United States and Northern Ireland, brought him into other relationships. In Berkeley, California, he got to know Jay Bakker; in Chicago, he spoke with Tony Jones; and in Belfast he spent time with Peter Rollins and later participated in a multiday gathering with a group staying at his home in Greenwich, Connecticut. While meetings with prominent leaders like these were important to understanding the ECM, his broad interactions with nonpublic participants in these and other settings were far more extensive.

In Gladys's case, her research was focused primarily on Ikon in Belfast. Gladys also has written about her American evangelical background, describing the insider/outsider dilemma in fieldwork in which one could be considered a member.[12] Gladys had relationships or acquaintances with some Ikon participants going back more than a decade, and when the time came for the more focused research for this book, almost everyone in a core group associated with Ikon knew her or were aware of her work at the Irish School of Ecumenics. Over the years, Gladys had attended many of Ikon's public gatherings, writing field notes and/or blog posts about some of them. Ikon events are usually full-on sensory experiences, engaging all the senses of the ethnographer. When she began the more focused phase of this research, Ikon's "Cyndicate" (planning committee) granted her permission to attend these meetings, which were usually held in people's homes. These meetings often took the form of brain-storming sessions; at times, Gladys took minutes or notes for the group. On occasions, Gladys contributed some perspective on how the particular event was developing but kept these contributions to a minimum. Not only was her relative silence meant to not unduly affect Ikon's internal processes, she also felt that her gifts were not in the same artistic, creative areas as many of those involved in Ikon. In other words, while she might be comfortable as a sociologist, Gladys is not comfortable as a choreographer, artist, or a poet!

Gladys was also aware that in the United States, Ikon is usually associated with Peter Rollins, and that the contributions of others in the collective (as founders and especially in later years when Rollins was living in the United States) are often obscured. That made it important to her to highlight the contributions of others in Ikon and how they distinguished themselves from Rollins's published work. So she asked participants in the research interviews if they would grant permission for their names to be used in the book. Most did, and their names are in the text of this book. For those who did not, their names and any identifying characteristics have been changed. Drawing on feminist and participatory traditions of research, Gladys also thought it was important that people from Ikon have the opportunity to read portions of the soon-to-be published text, especially when they were quoted directly.[13] So she distributed portions of the text to those participants, some of whom provided feedback that changed and enriched the analysis. While this does not fulfill the feminist-inspired ideal of "co-production" of texts between "researcher"

and "researched," it is an attempt to ensure that participants' voices are faith-
fully represented.

Gladys suspects that there were times throughout the research process when
she was viewed as either an insider or an outsider to Ikon. Indeed, researchers
are apt to shift back and forth between insider/outsider and other identities
throughout their fieldwork, assuming different identities at different times.[14]
She often joked that everyone in Ikon told her that they were on the "fringes"
of Ikon, and in that way she was no different than the rest. When the "Pyrotheology" website was being constructed, primarily as an initiative by Rollins,
she was asked to provide "testimonials" about some of Ikon's practices.[15] But
she was never deeply involved or invested in the planning of Ikon events like
the people she observed. Having said that, if asked, Gladys told people she was
sympathetic to Ikon as well as the ECM (even if most in Ikon were keen to distance themselves from the ECM). She usually received positive feedback from
people from Ikon about any posts about their activities that she wrote on her
blog. She also comes from an evangelical background, like many within Ikon
and the ECM. Although she was born and raised in the United States rather
than Northern Ireland, she shared many of the critiques of evangelicalism articulated by or embodied in Ikon. She now primarily attends a Catholic church
with her Catholic husband (in Northern Ireland, a "mixed marriage" between
Catholic and Protestant is quite rare). She occasionally visits the Presbyterian congregation she attended before marriage, whose congregation includes
some people from Ikon and whose pastor has some sympathies for the ECM.
Gladys is aware that her sympathy toward the ECM, friendships with people in
Ikon, and evangelical background are sure to affect her analysis of the ECM—
possibly making her predisposed to see significance in the movement where
others might see marginalization or irrelevance. Readers can judge for themselves whether the empirical data presented in the book supports its central
claims.

In addition to Gerardo's and Gladys's ethnographic fieldwork, Tony Jones
provided sets of field notes based on participant observation in the eight congregations he studied, including an additional observation from an ECM
church in London not included in his dissertation analysis. The eight emerging
congregations Jones visited across the United States in 2005 and 2006 were:
Cedar Ridge Community Church (Spencerville, Maryland), Solomon's Porch
(Minneapolis, Minnesota), House of Mercy (St. Paul, Minnesota), Journey
(Dallas, Texas), Pathways Church (Denver, Colorado), Church of the Apostles (Seattle, Washington), Jacob's Well (Kansas City, Missouri), and Vintage
Faith Church (Santa Cruz, California). As described above, his data supple-
mented our own.

# Focus Groups and In-Depth Interviews

Focus groups and in-depth interviews built on the insights we gained in our participant observation. Interviews, both formal and informal, as well as the structured conversational interactions of focus groups, allow researchers like us to access information that may not be available through observation alone.[16] Participant observation and background reading may help researchers formulate questions, but it is in the interaction of the interview where participants can make sense and put order on their everyday thoughts and actions. Researchers listen closely and ask follow up questions that might not have otherwise occurred to them. In-depth interviews allow researchers to solicit detailed life stories and life histories that cannot be gained by observing or hanging out.[17]

Gladys carried out seventeen interviews with people associated with Ikon between 2003–2013; some participants she interviewed in 2003 and then again almost a decade later, which provided perspective on Ikon over time. Interviews were semistructured, which meant that she prepared an interview guide but was content to allow conversation to move into other areas through follow-up questions if these areas were relevant. Participants were asked to sign a consent form for their names to be used in publication, while also being given the opportunity to remain anonymous. Interviews usually lasted about one hour, with the longest running to just over two hours. To help people get comfortable about telling stories about themselves, she first asked people to describe their religious background, then moved on to ask them about how they got involved in Ikon and what attracted them to the group. Other questions included (but were not limited to): What are your thoughts on church institutions? Do you think Ikon is an institution or could become institutionalized? How does Ikon approach liturgy, or the planning of its gatherings? How does Ikon have an impact on the way you live your life? What are your thoughts on the relationship between faith and doubt? How has postmodern philosophy influenced Ikon? Do you see Ikon as part of the wider Emerging Church Movement? In the wider picture of Christianity, what role do you see Ikon and other similar groups playing? All the interviews were transcribed, and Gladys coded them by hand, identifying common themes relevant to the project's broader research questions.

Gerardo helped facilitate two focus group conversations (sixteen participants total) that met on the campus of Catholic University of America in Washington, DC in 2008. These included leaders of emerging congregations in the region who answered a broad set of questions about their ministries as well as non-emerging congregational leaders who described their descriptions and reflections on the ECM. While Gerardo carried out only one extended, digitally recorded, semiformal interview with an ECM leader, Gerardo listened and selectively transcribed data from nearly 200 hours of digital recordings provided by Tony Jones, which added considerably more detail on the processes of joining and identifying with these communities. Jones conducted one-on-one interviews with the pastors and lay leaders, and facilitated focus group sessions, following an open-ended line of questioning. At each church, he conducted two focus groups (usually seven-five minutes long), two one-on-one interviews (forty-five minutes), and an interview with the pastor. Our analysis draws primarily on the focus group data, and secondarily on several one-on-one interviews. Jones's line of questioning in focus groups and individual interviews generally followed this pattern: Who are you? (What do you do? How do you want to define yourself?); What brought you to this church? (How did you find out about it? What got you in the door the first time?); What kept you at this church? (Why didn't you keep looking after you visited here?) Jones listened for ways people described their experiences in the congregations, paying special attention to recurring words and phrases. He also attended the church's primary worship service and any other activities of the community available during the visit, and he read the church's literature, both printed and online. In the end, fourteen focus groups and thirteen interviews from Jones's data were analyzed, which represented a total of 127 people who participated in one-on-one interviews and focus groups. Notes from the focus group meetings and interviews were made available for our research. Of the data from Jones's study, no demographics were gathered from these groups, but the best estimate based on names, character of people's voices, and inferences from interactions in the session, we estimate focus group participants were slightly majority female (57%) with a median age of mid-thirties, although it is clear from comments made by participants, their stated occupation, and the experiences they shared that those who were youngest were college age and completing their bachelor's degree while those who were oldest were approaching retirement age but still working. Focus group participants also varied in membership tenure in their congregation as sessions included a wide range of time frames from recent attendees who joined the congregation within the previous year to "charter members" present at the church from its first gathering.

## Congregational Surveys

Jones provided the results of surveys from eight emerging congregations described above. Jones essentially conducted a church census in each of the eight ECM congregations. These eight congregations define themselves (however uncomfortably) as part of the ECM and are recognized as part of the ECM by members of the broader network of authors, pastors, and lay leaders who participate in the movement. The congregations included are geographically diverse, ranging from Washington and California on the Pacific coast to Maryland on the Atlantic with congregations between in Colorado, Missouri, Minnesota, and Texas. The congregations varied in size from 31 to 537 respondents. Each congregational survey was administered during all of the Sunday worship services at all eight congregations in May 2006, resulting in 2,020 returned surveys that reveal quantitative data about these congregations.

The original ECM dataset included 2,020 cases. In collaboration with Paul Olson, the survey data was analyzed, but in order to make the data more comparable to the data gathered in the Baylor Religion Survey (BRS), we eliminated a number of cases.[18] First, the original ECM dataset included fifty-eight individuals who were under the age of eighteen. Because the BRS only included people who are eighteen and older, we removed the minors from the ECM dataset. Second, one of the options available for ECM survey respondents for church attendance was "first time," indicating that the respondent had not attended services at the church before and happened to be attending for the first time on the day of the survey. We did not consider it appropriate to include these respondents in the analysis, so they were excluded. When we removed the minors and first time attendees from the analysis, the final sample size was reduced to 1,771.

The data set yielded several demographic characteristics. In terms of male/female gender, 54.5% are female. In terms of age: 31.5% are 18–25, 36.9% are 26–35, 15.8% are 36–45, 10.3% are 46–55, and 5.5% are 56 and older (the oldest recorded age is 88). For race/ethnicity, the original survey included fifteen categories, the last one being "I don't know." Data show 92.8% indicated white, 2.4% Asian/Pacific Islander, 2.2% Hispanic, 1.3% black, 0.3% Native American, and 0.8% are other. Education is skewed toward higher degrees: 1% had some high school, 3.9% had only a high school diploma, 20.2% had some college or vocational schooling, 39.5% completed college or vocational schooling, 12.3% had some postcollege education, and 23.2% completed a graduate degree. In terms of marital status, 50.3% are single and 42.5% are married; also included are 1.3% cohabitating, 5.5% divorced, and 0.5% widowed. Sixty-eight percent had no children, 30.7% had minor children, and only 1.3% with grown children.

Religious characteristics drawn from the survey include respondents' past and current religious designation. Mainline Protestant "best described" 30.7% of respondents' religious background, followed by evangelical Christian 28.5%, independent/nondenominational 13.5%, Roman Catholic 12.6%, nonreligious/agnostic/atheist 9.2%, Pentecostal 3.4%, and other 2.1%. In terms of what best described their current religion, the great majority (63%) marked independent/nondenominational, followed by 21.2% evangelical Christian, 8.1% Mainline Protestant, 1.3% Roman Catholic, 1% Pentecostal, 0.9% nonreligious/agnostic/atheist, and 4.5% as other.

In addition, the survey indicates 37% of these ECM participants describe their church as "emergent," 27.5% as "independent," 11.7% as "evangelical," and 2% as "mainline." Additionally, 7.4% responded, "none of the above," and 14.2% indicated they were unclear on the terms used in the survey.

## Textual Sources

In addition to observation and interviews, other sources of data included published books representative of and reactive to the movement, as well as online documents, recorded lectures, blog and Facebook posts, audio podcasts, Twitter feeds, and other related online materials. Some leaders have published books and made podcasts or videos available online. By adding these additional sources, we sought "structural corroboration" described by Elliot Eisner as "a means through which multiple types of data are related to each other to support or contradict the interpretation and evaluation of a state of affairs."[19] All the material used for analysis is publicly accessible.

Throughout our project, we treated the publically accessible discourses of Emerging Christians like primary source texts, identifying patterns and themes across a range of this material. Such texts do not operate independently nor in isolation; rather, texts are adopted, selectively accentuated, and utilized in pursuit of particular ends. It is the authoring and use of texts that matters. We do not assume texts have singular or static meanings; our ethnographic orientation emphasizes that the texts selected here matter not because researchers have decided their importance but rather in observation these texts take on salience in the shaping and legitimation of ECM practices. Texts are symbolic representation evident in various documents, books, online media, interviews, speeches, and other forms of communication that are spoken, written, or otherwise depicted in a material form that is accessible to others.[20] The power of textual discourses is that they define what is normal, standard, and appropriate, and in the case of the ECM, they are integral to the way the movement defines itself—as far as it can be said to define itself (see chapter 4).[21]

We define discourse broadly as collections of interrelated texts that cohere to produce meanings and action in the world.[22] Discourses can shape strategies and rules for speaking and acting and can serve to constrain agency.[23] Maguire and Hardy write, "Discourse thus creates bodies of knowledge that normalize certain ways of believing, speaking, and behaving."[24] They not only make sense of the world but can generate experiences and practices.[25] Discourses can become reified and thus, in the relative coherence of their structure, appear to present a more cohesive presentation of an institution. This helps institutions conserve their power through their idealized and taken for granted presentation, a process which Emerging Christians say they are keen to subvert (see chapter 4).[26]

Because printed books are characterized by broad accessibility and, more importantly, are accepted as more substantive in establishing legitimacy of thought and practice, we draw on selected books, especially those of Brian McLaren, Rob Bell, Tony Jones, and Peter Rollins. These encode key viewpoints for the revision and even abandonment of conventional theology and spiritual practices within Christianity. Although it is not possible to analyze all possible sources of discourse within the ECM, our ethnographic immersion in emerging communities and networks suggested those which became focal points for analysis, and sources were added and the relative weighing of sources changed as our analysis developed. We juxtaposed accounts and rationale from different sources whenever possible to establish points of convergence. Such texts also often documented ongoing subsequent struggles around problematizations given by the ECM.

Social media also became an important avenue for engaging and understanding the ECM. Conferences and gatherings emphasized the use of social media as a means for connecting with people and sharing ideas. Twitter is especially prominent; for example, projection screens were commonly used to display ongoing tweets as they occurred during meetings to encourage broad interaction. Apart from meetings, the near constant microposts characteristic of Twitter provided an opportunity for observing ongoing discussions and self-expression among ECM participants. It became important to take advantage of this new form of interaction and public expression. From 2010 to 2012, we actively monitored a carefully curated Twitter feed of ECM insiders and ECM observers including (but not limited to): @peterrollins, @RealPeteRollins, @jaybakker, @jonestony, @adamwc, @realrobbell, @adamdmoore, @chadcrawford, @Shane_Claiborne, @emergentvillage, @zachjhunter, @moffou42, @shinabarger, @bigtentx, @kathyescobar, @ikonbelfast, @ikonnyc, @markvans, @nelsoncost, @u_r_epyc, @theotherjournal, @timconder, @orthopraxy, @pagitt, @SamirSelmanovic, @reverenddvince, @rbolger, @lloydchia, @postmodernegro, @trippfuller, @CreatingLove, @trans4m, @bobhyatt, @Sarcasticluther, @AndyRowell, @eliacin, @julieclawson, @Originsproject, @trippfuller, @warrenbird, @jrdkirk, @KSMoody, @mattgallion, @tallskinnykiwi, @duanalla, @kesterbrewin, @philsnider, @XochitlAlvizo. While this list of Twitter handles is not exhaustive (as Twitter accounts were sometimes added or dropped due to irrelevance or inactivity), it represents the most active and consistent individual accounts. These are people who made posting and engaging on Twitter regarding ECM and related issues a priority. The active monitoring of every tweet, retweet, and associated interactions and hyperlinks (most often to news sites or blog posts) provided additional information regarding issues, controversies, personalities, events, lists, and additional published pieces (both print and digital) regarding the ECM. Overall, monitoring Twitter feeds was a form of "digital ethnography" that allowed a unique window to the shape, hierarchy, and content of ECM relational networks.[27]

Finally, secondary sources with relevant observations from other scholars of the ECM were included as they became available. Some counter-texts against the ECM (or some caricature of it), usually in the form of books from Christian publishers, were also included. Counter-texts often present themselves as defending theology, especially in relation to ecclesiology and individual morality, using orthodox formulations to challenge the ECM. Since counter-texts were largely polemical in nature, they did not become the basis for understanding the ECM itself.

# NOTES

## Chapter 1

1. Throughout this book, we refer to Ikon Belfast as a product of the Northern Ireland context. Northern Ireland, which is a part of the United Kingdom, is a contested geographical space. Many people from "Catholic, nationalist, and/or republican" (and a very few from "Protestant, unionist, and/or loyalist" backgrounds) identify with the Republic of Ireland and advocate a "united Ireland." They would often rather refer to the "north of Ireland" rather than "Northern Ireland." Without delving into the dynamics of the Troubles and present peace process, we acknowledge that it is important to locate Ikon within both UK and Ireland developments in religion.

2. The Re-Emergence Conference was held March 16–18, 2010 at the Irish School of Ecumenics, Trinity College Dublin at Belfast, and various venues in Belfast. It was organized by Rollins and billed as a launch event for his "Insurrection" tour in pubs in ten North American cities. Poet/musician Pádraig Ó Tuama and musician/artist Jonny McEwen accompanied Rollins on the "Insurrection" tour. Speakers at the conference included Phyllis Tickle, Dave Tomlinson, and Samir Selmanovic. Rollins's book *Insurrection* was published in 2011 and explored many of the themes raised on the tour.

3. Bielo (2009, 2011), Chia (2010), Harrold (2006), Lee and Sinitiere (2009), Putnam and Campbell (2010), and Wollschleger (2012).

4. Elsewhere, we locate Ikon and Rollins on the margins of the ECM. Ikon stimulates the ECM to ask questions about how far it is willing to go in its anti-institutionalism and "leaderless" aspects, while Rollins pushes the boundaries in his work on language, anti-conversionism, doubt and "a/theism" (Ganiel and Marti, forthcoming). See also Gay (2011).

5. Carson (2005) and DeYoung and Kluck (2008).

6. Many Ikon participants urged us to distinguish between Rollins's work (located within the ECM) and Ikon (which they insisted is not part of the ECM). Although Rollins has used examples from Ikon in his published work, he also has written: "Some of my friends in Ikon Belfast were dismayed by my becoming an author and talking about the group in my work. Most had never heard of the emerging church and had no interest in what was going on in the church there or in the wider world. They were worried that we might be seen as something we were not." (See comment on Stephen Keating, "Neoliberal Church?" An Und Für Sich, April 10, 2013, http://itself.wordpress.com/2013/04/10/neoliberal-church, accessed July 18, 2013). Like Rollins, we do not want to portray Ikon as something it is not. We appreciate most describe it as an arts collective, and we would not call it a "congregation" in the most common sense of the word. Nevertheless, we locate it on the margins of the ECM and include examples from it in this book because we think it illustrates what some trends in the ECM might look like, if followed to their most radical conclusions.

7. Authors' field notes were compared with a blog entry by Devin Bustin ("In an Upper Room," Peter Rollins: To Believe is Human; To Doubt, Divine, April 7, 2010, http://peterrollins.net/?p=1074, accessed June 7, 2013). We quote directly in this section at several points from his written account.
8. Published as a poem in Ó Tuama (2010: 78).
9. Published as a poem in Ó Tuama (2012: 84).
10. McKnight (2007).
11. Bielo (2009, 2011), Carson (2005), Chia (2010), Drane (2006), Ganiel (2006), Webber (2007), and Lings (2006).
12. Drane (2006: 4).
13. Gibbs and Bolger (2005).
14. Examples of those critical of the ECM include Carson (2005), DeYoung and Kluck (2008), MacArthur (2007), and Oakland (2007). Of course, this does not include numerous blog posts, newsletters, and unpublished sermons over the years.
15. Labanow (2009: 126).
16. Caputo (2007: 129).
17. Jones (2011). As is clear throughout this book, Jones is an ECM "insider."
18. Quoted in Moynagh (2012: xxi).
19. Tickle (2008, 2012). Tickle has come to be seen as an advocate for the ECM; it is little exaggeration to conclude that she sees the ECM as the future of a renewed (Western) Christianity that will ultimately prove as significant as the Reformation.
20. Tickle (2012: 112).
21. Tickle (2012: 113–114).
22. Tickle (2012: 143).
23. Tickle (2012: 35).
24. Ó Tuama, personal e-mail, June 23, 2013.
25. See Ammerman (2005) and Warner (1994).
26. Packard (2012).
27. Pew Research Center, Pentecostal Resource Page, Pew Research: Religion and Public Life Project, October 5, 2006, http://www.pewforum.org/Christian/Evangelical-Protestant-Churches/Pentecostal-Resource-Page.aspx, accessed July 23, 2013.
28. Gibbs and Bolger (2005: 331–333).
29. Lynch (2003: 78).
30. Moynagh (2012: 71).
31. Packard (2012: 9). Packard cites figures that come from Graham Clay, an Anglican bishop associated with Fresh Expressions. Moynagh is a Church of England minister who is part of the UK's national Fresh Expressions team. Moynagh's figures are similar to Clay's.
32. Engelke (2013).
33. Packard (2012: 9).
34. Association with the ECM has been documented in Anglophone countries like Australia and New Zealand as well as European countries like Germany and the Netherlands in Doornenbal (2012). More insider reports of ECM communities beyond the United States and the United Kingdom, including Latin America, can be found in Bolger (2012).
35. Packard (2012: 9–10).
36. Bielo (2011: 26).
37. The ECM has spread from evangelicalism and influenced Christians among Mainline Protestant, Roman Catholic, and Greek Orthodox congregations. There are now emergent cohorts in every major city including Atlanta, Baltimore, Charlotte, Kansas City, and Seattle. The movement also has spawned many special interest emergent groups like Emergent Women, Globemerging, Presbymergent, and Queermergent. Since around 2005, Christian publishers have devoted entire book series, and Christian bookstores set apart entire bookshelves, for emerging products featuring bright, pop-culture echoes of style and colors. Most surprising, the spread of the movement is evident in recent moves towards recognizing "Emergent Jews" and even "Emergent Muslims."

38. See also Wollschleger (2012: 84).
39. See the description of Sanctus1's ministry run out of a bar in Manchester, UK (Edson 2006: 33) and Jesus at a Pub hosted at the Spiderhouse in Austin, Texas (Snyder 2011: 135–136).
40. Tickle (2012: 60).
41. Bolz-Weber (2012a: 52).
42. Bolz-Weber (2012a: 53).
43. Bolz-Weber (2012b: 258).
44. Snyder (2011: 135–136).
45. Snyder (2011: 136).
46. Berghoef (2012).
47. See http://www.pubchurch.co.uk/.
48. Edson (2006: 33).
49. Bakker (2001).
50. Lynch (2003: 56).
51. See chapter 7.
52. Labanow (2009: 5–6).
53. A source of ECM twitter feeds can be found using the "following" and "list" functions http://twitter.com/emergentvillage and http://twitter.com/trans4m. For more on the Internet and the Emerging Church, see Drane (2006).
54. http://www.patheos.com/blogs/emergentvillage/, accessed December 6, 2011.
55. http://www.facebook.com/groups/191109674243204/, accessed December 6, 2011.
56. http://pyrotheology.com/.
57. http://www.eastcentralministries.org.
58. Perkins (1993).
59. Some "dispersed" communities, such as the Iona Community in Scotland and the Corrymeela Community in Northern Ireland, are neo-monastic. Dispersed communities usually require members—who may not be able to move geographically to the site where the community is located—to identify with the ideals of the community, maintain regular contact with other members, and to return to community headquarters on a regular basis, such as once per year.
60. Moynagh (2012: xi–xiii) also argues that "new monasticism" informs the wider ECM.
61. Bielo (2011: 109).
62. Power (2007: 118–164).
63. Hurley (1998: 317–340).
64. Ganiel (2011).
65. Pagitt and Jones (2007).
66. Gay (2011).
67. Higgins locates Church Without Walls within the ECM (2013: 179–181). The Church of Scotland website has sections for "Church Without Walls" and for "Emerging Church." The Emerging Church section is linked on the site to Church Without Walls and also references the Anglican/Methodist Fresh Expressions initiative. See http://www. churchofscotland.org.uk/connect, accessed June 1, 2013 and Drane (2006).
68. Moynagh (2012: 81).
69. Ganiel (2008: 97–99, 123–126, 2006).
70. Bielo (2009) and Wollschleger (2012). See also Marti (2005).
71. Bielo (2009).
72. Ammerman (1987) and Marti (2005).
73. Harrold (2006).
74. While from the standpoint of a "lived religion" perspective there is no singular evangelicalism in the world, we might say that the ECM crafts an imaginary other in a conservative, fundamentalist, evangelicalism as its common base of comparison and action. One of the ironies of the ECM is how it embraces the complexity of standpoints within its own community while ignoring the complexity of evangelicalism as a whole.
75. See Appendix: Research Methodology.
76. See Appendix: Research Methodology.

77. Stuart Brown, "The Without Walls Story," Without Walls Cohort, May 31, 2013, http://withoutwallscohort.wordpress.com/2013/05/31/the-withoutwalls-cohort-story-version-1-0, accessed June 1, 2013.

78. Packard (2012: 141).

79. In terms of gender, while the ECM welcomes women and has a more egalitarian ethos in the gatherings, we consistently find a greater weight toward men as speakers and as interlocutors in formal workshops and informal conversations. Thus for men, it may be speculated that the movement provides a male-oriented space that combines an opinionated bravado on spiritual matters with a nerdish vulnerability to doubt and uncertainty. In addition, while the movement is based on mostly white, urban/suburban, and middle-class constituents, there is an earnest attempt to expand that base to become more "multicultural." The movement is recently taking on transnational concerns, discovering church leaders and championing social concerns outside the United States as a means to lift themselves from an overidentification with American pop culture (McLaren 2007).

80. McLaren (2004).

81. Tickle (2012: 101).

82. See chapter 3.

83. Gay (2011).

84. Gay (2011: 6). Such experiments include the English-based radical orthodoxy movement, the liturgical movement, and the influence of ecumenical communities like Iona in Scotland and Taizé in France.

85. Gay (2011: 16).

86. Gay (2011: 93–94).

87. See chapter 7.

88. For an example of a critique of conventional Christianity through the philosophical lens of deconstruction, see Caputo (2006, 2007, 2013).

89. Fuchs and Ward (1994: 481–500).

90. Labanow (2009: 124).

91. Fuchs and Ward (1994: 483).

92. Goffman (1961: 199–201).

93. Goffman (1961: 320).

94. Goffman (1961: 199).

95. Tickle (2012: 130).

96. Bielo (2009), Packard (2012).

97. While Jones's microposting on Twitter was abbreviated, the quote provided here is the full text. Khomiakov and Kireevsky (1998: 171).

98. See Kimball (2004) and Morgenthaler (1999).

99. Packard and Sanders (2013).

100. Packard (2012).

101. Packard and Sanders (2013).

102. There is a growing stream of scholarly literature including Bielo (2009, 2011), Chia (2010), Harrold (2006), Jones (2011), Lee and Sinitiere (2009), Packard (2011, 2012), Packard and Sanders (2013), Pally (2011), and Putnam and Campbell (2010).

103. See chapter 7.

104. McCracken (2010).

105. On the concept of "haven" as a place for valuing core aspects of self-identity, see Marti (2005, 2010b) and Ganiel's (2010) application of the concept to Ikon.

106. For more detail, see Appendix: Research Methodology.

## Chapter 2

1. Beck (2010: 152).

2. Packard (2012: 146).

3. Some research emphasizes that people adopt "hybrid" identities that draw on different logics simultaneously (Meyer and Hammerschmid, 2006, Rao et al., 2003, Lok, 2010).

4. Packard (2012).

5. Other scholars have noted a lack of denominational loyalty among Protestants, for example, Schwadel (2013).
6. Guest and Taylor (2006: 52).
7. Moody (2010: 501).
8. Beck (2010: 141).
9. Berghoef (2012).
10. Beck (2010: 141).
11. See Beck (2010: 68–71).
12. Beck (2010: 160).
13. Beck (2010: 41).
14. Beck (2010: 71).
15. Beck (2010: 71).
16. Beck (2010: 71).
17. Guest and Taylor (2006).
18. Labanow (2009: 48).
19. Packard (2012). Regarding cultivating affinities in congregations, see Marti (2005, 2008).
20. Packard (2012: 130).
21. Blatt (2009). See also Clark and Mills (1979) and Fiske (1992).
22. Shepherd, Douglas, and Shanley (2000).
23. Blatt (2009: 533).
24. Sluss and Ashforth (2007).
25. Clark & Mills (1979), Poppo and Zenger (2002).
26. Marti (2008: 137–140).
27. Ammerman (1997b: 208).
28. Drane (2006: 4).
29. Jamieson (2006).
30. Jamieson (2006: 69).
31. Bielo (2009: 240).

## Chapter 3

1. Kathy Escobar, "rebuilding after deconstructing," Kathy Escobar: pastor. writer. mommy. advocate. rule-breaker. dreamer., April 16, 2012, http://kathyescobar.com/2012/04/16/rebuilding-after-deconstructing, accessed December 8, 2013. While the lack of capitalization is Escobar's form of writing, this is not preserved in the quotes from her post.
2. Lynch (2003).
3. Bielo (2011) and Harrold (2006).
4. Beck (2010: 16).
5. Jones discussed this in a transcribed interview with Brian McLaren.
6. See also Bielo (2009).
7. There are varying percentages across the eight emerging congregations surveyed. On the low end, only 16.5% of the respondents in one of the congregations said that their church was emergent; on the other end of the spectrum, 68.5% of the respondents in another identified it as emergent. The inconsistency is due in part with the degree to which emerging congregational leaders promote "emergent" as a salient label to describe their churches. It should be noted that 27.5% labeled their church "independent," and an additional 14.2% of respondents indicated that they were "unclear on terms" for describing their church.
8. Tickle (2012: 101).
9. Anonymous message posted on the personal blog of Brian McLaren, "Q&R: Is the Emerging Church Movement Fizzling Out?," Brian D. McLaren: Author, Speaker, Activist, April 14, 2012, http://brianmclaren.net/archives/blog/i-am-a-former-christian.html, accessed December 8, 2013).
10. Harrold (2006: 80).
11. Jamieson (2006: 69).

12. Meyer and Jepperson (2000: 111).
13. The rise of individual action is partly associated with the development of neoliberalism. Meyer and Jepperson (2000: 109) write, "The liberal model is distinctive in foregrounding 'action,' creating extensive psychological, biographical, organizational theory about this action, and focusing upon proper agency arrangements and enactment." In our discussion, we focus more on the organization and the need for organizations to bolster individual action; specifically, religious organizations for religious action. Accordingly, "the properly agentic actor is always partly an agent of the broader historical telos of the modern system such that newly formed religious imperatives and identities inevitably reveal aspects of the direction of broader social change" (Meyer and Jepperson 2000: 112).

## Chapter 4

1. Bader-Saye (2006).
2. Harrold (2006: 80).
3. Lawrence and Suddaby (2006).
4. Tsoukas and Chia (2002: 567), Hardy and Maguire (2008).
5. Our understanding here and elsewhere is informed by the burgeoning literature on institutional entrepreneurship. See Hardy and Maguire (2008). Institutional entrepreneurs are those responsible for these new or changed institutions. The term emerged in part from the work of Paul DiMaggio (1988: 14) who argued that new institutions emerge through organized actors with resources to accomplish their interests. This literature is a subset of the broader literature on institution building and accentuates agency, power, interests, and the capacity for change in the analysis of institutional fields (Lawrence and Suddaby 2006).
6. Leca, Battilana and Boxebaum (2008: 3).
7. Van Dijk et al. (2011: 1509).
8. See Weik (2011).
9. For a recent effort to discuss religious entrepreneurialism, see Lee and Sinitiere (2009).
10. See Stark and Finke (2000: 163).
11. Battilana, Leca, and Boxenbaum (2009: 94), Morrill and Owen-Smith (2002), Munir and Phillips (2005), Phillips et al. (2004).
12. Strang and Meyer (1993, 1994), Battilana, Leca, and Boxenbaum (2009: 82), Morrill and Owen-Smith (2002), Greenwood et al. (2002), Maguire et al. (2004), Rao et al. (2003), Suchman (1995).
13. Mutch (2007), Leca and Naccache (2006).
14. Giddens (1991: 20), Beck et al. (1994), Tsoukas and Chia (2002: 575), Emirbayer and Mische (1998: 1010).
15. Battilana, Leca, and Boxenbaum (2009: 94).
16. Hjorth and Steyaert (2004: 4).
17. Czarniawska-Joerges (1998: 18).
18. Martens et al. (2007: 1109), Navis and Glynn (2011: 494–495).
19. Bruner (1986).
20. Polkinghorne (1988).
21. Weick (1995: 61).
22. Rhodes and Brown (2005).
23. Lounsbury and Glynn (2001), Zilber (2007: 1038).
24. Leca, Battilana, and Boxenbaum (2008). Brown and Duguid (1991: 41). See also: Wenger (1998), Chia (2004), Jarzabkowski (2004), Whittington (1996). See also Bourdieu's (1977) notion of habitus, and actor network-theory, Callon (1986) Latour (1987).
25. Battilana, Leca, and Boxenbaum (2009: 84–85).
26. Battilana, Leca, and Boxenbaum (2009: 84).
27. Perkmann and Spicer (2007), Fligstein (2001a: 112, 2001b).
28. Battilana, Leca, and Boxenbaum (2009: 74), Child et al. (2007), Fligstein (1997, 2001b), Greenwood et al. (2002), Holm (1995).

29. Packard (2011, 2012).
30. Packard and Sanders (2013).
31. Harrold (2006: 80).
32. Harrold (2006: 80).
33. Engelke (2013: 27).
34. Langenohl (2008: 70), Greenwood et al. (2002), Lawrence and Phillips (2004), Maguire and Hardy (2006), Munir and Phillips (2005), Phillips et al. (2004), Rao et al. (2000), Zilber (2007: 1050).
35. Bird (2010: 682), quoted in Jones (2011: 5).
36. Rao et al. 2000, Zilber (2002, 2007).
37. Snow, Rochford, Worden, and Benford (1986).
38. Suddaby and Greenwood (2005) are among the organizational theorists who describe the framing of problems and solutions into accessible packages as part of a rhetorical strategy that directs attention to the inadequacies of conventional institutional vocabularies and exposes contradictions in the standard symbolic coding of institutional behavior. See also Rao and Giorgi (2006: 272).
39. Beck (2010: 9).
40. Jones (2009: 155).
41. Jones (2009: 156).
42. Jones (2009: 157).
43. McLaren (2001, 2003, 2008).
44. Rollins (2009).
45. This term is borrowed from Ikon's 2011 Greenbelt performance. See Gladys Ganiel, "Ikon at Greenbelt: Reconstructing the De-Construction," Gladys Ganiel: Building a Church Without Walls, September 2, 2011, http://www.gladysganiel.com/social-justice/ikon-at-greenbelt-reconstructing-the-de-construction, accessed October 22, 2012.
46. Bolz-Weber (2013: 38–39).
47. Rollins (2006: 12–13).
48. Wellman (2012: 150).
49. Wellman (2012: 57; 58).
50. Engelke (2013: 22).
51. Brewin (2012).
52. Rollins (2009).
53. For a classic statement on dispensationalism, see Ryrie (1995).
54. The full text of this tract is on Rollins's website: Peter Rollins, "Left Behind," Peter Rollins: To Believe is Human; To Doubt, Divine, May 21, 2011, http://peterrollins.net/?p=2854, accessed October 24, 2012. On Chick tracts, see Bivins (2008).
55. Mitchell and Ganiel (2011).
56. Harrold (2006). See chapter 3.
57. Gladys Ganiel, interview with Lindsey Mitchell, September 17, 2012.
58. Field notes from talk given at Emerging Cohort meeting in Charlotte, September 11, 2012.
59. Leca, Battilana and Boxebaum (2008: 20), Leca also cites Rao et al. (2000) and Dorado (2005).
60. Battilana, Leca, and Boxenbaum (2009: 70).
61. Beck (2010: 11).
62. Beck (2010: 11).
63. Beck (2010: 11).
64. Packard and Sanders (2013: 438).
65. Bell (2011).
66. See chapter 3.
67. Wellman (2012: 115).
68. Mitchell and Ganiel (2011: 33).
69. See chapter 3.
70. Gladys Ganiel, interview with Lindsey Mitchell, September 17, 2012.
71. Guest and Taylor (2006: 59).

72. Davie (1994).
73. Beck (2010: 130).
74. McLaren (2010: 254). See also McLaren (2007).
75. Scot McKnight, "Brian McLaren's *A New Kind of Christianity*. Brian McLaren's "New" Kind of Christianity is not so much Revolutionary and Evolutionary." *Christianity Today*, February 26, 2010, http://www.christianitytoday.com/ct/2010/march/3.59. html?start=1, accessed October 24, 2012.
76. Jones (2009: 162).
77. Engelke (2013: 101).
78. Tickle (2012: 161).
79. Tickle (2012: 161).
80. Bielo (2011: 55).
81. Bielo (2011: 57).
82. Bielo develops his idea of the ECM's "language ideology" through a further, illuminating discussion of irony and how people in the ECM view irony as "a treasure" (2011: 61). He observes that "conservative Evangelicals find this reliance on irony infuriating. It is interpreted as a smokescreen for theological waffling and a lack of spiritual reverence" (2011: 67).
83. Pagitt (2008: 30).
84. McKnight (2011: 116).
85. McKnight (2011: 117).
86. McKnight (2011: 117).
87. McKnight (2011: 118).
88. Rollins (2008).
89. Quoted in Lynch (2003: 65).
90. Beck (2010: 89).
91. Beck (2010: 89).
92. Rollins (2011).
93. Harrold (2006: 81).
94. Caputo (2007: 126).
95. Wellman (2012: 119).
96. Rollins (2006).
97. Peter Rollins, "Changing the Structure," Vimeo, July 14, 2011, http://vimeo.com/26423428, accessed on November 6, 2012.
98. Bonheoffer (2001).
99. Rollins (2011: 76ff).
100. Rollins (2011: 77).
101. Bakker (2013: 25).
102. Bakker (2013: 27).
103. Beck (2010: 127–128).
104. The poem is "Creed" in Henderson (1993).
105. Gladys Ganiel, interview with Pádraig Ó Tuama, June 16, 2011.
106. Harrold (2006: 81).
107. David Masters, "Why Proof of God's Existence Would Destroy My Faith," November 5, 2012, http://davidmasters.posterous.com, accessed November 6, 2012.
108. Rollins (2011: 21).
109. Bakker (2013: 24–25).
110. Rollins (2013).
111. Rollins (2013: back cover).
112. Bakker (2013: 31).
113. Bakker (2013: 185).
114. The William Belden Nobel Lectures of 1969 were published as Frederick Buechner (1970: 47).
115. Brandon Ambrosino. "Giving Up God for Lent." Huffington Post religion blog, February 16, 2013, http://www.huffingtonpost.com/brandon-ambrosino/why-im-giving-up-god-for-_b_2,683,164.html, accessed on April 3, 2013.

116. Tomlinson (2008: 2).
117. Tickle (2012: 197).
118. A book countering *The Lost Message of Jesus* is *Pierced for our Transgressions* (Jeffrey, Ovey, and Sach 2007).
119. Tickle (2012: 197).
120. Tickle (2012: 198).
121. Bell (2013: 2).
122. Bell (2013: 8).
123. Bell (2013: 153–173).
124. Bakker (2011: 65–66).
125. Bakker (2011: 71).
126. Bolz-Weber (2013: 185).
127. Bakker (2011: 72).
128. Tickle (2012: 172).
129. Higgins (2013: 104–105).
130. Jones (2011: 147).
131. Moynagh and Harrold (2012: 114, see also 105–114).
132. Bolz-Weber (2013: 185).
133. Jones (2009: 141).
134. Carson (2005: 132–138).
135. Jones (2009: 233).
136. Shults quoted in Jones (2009: 235).
137. Packard and Sanders (2013: 444).

## Chapter 5

1. DiMaggio (1988: 15); see also Aldrich and Fiol (1994), DiMaggio (1991), Hinings and Greenwood (1988), Suchman (1994).
2. While it is possible to trace a wide range of influences on the practices of the ECM (as in Gay 2011), our observations reveal a consistent pattern of responses to entities labeled "the megachurch" and "the mainline," although these are often collapsed into more ambiguous criticisms of "the church."
3. Packard (2012: 33–59).
4. An example of such critique comes from Higgins (2013: 89), writing out of the Irish context: "The challenge for the Catholic Church, at the present time, is to move beyond institutionalism and, with the help of the wider community, recover the centrality of kingdom values. The challenge for those Protestant churches who have interpreted mission as evangelism is to recognise that the Spirit of God is at work in all spheres of life, and God's kingdom is broader than any church and includes 'all things in heaven and earth' (Eph 1:10)."
5. Ganiel (2006, 2008).
6. For more on the "seeker model" of congregations, see Sargeant (2000) and Marti (2005).
7. Bielo (2009: 229).
8. Jamieson (2006: 68).
9. Popular books by Dan Kimball et al., *The Emerging Church: Vintage Christianity for New Generations* (2003) and Robert E. Webber, *Ancient-Future Faith: Rethinking Evangelicalism for a Postmodern World* (1999) have looked back to premodern and ancient church liturgical practices as a means to jolt Christian worship from more recent Western traditions.
10. Higgins locates the "Women-Church" movement as part of the ECM, seeing it as a paradigmatic example of women taking action to try and transform churches (2013: 157–161). But it is not entirely clear the extent that Women-Church, with its primarily Catholic origins, is in dialogue with the key leaders and communities usually associated with the ECM, especially those coming from American evangelical backgrounds.
11. Our descriptions of the public worship of three emerging congregations in chapter 2 illustrate this.

12. Engelke (2013), Bielo (2011), Gay (2011).
13. Kimball (2003).
14. Bielo (2011), chapter 3 "Ancient-Future I: Experiencing God" and chapter 4–"Ancient-Future II: Everyday Monastics."
15. This corresponds to the processes of "institutional isomorphism." See DiMaggio and Powell (1983).
16. Jones (2011: 57).
17. Jones (2011: 58). See also Pagitt (2005).
18. For a review of the relation between preaching and church architecture, see Kilde (2002) and Marti (2008: 112–115).
19. For a description of a "communitarian hermeneutic" by prominent ECM leaders, see Conder and Rhodes (2009).
20. Jones (2009: 216).
21. Moody (2012: 193).
22. Audio files of Jay Bakker's preaching can be found at his congregation's website, http://www.revolutionnyc.com. In 2013, Bakker moved his ministry to Minneapolis, Minnesota.
23. One of McManus's most popular messages became a bestselling book, *The Barbarian Way: Unleash the Untamed Faith Within* (2005). More on McManus and his preaching can be found in Marti (2005).
24. For more on Bell, see Wellman (2012).
25. Lenin (1940).
26. For more on "de-facto congregationalism," and its consequence for the structure of religious gatherings, see Warner (1994, 1998).
27. On Weber's notion of charisma, see Weber (1978).
28. Packard (2012: 95–121).
29. Packard (2012: 95–121).
30. Tickle (2012: 125).
31. Jones (2011).
32. The term "Cyndicate" reflects "both the self-organization, diversity and common purpose of a syndicate, and the counter-culturalism of the Greek cynics" (Moody 2012: 188).
33. Some people in Ikon insist it does not have leaders. Others say that there are people who are seen as leaders (by some people who attend or know about Ikon events).
34. Michels (1915).
35. Snider (2011: xix).
36. Bielo (2009: 219–232).
37. Bolz-Weber (2011: 7).
38. Drane (2006).
39. Gay (2011: 38–45); Bielo (2011: 15).
40. Tomlinson (2008: x).
41. Sargeant (2000).
42. See chapter 2.
43. Jones (2011: 100).
44. The ECM has an interesting and still developing connection to Pentecostalism. Tony Jones was asked to present his thoughts on the connections between the ECM and Pentecostalism at the annual meeting of the Society for Pentecostal Studies in 2010. Jones's tentative remarks are less a summary evaluation than an indication that Pentecostalism is, as yet, not a true conversational partner among emerging church leaders. So, while Pentecostalism and the ECM both critique similar religious developments within Christianity, they do so out of different histories, different priorities, and different conceptual developments in their theology. A recent overview of Pentecostalism and its manifestation in a local church can be found in Marti (2008).
45. Guest and Taylor (2006: 60).
46. Bielo (2011: 130).
47. See http://www.solomonsporch.com, accessed February 8, 2012.

48. All three events are described by Bielo in some detail (2011: 76–94).
49. See Luhr (2009).
50. Megachurches are defined as congregations with 2,000 or more weekly attendees. See Thumma and Travis (2007).
51. Tracey, Phillips, and Jarvis (2011: 63).
52. Dyck and Starke (1999) describe "breakaway organizations," churches that split from a parent church due to intense resistance and failure to resolve it. See also Miller (2002).
53. Lounsbury and Crumley (2007).
54. Hervieu-Leger (2006: 64).

## Chapter 6

1. McKnight (2007).
2. Bielo (2011). For an insider perspective, see Faix (2012).
3. Caputo (2007: 137).
4. Bielo (2011: 12).
5. Quoted in Croft (2008: 10).
6. Cray (2010: 5–6).
7. Bielo (2011: 160).
8. Hansen (2008).
9. Wollschleger's (2012) study of congregations in the Pacific Northwest supports our conclusion. He found that some congregations that originally seemed to be "emerging" should be, on closer analysis, identified with older evangelicalism, or neo-Calvinism. He labels such congregations "relevant," as opposed to "emerging," and introduces a third category of "wilderness" congregations that are seemingly straddling the emerging and relevant universes, walking the tightrope of tension between postmodernity and modernity that Bielo describes.
10. Wollschleger (2012: 82–84).
11. Harland and Wolff still operate in Belfast, but in a much diminished capacity from the days when Belfast was one of the main shipbuilding cities of the British Empire.
12. "Life in the Titanic Quarter," http://www.the-dock.org/blog/the-chaplains/, accessed December 22, 2013.
13. Gladys Ganiel, "All Aboard for the Dock?" June 25, 2011, Slugger O'Toole: Conversation, Politics, and Stray Insights, http://sluggerotoole.com/2011/06/25/all-aboard-for-the-dock-church/, accessed August 2, 2012.
14. See http://the-dock.org/, accessed August 2, 2012.
15. Jones (2011).
16. Wollschleger (2012: 82); and (2012: 81–82).
17. Gladys Ganiel, interview with Jon Hatch, May 21, 2004.
18. Yukich (2010: 174).
19. The Catholic Worker movement predates, but in many ways foreshadows, the neo-monastic movement that is analyzed in this book. The practices of neo-monastic communities we discuss later in this chapter resonate with the way people in Catholic Worker houses live.
20. Yukich (2010: 172).
21. Yukich (2010: 187–189).
22. Yukich (2010: 189–191).
23. Yukich (2010: 191–193).
24. Yukich (2010: 190).
25. See chapter 2.
26. Gladys Ganiel, interview with Jonny McEwen, June 24, 2011.
27. Gladys Ganiel, interview with Jonny McEwen, June 24, 2011.
28. Gladys Ganiel, "What Troubles You about Peter Rollins?," Gladys Ganiel: Building a Church Without Walls, November 28, 2011, http://www.gladysganiel.com/social-justice/what-troubles-you-about-peter-rollins, accessed August 10, 2012.
29. See Jones's (2011: 148–155) discussion of Hauerwas.

30. Gladys Ganiel, "Is Peter Rollins on a Mission?," Gladys Ganiel: Building a Church With-out Walls, December 5, 2011, http://www.gladysganiel.com/social-justice/is-peter-rollins-on-a-mission-towards-an-assessment-part-iv, August 10, 2012.

31. Aldous (2012).

32. See Ganiel (2008: 123–126).

33. The Wild Goose Festival is a Christian arts festival in North Carolina, which has been inspired and influenced by the UK's Greenbelt Festival.

34. Gladys Ganiel, interview with Jackson, March 12, 2004.

35. Kyle quoted in Orr (2008: 76). Some have criticized Kyle for what they see as a naive en-gagement with the UVF. See Gladys Ganiel, "The UVF and the PUP: Is Transformation Possible?" Gladys Ganiel: Building a Church Without Walls, June 7, 2010, http://www.gladysganiel.com/churches-reconciliation/the-uvf-and-the-pup-is-transformation-possible-john-kyle-on-the-nolan-show, accessed August 8, 2012. It also should be noted that Kyle's primary involvement was with Zero28 rather than Ikon, and that he maintains involvement in a charismatic church.

36. Einolf (2011: 437).

37. Rollins (2012: 64, 67).

38. Brian McLaren, for example, is an occasional author on the Sojourners blog, see http://sojo.net/biography/brian-mclaren, accessed June 18, 2013. Others, like Tony Jones, have been critical of Jim Wallis of Sojourners for failing to speak out on LGBTQ issues, see Tony Jones, "What Jim Wallis Might Be Missing," Theoblogy, May 10, 2011, http://www.patheos.com/blogs/tonyjones/2011/05/10/what-jim-wallis-might-be-missing, accessed June 18, 2013.

39. Bakker (2011).

40. Bakker (2011: 169).

41. Bakker (2011: 170).

42. Bakker (2013: 107).

43. Bakker (2013: 110–111).

44. Carol Kuruvilla, "Minneapolis Church Celebrates Gay Marriage Bill with Rainbow Communion Bread," New York Daily News, May 18, 2013, http://www.nydailynews.com/life-style/eats/church-celebrates-gay-marriage-rainbow-communion-bread-article-1.1347952, accessed May 23, 2013.

45. Melissa Steffan, "Brian McLaren Leads Commitment Ceremony At Son's Same-Sex Wedding," Christianity Today, September 24, 2012, http://www.christianitytoday.com/gleanings/2012/september/brian-mclaren-leads-commitment-ceremony-at-sons-same-sex.html, accessed December 8, 2013.

46. Bolz-Weber (2013: 119).

47. Claiborne has not only been considered a leader within the ECM, he has spoken at con-ferences and has relationships with other prominent ECM leaders. One label Claiborne has identified himself with is "Red Letter Christians," a term usually credited to Tony Campolo (2008). Red Letter refers to a convention in Bible printing in which the words of Jesus are printed in red letters. Claiborne and Campolo (2012) have written an ex-tended dialogue on "Red Letter Christianity."

48. Bielo (2011: 98–117), and (2011: 111).

49. Moving to deprived urban areas is not without its critics. Bielo quotes Dr Soong-Chan Rah, speaking at a conference of the Christian Community Development Association: "Much of his talk was a criticism of mono-ethnic Christianity and how white Evangeli-cals conduct urban ministry. Midway through his talk he boldly asserted, 'If you, as a white person, want to move into an urban setting and do ministry, and you don't have any nonwhite mentors, you're not a missionary, you're a colonialist'" (Bielo 2011: 133).

50. Bielo (2011: 102–103).

51. Claiborne (2006), Claiborne and Haw (2008).

52. Escobar (2012: 90).

53. Bielo (2011: 136).

54. On the concept of "havens," see Marti (2005, 2010b).

55. Bean (2012: 310).

56. "Relocation to the abandoned places of empire" is the first of the "Twelve Marks of New Monasticism" on The Simple Way's website (see http://www.thesimpleway.org/about/12-marks-of-new-monasticism, accessed June 18, 2013). The remaining marks are (2) Sharing economic resources with fellow community members and the needy among us. (3) Hospitality to the stranger. (4) Lament for racial divisions within the church and our communities combined with the active pursuit of a just reconciliation. (5) Humble submission to Christ's body, the church. (6) Intentional formation in the way of Christ and the rule of the community along the lines of the old novitiate. (7) Nurturing common life among members of intentional community. (8) Support for celibate singles alongside monogamous married couples and their children. (9) Geographical proximity to community members who share a common rule of life. (10) Care for the plot of God's earth given to us along with support of our local economies. (11) Peacemaking in the midst of violence and conflict resolution within communities along the lines of Matthew 18. (12) Commitment to a disciplined contemplative life.

57. Brewin (2010: 146).

58. Brewin (2010: 147).

59. Brewin (2010: 195).

60. Aldous (2012: 60–68).

61. Rollins (2011: 63–80).

62. Moody (2014a, 2014b).

63. Brewin (2012: 137–154).

64. Brewin (2012: 19ff).

65. Brewin (2012) attempts to avoid glorifying pirates, especially the cruelty and violence for which they are known, in caveats throughout the book. See especially page 134.

66. Brewin (2012: 139–140).

67. Brewin (2012: 157).

68. Packard (2012).

69. Wollschleger (2012: 82).

70. Einolf (2011).

71. Florida (2003). See also Marti (2008, 2010a).

72. Josh Lujan Loveless, "Is Rob Bell a Universalist?," Relevant Magazine, December 29, 2011, http://www.relevantmagazine.com/god/church/features/25030-is-rob-bell-a-universalist, accessed July 23, 2013.

73. Bell (2011: 178–179).

74. Josh Packard, personal e-mail communication, June 20, 2013.

## Chapter 7

1. McCracken (2010).

2. Luhrmann (2012), Marti (2008), Cox (1995).

3. Blake Huggins, "Misusing Deconstruction: On Belief and the Emergent Church," September 14, 2011, http://blakehuggins.com/2011/09/14/misusing-deconstruction-on-belief-and-the-emergent-church/, accessed September 20, 2011 (webpage no longer available).

4. Negative theology concentrates on describing what God is not. It is often referred to as apophatic (from the Greek "to deny") theology and associated with historical figures such as John Scot Erigena, Meister Eckhart, and St John of the Cross. Some have associated Peter Rollins's work with negative theology, though he prefers to locate his wider project within radical theology.

5. Heelas and Woodhead (2005).

6. Luhrmann (2012).

7. Turner (2011).

8. Alexander (2003, 2009), Lynch and Sheldon (2013).

9. Lynch (2012).

10. Lynch (2012: 35).

11. Lynch (2012: 49).

12. Lynch (2012: 5).
13. Beck (2010: 25).
14. Beck (2010: 26).
15. Maguire and Hardy (2009: 156).
16. Brunsson and Olsen (1993: 34).
17. Emirbayer and Mische (1998: 1009).
18. Maguire and Hardy (2009: 168).
19. See comments regarding Gladys Ganiel, "Heresies and How to Avoid Them?: Thoughts on Ikon, Heretics and a Plea to Listen to Them," Gladys Ganiel: Building a Church Without Walls, February 5, 2011, http://www.gladysganiel.com/irish-catholic-church/heresies-and-how-to-avoid-them-thoughts-on-ikon-heretics-and-a-plea-to-listen-to-them/#comment-7806, accessed April 10, 2013.
20. "The 8 Points," Progressive Christianity.Org: Spiritual Networking and Resources for an Evolving Faith, http://progressivechristianity.org/the-8-points/, accessed April 10, 2013.
21. Heelas and Woodhead (2005: 18).
22. Moody (2014a). Radical theologian Mark C. Taylor has employed the term extensively, as has Peter Rollins in his popular writings.
23. Katharine Sarah Moody, "Introducing the Network," Philosophy and Religious Practices: An AHRC Network for Philosophers of Religion and Other Researchers on Religion, April 12, 2013, http://philosophyreligion.wordpress.com/tag/ikon-belfast, accessed April 15, 2013.
24. Peter Rollins, "Is It Possible for a Christian to Give up Atheism for Lent?" Peter Rollins: To Believe is Human, to Doubt Divine, March 15, 2011, http://peterrollins.net/ ?p = 2428, accessed July 18, 2013.
25. Christian Piatt, "The Problem Isn't God; It's Certainty," Christian Piatt: Father, Son, and Holy Heretic, April 6, 2013, http://www.patheos.com/blogs/christianpiatt/2013/04/the-problem-isnt-god-its-certainty, accessed April 11, 2013.
26. Moody (2014b).
27. Ammerman (1997a).
28. Macquarrie (1972: 215).
29. Macquarrie (1972: 223).
30. Packard (2012: 142).
31. Bolz-Weber (2013: 181).
32. See Appendix: Research Methodology; see Marti and Olson (2013).
33. Bolz-Weber (2013: 182).
34. Bolz-Weber (2013: 187).
35. Williams (2012: 1).
36. Cray, Kennedy and Mobsby (2012).
37. Stephen Keating, "Neoliberal Church?" An Und Für Sich, April 10, 2013, http://itself.wordpress.com/2013/04/10/neoliberal-church, accessed April 15, 2013.
38. Garud, Hardy, and Maguire (2007: 957–958), Reay, Golden-Biddle, and Germann (2006: 993).
39. King et al. (2011: 567). See also McKendrick et al. (2003).
40. See for example: Url Scaramanga, "R.I.P. Emerging Church," Out of Ur, September 8, 2008, http://www.outofur.com/archives/2008/09/rip_emerging_ch.html; Scott Daniels, "The Death of the Emerging Church," Pastor Scott's Thoughts, April 10, 2010, http://drtscott.typepad.com/pastor_scotts_thoughts/2010/08/the-death-of-the-emerging-church.html; Anthony Bradley, "Farewell Emerging Church, 1989–2010," World Magazine, April 14, 2010, http://www.worldmag.com/2010/04/farewell_emerging_church_1989_2010.
41. Brian McLaren, "Q&R: Is the Emerging Church Movement Fizzling Out?," posted April 14, 2012, http://brianmclaren.net/archives/blog/i-am-a-former-christian.html, accessed December 20, 2013.
42. King et al. (2011: 567).
43. King et al. (2011: 568). See also Thornton and Ocasio (2008).

44. Battilana, Leca, and Boxenbaum (2009: 89). See also Delbridge and Edwards (2008), Garud et al. (2007), Reay and Hinings (2005).
45. Beck (2010: 19).
46. "What is the Mixed Economy?," Fresh Expressions, http://www.freshexpressions.org.uk/guide/about/mixedeconomy, accessed July 24, 2013. There has been considerable debate about the viability and desirability of a "mixed economy" in the UK; it is an important theme in Moynagh (2012) as well as Nelstrop and Percy (2008) and Cray, Kennedy and Mobsby (2012).
47. Beck (2010: 81).
48. Castells (2000).
49. Castells (2012).
50. Castells (2012: 221), and (2012: 230).
51. Castells (2012: 231).
52. Castells, (2012: 229).
53. Campbell (2012).
54. Drescher (2011). Drescher laments that mainline churches have not effectively engaged with social media.
55. Campbell (2012: 68).
56. Drescher (2011).
57. Campbell (2012: 68).
58. Kim and Pfaff (2012).
59. Packard and Sanders (2013).
60. Beck (2010: 15).
61. Beck (2010: 84).
62. Beck (2010: 124).
63. Beck is far less convinced that individuals become god-like. He instead draws out the oppressive system that demands reconsideration of the self in relation to market and governmental structures, and places the burden of positioning the self to avoid risk and sustain personal well-being. See Marti (2012a, 2012b, 2012c).
64. Beck (2010: 95).
65. Beck (2010: 94).
66. Beck (2010: 124).
67. Beck and Beck-Gernsheim (2002).
68. Eagleton (2003: 162).
69. Beck (2010: 140).
70. Lynch (2012: 135).
71. Beck (2010: 14).
72. Beck (2010: 140).
73. Beck (2010: 140).
74. Beck (2010: 79).
75. "Sheila" was made famous in the study of religion for her self-legitimated religiosity, which she called "Sheilaism." See Bellah et al. (1985).
76. Meyer and Jepperson (2000:105), Zilber (2007).
77. Beck (2010: 89).
78. Johnson, Dowd, and Ridgeway (2006).
79. Miller (2003).
80. Paul O'Donnell, "*Blue Like Jazz*: A Movie about When Christians Go to College," Huff Post Religion, March 30, 2012, http://www.huffingtonpost.com/paul-odonnell/when-christians-go-to-college_b_1377231.html, accessed June 29, 2013.
81. Rebecca Cusey, "A Christian Fatwa Against *Blue Like Jazz Movie*?," Tinsel: Gold and Glitter from Tinsel Town, March 22, 2012, http://www.patheos.com/blogs/tinseltalk/2012/03/a-christian-fatwa-against-blue-like-jazz, accessed June 29, 2013.
82. On "being reasonable" in modern religion, see Wuthnow (2012).
83. Bell (2013: 21–80).
84. Bell (2013: 22).
85. Engelke (2013: 190–191).

86. Engelke (2013: 191).
87. Engelke (2013: 201).
88. On organizational fields, see DiMaggio and Powell (1983: 148).
89. Friedland and Alford (1991). Structuration theory (Giddens 1984) defines structure as composed of rules and resources, which are perpetuated through the social processes that invoke them and by that invocation, are legitimated.
90. Rao and Giorgi (2006: 270).
91. Scott and Meyer (1994).
92. Martin (2003), Barman (2002), Dorado (2005), Mohr and Friedland (2008), Scott et al. (2000: 170), Purdy and Gray (2009), Friedland (2002), Lounsbury (2002), Thornton (2004).
93. Lok (2010: 1308).
94. Hargadon and Yellowlees (2001), Hardy and Phillips (1999), Rao (1998), Rao et al. (2000).
95. Weber (1978).
96. Eisenstadt (1986).
97. Meyer and Jepperson (2000: 103).
98. Meyer and Jepperson (2000: 109).
99. Meyer and Jepperson (2000).
100. Beck (2010: 94).
101. Meyer and Jepperson (2000: 105).
102. Durkheim (1969: 25–26).
103. Beck (2010: 98).
104. Joas (2013).
105. Durkheim quoted in Joas (2013: 53).
106. Joas (2013: 53).
107. Joas (2013: 51).
108. For footnoted references, see Meyer and Jepperson (2000: 102), which include Weber, Parsons, and Eisenstadt.
109. Brewin (2013).
110. Brewin (2013: 74).
111. Brewin (2013: 78).
112. Brewin (2013: 81).
113. Luhrmann (2012).
114. "Outlaw entrepreneurs" is a term from Suchman (1995: 594). See also Hannan (1986), Powell (1991).
115. Beck (2010: 68).
116. Beck (2010: 15).
117. Beck (2010: 71).
118. Berger (1997).
119. Beck (2010: 41).
120. Lynch (2012: 44–45).
121. Beck (2010: 41).
122. Beck (2010: 41).
123. Meyer and Jepperson (2000: 111).
124. Beck (2010: 136).
125. On competing logics, see D'Aunno, Sutton, and Price (1991), Friedland and Alford (1991), and Lounsbury (2008).
126. Meyer and Rowan (1977: 356).
127. Purdy and Gray (2009).
128. Schneiberg (2007: 48).
129. Lounsbury (2007), Schneiberg (2007), Thornton and Ocasio (2008).
130. Khan et al. (2007).
131. See Ammerman (2013).
132. Beck and Willms (2004: 77).
133. Beck and Willms (2004: 77).

134. Alexander (2006).
135. Beck and Willms (2004: 77).
136. Beck and Willms (2004: 78).
137. Beck and Willms (2004: 76).
138. Beck and Willms (2004: 77).
139. Packard (2012: 162).
140. Jones (2011).
141. A popular example can be found in Friesen (2009).
142. Beck (2010: 40).
143. Beck (2010: 39).
144. Beck (2010: 139).
145. On the "paradox of embedded agency," see Battilana (2006), Holm (1995), Seo and Creed (2002), DiMaggio and Powell (1991), Friedland and Alford (1991), Sewell (1992).
146. Following Bourdieu, actors are products of fields; indeed, subject positions are limited and there are only some legitimated identities within a field. See Oakes et al. (1998), Maguire et al. (2001), Bourdieu (1990).
147. Maguire (2007).
148. North (1990).
149. Bonchek and Shepsle (1996).
150. Jepperson (1991).
151. Meyer and Rowan (1977).
152. Jepperson, (1991: 145). On normative institutional regulations, see Wicks (2001), Caronna (2004), Hoffman et al. (2002), Scott (2001).
153. Friedland and Alford (1991), Zucker (1988, 1983). Whereas the "Stanford School" models of neoinstitutionalism initially framed by Meyer, Rowan, and Scott privileged widely shared symbolic models, DiMaggio and Powell (1983) stressed the importance of palpable network connections that transmitted coercive or normative pressures from institutional agents.
154. Brian Berghoef, "Beer, Conversation and God: Pursuing Faith Over a Pint," religion blog, Huffington Post, March 18, 2013, http://www.huffingtonpost.com/bryan-berghoef/beer-conversation-and-god_b_2885329.html, accessed March 20, 2013.
155. Navis and Glynn (2011: 479).
156. Seo and Creed (2002: 236–237), Clemens and Cook (1999).

## Appendix

1. Cox (1972: 13).
2. Reimer (1977).
3. Hayano (1979: 100).
4. See his dissertation listed under his full name, Anthony Hawthorne Jones (2011). Jones's dissertation was self-published under his shorter name as *The Church is Flat* (Jones 2011).
5. Examples can be drawn from a range of scholars including old-school phenomenologists like Alfred Schutz, prototypical symbolic interactionists like Herbert Blumer, and contemporary qualitative researchers like Norman Denzin.
6. Becker and Geer (1982).
7. Van Maanen (1988: 3).
8. Jorgensen (1989: 21).
9. Marti (2005: 197–210).
10. See Marti (2005).
11. Sweet (2003).
12. Mitchell and Ganiel (2006).
13. Reinharz (1992), Burns and Walker (2005), McIntyre (2008).
14. Mitchell and Ganiel (2006), Poloma (2003).
15. See http://pyrotheology.com/, testimonial sections on the Last Supper, the Evangelism Project, and Atheism for Lent.

16. This continues a tradition within sociology that includes Max Weber, Alfred Schutz, George Herbert Mead, and Peter Berger that the ways in which people make sense of themselves and their worlds is critical to understanding the dynamics of any social setting.
17. Minkin (1997: 122).
18. See Marti and Olson (2013).
19. Eisner (1991: 110).
20. Taylor et al. (1996: 7).
21. Merilänen et al. (2004: 544), Hall (2001).
22. Parker (1992), Carabine (2001: 268).
23. Reed (1998: 196).
24. Maguire and Hardy (2009: 151). See also Barge and Oliver (2003), Knights (1992), Townley (1993).
25. Phillips, Lawrence, and Hardy (2004: 636).
26. Knights and Morgan (1991: 262).
27. On the potential of "digital ethnography," see Murthy (2008).

# BIBLIOGRAPHY

Ahmadjian, Christina L., and Patricia Robinson. 2001. Safety in Numbers: Downsizing and the Deinstitutionalization of Permanent Employment in Japan. *Administrative Science Quarterly*, 46.4: 622–654.

Aldous, Benjamin James. 2012. Roots, Shoots and Fruits: Towards an Assessment of the Work of Peter Rollins. PhD diss., Redcliffe College.

Aldrich, H. E., and C. M. Fiol. 1994. Fools Rush In? The Institutional Context of Industry Creation. *Academy of Management Review*, 19: 645–670.

Alexander, Jeffrey C. 2003. *The Meanings of Social Life: A Cultural Sociology*. New York: Oxford University Press.

———. 2006. *The Civil Sphere*. Oxford: Oxford University Press.

———. 2009. *Remembering the Holocaust: A Debate*. New York: Oxford University Press.

Ammerman, Nancy Tatom. 1987. *Bible Believers: Fundamentalists in the Modern World*. New Brunswick, NJ: Rutgers University Press.

———. 1997a. Golden Rule Christianity: Lived Religion in the American Mainstream. In David D. Hall, ed. *Lived Religion in America: Toward a History of Practice*, Princeton, NJ: Princeton University Press. 196–216.

———. 1997b. Organized Religion in a Voluntaristic Society. *Sociology of Religion*, 58: 203–215.

———. 2005. *Pillars of Faith: American Congregations and Their Partners*. Berkeley: University of California Press.

———. 2013. *Sacred Stories, Spiritual Tribes: Finding Religion in Everyday Life*. New York: Oxford University Press.

Anand, N., and M. R. Watson. 2004. Tournament Rituals in the Evolution of Fields: The Case of the Grammy Awards. *Academy of Management Journal*, 47: 59–80.

Andrews, Kenneth, and Michael Biggs. 2006. The Dynamics of Protest Diffusion. *American Sociological Review*, 71: 752–777.

Ashforth, Blake E., and Barrie W. Gibbs. 1990. The Double-edge of Organizational Legitimation. *Organization Science*, 1: 177–194.

Bader-Saye, Scott. 2006. Improvising Church: An Introduction to the Emerging Church Conversation. *International Journal for the Study of the Christian Church*, 6.1 (March): 12–23.

Bakker, Jay. 2001. *Son of a Preacher Man: My Search for Grace in the Shadows*. San Francisco: HarperCollins.

———. 2011. *Fall to Grace: A Revolution of God, Self and Society*. London: Hodder and Stoughton.

———. 2013. *Faith, Doubt and Other Lines I've Crossed: Walking with the Unknown God*. New York: Jericho Books.

Barge, J. Kevin, and Christine Oliver. 2003. Working with Appreciation in Managerial Practice. *Academy of Management Review*, 28: 124–142.

Barley, Stephen R., and Pamela S. Tolbert. 1997. Institutionalization and Structuration:
Studying the Links Between Action and Institution. *Organization Studies*, 18: 93–117.

Barman, Emily. 2002. Asserting Difference: Strategic Response of Nonprofit Organizations to
Competition. *Social Forces*, 80.4: 1191–1222.

Battilana, Julie. 2006. Agency and Institutions: The Enabling Role of Individuals' Social Position. *Organization*, 13: 653–676.

Battilana, Julie, Bernard Leca, and Eva Boxenbaum. 2009. How Actors Change Institutions:
Towards a Theory of Institutional Entrepreneurship. *Academy of Management Annals*,
3.1: 65–107.

Bean, Kelly. 2012. Urban Abbey: The Power of Small, Sustainable, Nimble Micro-Communities
of Jesus. In Bolger, 303–312.

Beck, Ulrich. 2010. *A God of One's Own: Religion's Capacity for Peace and Potential for Violence.*
Cambridge, UK: Polity Press.

Beck, Ulrich, and Elisabeth Beck-Gernsheim. 2002. *Individualization: Institutionalized Individualism and Its Social and Political Consequences.* London: Sage.

Beck, Ulrich, Anthony Giddens, and Scott Lash. 1994. *Reflexive Modernization. Politics, Tradition and Aesthetics in the Modern Social Order.* Cambridge, UK: Polity Press.

Beck, Ulrich, and Johannes Willms. 2004. *Conversations with Ulrich Beck.* Cambridge, UK:
Polity Press.

Becker, Howard S., and Blanche Geer. 1982. Participant Observation: The Analysis of Qualitative Field Data. In R. Burgess, ed. *Field Research: A Sourcebook and Field Manual.* London:
Allen and Unwin, 239–250.

Bell, Rob. 2011. *Love Wins: A Book About Heaven, Hell, and the Fate of Every Person Who Ever
Lived.* San Francisco: HarperOne.

_____. 2013. *What We Talk About When We Talk About God: Finding a New Faith for the
Twenty-first Century.* London: Collins.

Bellah, Robert N., Richard Madsen, William M. Sullivan, Ann Swidler, and Steven M. Tipton.
1985. *Habits of the Heart: Individualism and Commitment in American Life.* Berkeley: University of California Press.

Benford, Robert D., and David A. Snow. 2000. Framing Processes and Social Movements: An
Overview and Assessment. *Annual Review of Sociology*, 26: 611–639.

Berard, T. J. 2005. Rethinking Practices and Structures. *Philosophy of the Social Sciences*, 35.2
(June): 196–230.

Berger, Peter L. 1997. Pluralism, Protestantization and the Voluntary Principle. In Thomas
Banchoff, ed., *The New Religious Pluralism and Democracy*, New York: Oxford University
Press, 19–30.

Berger, Peter, and Thomas Luckman. 1966. *The Social Construction of Reality: A Treatise in the
Sociology of Knowledge.* Garden City, NY: Anchor Books.

Berghoef, Bryan. 2012. *Pub Theology: Beer, Conversation, and God.* Eugene, OR: Cascade
Books.

Bielo, James S. 2009. The "Emerging Church" in America: Notes on the Interaction of Christianities. *Religion*, 39.3: 219–232.

_____. 2011. *Emerging Evangelicals: Faith, Modernity, and the Desire for Authenticity.* New
York: New York University Press.

Bird, Warren. 2010. Emerging Church Movement. In C. H. Lippy and P. W. Williams, eds.,
*Encyclopedia of Religion in America.* Washington, DC: CQ Press, 682.

Bivins, Jason C. 2008. *Religion of Fear: The Politics of Horror in Conservative Evangelicalism.*
New York: Oxford University Press.

Blatt, Ruth. 2009. Tough Love: How Communal Schemas and Contracting Practices Build
Relational Capital in Entrepreneurial Teams. *Academy of Management Review*, 34.3:
533–551.

Bolger, Ryan. 2012. *The Gospel After Christendom: New Voices, New Cultures, New Expressions.* Grand Rapids, MI: Baker Academic.

Bolz-Weber, Nadia. 2011. Innovating with Integrity: Exploring the Core and Innovative Edges of Postmodern Ministry. In Snider, 1–11.

———. 2012a. Operation: Turkey Sandwich. In Graham Cray, Aaron Kennedy, and Ian Mobsby, eds., *Fresh Expressions of Church and the Kingdom of God.* Norwich, UK: Canterbury Press. 51–58.

———. 2012b. House for All Sinners and Saints. In Bolger, 251–259.

———. 2013. *Cranky, Beautiful Faith: For Irregular (and Regular) People.* Norwich: Canterbury Press. Published in the United States as *Pastrix: The Cranky, Beautiful Faith of a Sinner & Saint.* New York: Jericho Books.

Bonchek, Marks S., and Kenneth A. Shepsle. 1996. *Analyzing Politics: Rationality, Behavior and Institutions.* New York: W.W. Norton.

Bonheoffer, Dietrick. 2001 (SCM Classics Edition) with Peter Sellby. *Letters and Papers from Prison.* London: SCM.

Bourdieu, Pierre. 1977. *Outline of a Theory of Practice.* Cambridge: Cambridge University Press.

———. 1990. *The Logic of Practice.* Trans. R. Nice. Cambridge, UK: Polity.

Boxenbaum, Eva. 2006. Lost in Translation? The Making of Danish Diversity Management. *American Behavioral Scientist,* 49.7: 939–948.

Boxenbaum, Eva, and T. Daudigeos. 2008. Institutional Factors in Market Creation: Concrete Theorization of a New Construction Technology. Best Paper Proceedings of the 2008 Academy of Management Annual Meeting, August. Anaheim, CA, 1–6.

Brewin, Kester. 2010. *Other: Loving God, Self and Neighbour in a World of Fractures.* London: Hodder and Stoughton.

———. 2012. *Mutiny: Why We Love Pirates, and How They Can Save Us.* Self-published.

———. 2013. *After Magic: Moves Beyond Super-nature from Batman to Shakespeare.* Self-published.

Brown, John Seely, and Paul Duguid. 1991. Organizational Learning and Communities-of-Practice: Toward a Unified View of Working, Learning, and Innovation. *Organization Science,* 2.1: 40–57.

Bruner, Jerome. 1986. *Actual Minds, Possible Worlds.* Cambridge, MA: Harvard University Press.

———. 1996. *The Culture of Education.* Cambridge, MA: Harvard University Press.

Brunsson, Nils, and Johan P. Olsen. 1993. *The Reforming Organization.* London and New York: Routledge.

Buechner, Frederick. 1970. *The Alphabet of Grace.* San Francisco: HarperSanFrancisco.

Burns, Diane, and Melanie Walker. 2005. Feminist Methodologies. In Bridget Somekh and Cathy Lewin, eds. *Research Methods in the Social Sciences.* London: Sage, 66–73.

Burt, Ronald S. 2005. *Brokerage and Closure.* New York: Oxford University Press.

Callon, Michel. 1986. Some Elements of a Sociology of Translation: Domestication of the Scallops and the Fishermen of St Brieuc Bay. In John Law ed., *Power, Action and Belief: A New Sociology of Knowledge,* London: Routledge and Kegan Paul, 196–233.

———. 1991. Techno-economic Networks and Irreversibility. In John Law ed., *A Sociology of Monsters: Essays on Power, Technology and Domination,* London: Routledge, 132–165.

Campbell, Heidi. 2012. Understanding the Relationship Between Religion Online and Offline in a Networked Society. *Journal of the American Academy of Religion,* 80.1: 64–93.

Campolo, Tony. 2008. *Red Letter Christians: A Citizen's Guide to Faith and Politics.* Ventura, CA: Regal Books.

Canales, R. J. 2008. From Ideals to Institutions: Institutional Entrepreneurship in Mexican Small Business Finance. PhD diss., Massachusetts Institute of Technology.

Caputo, John D. 2006. *The Weakness of God: A Theology of the Event.* Bloomington: Indiana University Press.

Caputo, John D. 2007. *What Would Jesus Deconstruct? The Good News of Post-modernism for the Church*. Grand Rapids, MI: Baker Academic.

_____. 2013. *The Insistence of God: A Theology of Perhaps*. Bloomington: Indiana University Press.

Carabine, Jean. 2001. Unmarried Motherhood 1830–1990: A Genealogical Analysis. In M. Wetherell, S. Taylor, and S. Yates, eds., *Discourse as Data: A Guide for Analysts*. London: Sage, 267–310.

Caronna, Carol A. 2004. The Misalignment of Institutional "Pillars": Consequences for the U.S. Health Care Field. *Journal of Health and Social Behavior*, 45: 45–59.

Carson, D. A. 2005. *Becoming Conversant with the Emerging Church: Understanding a Movement and Its Implications*. Grand Rapids, MI: Zondervan.

Castells, Manuel. 2000. *The Rise of the Network Society: Economy, Society and Culture*. Vol. 1. Oxford: Wiley-Blackwell.

_____. 2012. *Networks of Outrage and Hope: Social Movements in the Internet Age*. Cambridge, UK: Polity.

Chia, Lloyd. 2010. Emerging Faith Boundaries: Bridge-Building, Inclusion, and the Emerging Church Movement in America. PhD diss., University of Missouri.

Chia, Robert. 2004. Strategy-as-Practice: Reflections on the Research Agenda. *European Management Review*, 1.1: 29–34.

Child, J., Y. Lua, and T. Tsai. 2007. Institutional Entrepreneurship in Building an Environmental Protection System for the People's Republic of China. *Organization Studies*, 28.7: 1013–1034.

Claiborne, Shane. 2006. *The Irresistible Revolution: Living as an Ordinary Radical*. Grand Rapids, MI: Zondervan.

Claiborne, Shane, and Tony Campolo. 2012. *Red Letter Christianity: Living the Words of Jesus No Matter the Cost*. London: Hodder and Stoughton.

Claiborne, Shane, and Chris Haw. 2008. *Jesus for President: Politics for Ordinary Radicals*. Grand Rapids, MI: Zondervan.

Clark, M. S., and J. Mills. 1979. Interpersonal Attraction in Exchange and Communal Relationships. *Journal of Personality and Social Psychology*, 37: 12–24.

Clegg, S. R., C. Hardy, T. B. Lawrence., W. R. Nord, eds., 2006. *Handbook of Organization Studies*. London: Sage, 215–254.

Clemens, Elizabeth S., and James M. Cook. 1999. Politics and Institutionalism: Explaining Durability and Change. *Annual Review of Sociology*, 25: 441–466.

Collinge C., and J. Gibney. 2010. Connecting Place, Policy and Leadership. *Policy Studies*, 31: 379–391.

Colomy, Paul. 1998. Neofunctionalism and Neoinstitutionalism: Human Agency and Interest in Institutional Change. *Sociological Forum*, 13. 2: 265–300.

Colomy, Paul, and G. Rhoades. 1994. Toward a Micro Corrective of Structural Differentiation Theory. *Sociological Perspectives*, 37: 54.7–83.

Conder, Tim, and Daniel Rhodes. 2009. *Free for All: Rediscovering the Bible in Community*. Grand Rapids, MI: Baker Books.

Cox, Harvey. 1972. *The Seduction of the Spirit: The Use and Misuse of People's Religion*. New York: Simon and Schuster.

_____. 1995. *Fire from Heaven: The Rise of Pentecostal Spirituality and the Reshaping of Religion in the Twenty-first Century*. Cambridge, MA: Da Capo.

Cray, Graham. 2010. Why Is New Monasticism Important to Fresh Expressions? In Graham Cray, Ian Mobsby, and Aaron Kennedy eds., *New Monasticism as Fresh Expression of Church*. Norwich, UK: Canterbury Press, 1–11.

Cray, Graham, Aaron Kennedy, and Ian Mobsby, eds. 2012. *Fresh Expressions of Church and the Kingdom of God*. Norwich, UK: Canterbury Press.

Creed, W. E. D., M. A. Scully, and J. A. Austin. 2002. Clothes Make the Person? The Tailoring of Legitimating Accounts and the Social Construction of Identity. *Organization Science*, 13. 5: 475–496.

Croft, Steve. 2008. What Counts as a Fresh Expression of Church? In Louise Nelstop and Martyn Percy, eds., *Evaluating Fresh Expressions: Explorations in Emerging Church*. Norwich, UK: Canterbury Press, 3–14.

Czarniawska, Barbara. 2009. Emerging Institutions: Pyramids or Anthills? *Organization Studies*, 30: 423–441.

Czarniawska-Joerges, Barbara. 1998. *Narrative Approach in Organization Studies*. Thousand Oaks, CA: Sage.

D'Aunno, T., M. Succi, and J. A. Alexander. 2000. The Role of Institutional and Market Forces in Divergent Organizational Change. *Administrative Science Quarterly*, 45: 679–703.

D'Aunno, Thomas, Robert I. Sutton, and Richard N. Price. 1991. Isomorphism and External Support in Conflicting Institutional Environments: A Study of Drug Abuse Treatment Units. *Academy of Management Journal*, 34: 636–661.

Dacin, M. T., J. Goodstein, and W. R. Scott. 2002. Institutional Theory and Institutional Change: Introduction to the Special Research Forum. *Academy of Management Journal*, 45: 45–57.

Dacin, M. T., M .J. Ventresca, and B. D. Beal. 1999. The Embeddedness of Organizations: Dialogue & Directions. *Journal of Management*, 25: 317–356.

Davie, Grace. 1994. *Religion in Britain since 1945: Believing without Belonging*. Oxford and Cambridge, MA: Blackwell.

Davis, Gerald F., Kristen A. Diekmann, and Catherine H. Tinsley. 1994. The Decline and Fall of the Conglomerate Firm in the 1980s: The Deinstitutionalization of an Organizational Form. *American Sociological Review*, 59.4: 547–570.

Davis, Gerald F., and Christopher Marquis. 2005. The Globalization of Stock Markets and Convergence in Corporate Governance. In Richard Swedberg and Victor Nee eds., *The Economic Sociology of Capitalism*. Princeton, NJ: Princeton University Press, 352–390.

DeYoung, Kevin, and Ted Kluck. 2008. *Why We're Not Emergent (By Two Guys Who Should Be)*. Chicago: Moody.

Delbridge, Rick, and Tim Edwards. 2007. Reflections on Developments in Institutional Theory. *Scandinavian Journal of Management*, 23.2: 191–205.

_____. 2008. Challenging Conventions: Actors and Roles in Processes of a Non-isomorphic Institutional Change. *Human Relations*, 61.3: 299–326.

Dialdin, D. A., and Wang, L. 2002. Organizational Networks. In J. A. C. Baum ed., *Companion to Organizations*. Oxford, UK: Blackwell, 281–303.

Dimaggio, Paul. 1988. Interest and Agency in Institutional Theory. In L. Zucker ed., *Institutional Patterns and Culture*. Cambridge, MA: Ballinger, 3–22.

_____. 1991. Constructing an Organizational Field as a Professional Project: U.S. Art Museums, 1920–1940. In Powell and DiMaggio, 267–292.

DiMaggio, Paul J., and Walter W. Powell. 1983. The Iron Cage Revisited: Institutional Isomorphism and Collective Rationality in Organizational Fields. *American Sociological Review*, 48: 147–60.

_____. 1991. Introduction. In Powell and DiMaggio, 1–38.

Doornenbal, Robert. 2012. *Crossroads: An Exploration of the Emerging-Missional Conversation with a Special Focus on "Missional Leadership" and Its Challenges for Theological Education*. Delft, The Netherlands: Eburon Academic.

Dorado, Silvia. 2005. Institutional Entrepreneurship, Partaking, and Convening. *Organization Studies*, 26.3: 383–413.

Drane, John. 2006. Editorial: The Emerging Church. *International Journal for the Study of the Christian Church*, 6.1: 3–11.

Drescher, Elizabeth. 2011. *Tweet If You Love Jesus: Practicing Church in the Digital Reformation*. New York: Morehouse.

Dunn, M. B., and C. Jones. 2010. Institutional Logics and Institutional Pluralism: The Contestation of Care and Science Logics in Medical Education, 1967–2005. *Administrative Science Quarterly*, 55: 114–149.

Durand, R., and J. McGuire. 2005. Legitimating Agencies in the Face of Selection: The Case of AACSB. *Organization Studies*, 26: 165–196.

Durkheim, Emile. 1969. Individualism and the Intellectuals, translated by Steven Lukes. *Political Studies*, 17.1: 19–30.

Dyck, Bruno, and Frederick A. Starke. 1999. The Formation of Breakaway Organizations: Observations and a Process Model. *Administrative Science Quarterly*, 44: 792–822.

Eagleton, Terry. 2003. *After Theory*. New York: Basic Books.

Edson, Ben. 2006. "An Exploration into the Missiology of the Emerging Church in the UK through the Narrative of *Sanctus1*." *International Journal for the Study of the Christian Church*, 6:1 (March): 24–37.

Einolf, Christopher J. 2011. The Link Between Religion and Helping Others: The Role of Values, Ideas, and Language. *Sociology of Religion*, 72: 4, 435–455.

Eisenstadt, Shmuel N. 1980. Cultural Orientations, Institutional Entrepreneurs, and Social Change: Comparative Analysis of Traditional Civilizations. *American Journal of Sociology*, 85: 840–869.

———. 1986. *The Origins and Diversity of Axial Age Civilizations*. Albany, NY: State University of New York Press.

Eisner, Elliot W. 1991. *The Enlightened Eye: Qualitative Inquiry and the Enhancement of Educational Practice*. New York: Macmillan.

Emirbayer, Mustafa, and Ann Mische. 1998. What Is Agency? *American Journal of Sociology*, 103.4 (Jan.): 962–1023.

Engelke, Matthew. 2013. *God's Agents: Biblical Publicity in Contemporary England*. Berkeley, CA: University of California Press.

Escobar, Kathy. 2012. Actually Living the Truth. In Chris Lewis ed., *Letters to a Future Church: Words of Encouragement and Prophetic Appeals*. Downers Grove, IL: IVP Books, 88–91.

Faix, Tobias. 2012. Toward a Holistic Process of Transformational Mission. In Bolger, 206–218.

Fiske, Alan Page. 1992. The Four Elementary Forms of Sociality: Framework for a Unified Theory of Social Relations. *Psychological Review*, 99: 689–723.

Fligstein, Neil. 1997. Social Skill and Institutional Theory. *American Behavioral Scientist* 40: 397–405.

———. 2001a. Institutional Entrepreneurs and Cultural Frames: The Case of the European Union's Single Market Program. *European Societies*, 3.3: 261–287.

———. 2001b. Social Skill and the Theory of Fields. *Sociological Theory*, 19.2: 105–125.

Florida, Richard. 2003. *The Rise of the Creative Class . . . and How It's Transforming Work, Leisure, Community and Everyday Life*. New York: Basic Books.

Friedland, Roger. 2002. Money, Sex and God: The Erotic Logic of Religious Nationalism. *Sociological Theory*, 20.3, 381–424.

Friedland, Roger, and Robert R. Alford. 1991. Bringing Society Back In: Symbols, Practices, and Institutional Contradictions. In Powell and DiMaggio, 232–263.

Friesen, Dwight J. 2009. *Thy Kingdom Connected: What the Church Can Learn from Facebook, the Internet and Other Networks*. Grand Rapids, MI: Baker Books.

Fuchs, Stephan, and Steven Ward. 1994. What Is Deconstruction, and Where and When Does It Take Place? Making Facts in Science, Building Cases in Law. *American Sociological Review*, 59.4 (Aug.): 481–500.

Gamson, W. A. 1992. The Social Psychology of Collective Action. In A. Morris and C. M. Mueller eds., *Frontiers in Social Movement Theory*. New Haven, CT: Yale University Press, 53–76.

Ganiel, Gladys. 2006. Emerging from the Evangelical Subculture in Northern Ireland: A Case Study of the Zero28 and Ikon Community. *International Journal for the Study of the Christian Church*, 6.1: 38–48.

———. 2008. *Evangelicalism and Conflict in Northern Ireland*. New York: Palgrave.

_____. 2010. Ethno-Religious Change in Northern Ireland and Zimbabwe: A Comparative Study of How Religious Havens Can Have Ethnic Significance. *Ethnopolitics*, 9.1: 103–120.

_____. 2011. The End of Irish Catholicism? Paper presented at the Annual Meeting of the European Sociological Association, September 5–7, 2011, Geneva.

Ganiel, Gladys, and Gerardo Marti. 2014. Northern Ireland, America, and the Emerging Church Movement: Exploring the Significance of Peter Rollins and the Ikon Collective. *Journal of the Irish Society for the Academic Study of Religions*, forthcoming.

Garud, R., and P. Karnøe. 2001. Path Creation as a Process of Mindful Deviation. In R. Garud and P. Karnøe eds., *Path Dependence and Creation*. Lawrence Erlbaum Associates, 1–38.

Raghu Garud, Sanjay Jain, and Arun Kumaraswamy. 2002. Institutional Entrepreneurship in the Sponsorship of Common Technological Standards: The Case of Sun Microsystems and Java. *The Academy of Management Journal*, 45.1: 196–214.

Garud, R., C. Hardy, and S. Maguire. 2007. Institutional Entrepreneurship as Embedded Agency. *Organization Studies*, 28.7: 957–969.

Gay, Doug. 2011. *Remixing the Church: Towards an Emerging Ecclesiology*. London: SCM Press.

Gibbs, Eddie, and Ryan Bolger. 2005. *Emerging Churches: Creating Christian Community in Postmodern Cultures*. Grand Rapids, MI: Baker.

Gibney J, S. Copeland, A. Murie. 2009. Toward a "New" Strategic Leadership of Place for the Knowledge-based Economy. *Leadership*, 5: 5–23.

Giddens, Anthony. 1984. *The Constitution of Society Outline of the Theory of Structuration*. Cambridge: Blackwell/Polity Press.

_____. 1991. *Modernity and Self-Identity: Self and Society in the Late Modern Age*. Stanford, CA: Stanford University Press.

Goffman, Erving. 1961. *Asylums: Essays on the Social Situation of Mental Patients and Other Inmates*. Garden City, NY: Anchor Books, 199–201.

Gray-Reeves, Mary, and Michael Perham. 2011. *The Hospitality of God: Emerging Worship for a Missional Church*. London: SPCK.

Greenwood, Royston, and C. R. Hinings. 2006. Radical Organizational Change. In Clegg et al., 814–842.

Greenwood, Royston, C.R. Hinings, and Roy Suddaby. 2002. Theorizing Change: The Role of Professional Associations in the Transformation of Institutionalized Fields. *Academy of Management Journal*, 45.1: 58–80.

Greenwood, Royston, Mia Raynard, Farah Kodeih, Evelyn R. Micelotta, Michael Lounsbury. 2011. Institutional Complexity and Organizational Responses. *Academy of Management Annals*, 5.1: 317–371.

Greenwood, Royston, and Roy Suddaby. 2006. Institutional Entrepreneurship in Mature Fields: The Big Five Accounting Firms. *Academy of Management Journal*, 49: 27–48.

Guest, Matthew, and Steve Taylor. 2006. The Post-Evangelical Emerging Church: Innovations in New Zealand and the UK. *International Journal for the Study of the Christian Church*, 6:1 (Mar.): 49–64.

Gulati, Ranjay, Dania Dialdin, and Lihua Wang. 2002. Organizational Networks. In J. A. C. Baum, ed., *Companion to Organizations*. Oxford: Blackwell, 281–303.

Hall, Stuart. 2001. Foucault: Power, Knowledge and Discourse. In M. Wetherell, S. Taylor, and S. Yates, eds., *Discourse Theory and Practice: A Reader*. London: Sage, 72–81.

Hannan, Michael T. 1986. Uncertainty, Diversity and Organizational Change. In N. Smelser and D. Gerstein, eds., *Behavioral and Social Sciences: Fifty Years of Discovery*. Washington, DC: National Academy Press, 73–94.

Hansen, Collin. 2008. *Young, Restless, Reformed*. Wheaton, IL: Crossway.

Hardy, Cynthia, and Steve Maguire. 2008. Institutional Entrepreneurship. In R. Greenwood, C. Oliver, R. Suddaby, and K. Sahlin-Andersson, eds. *The SAGE Handbook of Organizational Institutionalism*. Thousand Oaks, CA: Sage, 198–217.

Hardy, Cynthia, and Nelson Phillips. 1999. No Joking Matter: Discursive Struggle in the Canadian Refugee System. *Organization Studies*, 20.1: 1–24.

Hargadon, Andrew B., and Douglas Yellowlees. 2001. When Innovations Meet Institutions: Edison and the Design of the Electric Light. *Administrative Science Quarterly*, 46.3 (Sep.): 476–501.

Harrold, Philip. 2006. Deconversion in the Emerging Church. *International Journal for the Study of the Christian Church*, 6.1: 79–90.

Haveman, Heather A., and Hayagreeva Rao. 1997. Structuring a Theory of Moral Sentiments: Institutional and Organizational Coevolution in the Early Thrift Industry. *American Journal of Sociology*, 102: 1606–1651.

Hayano, David M. 1979. Auto-ethnography: Paradigms, Problems, and Prospects. *Human Organization*, 38.1: 99–104.

Heelas, Paul, and Linda Woodhead. 2005. *The Spiritual Revolution: Why Religion Is Giving Way to Spirituality*, Oxford: Blackwell.

Henderson, Stewart. 1993. *Homeland*. London: Hodder and Stoughton.

Hensmans, Manuel. 2003. Social Movement Organizations: A Metaphor for Strategic Actors in Institutional Field. *Organization Studies*, 24.3: 355–381.

Hervieu-Leger, Daniele. 2006. In Search of Certainties: The Paradoxes of Religiosity in Societies of High Modernity. *Hedgehog Review* 8.1–2: 59–68.

Higgins, Cathy. 2013. *Churches in Exile: Alternative Models of Church for Ireland in the 21st Century*. Dublin: Columba.

Hinings, C. R., and Royston Greenwood, R. 1988. The Normative Prescription of Organizations. In L. G. Zucker, ed., *Institutional Patterns and Organization*. Cambridge, MA: Ballinger, 53–70.

Hirsch, Paul M., Michael, Lounsbury, and Marc J. Ventresca. 2003. Social Movements, Field Frames and Industry Emergence: A Cultural-Political Perspective on US Recycling. *Socio-Economic Review*, 1: 71–104.

Hjorth, Daniel, and Chris Steyaert. 2004. *Narrative and Discursive Approaches in Entrepreneurship*. Cheltenham, UK: Edward Elgar.

Hoffman, A. J. 1999. Institutional Evolution and Change: Environmentalism and the U.S. Chemical Industry. *Academy of Management Journal*, 42: 351–371.

Hoffman, Andrew J., Hannah, C. Riley, John G. Troast, Jr., and Max H. Bazerman. 2002. Cognitive and Institutional Barriers to New Forms of Cooperation on Environmental Protection: Insights from Project XL and Habitat Conservation Plans. *American Behavioral Scientist*, 45: 820–845.

Hoffman, A. J,. and M. Ventresca. 1999. The Institutional Framing of Policy Debates: Economics Versus the Environment. *American Behavioral Scientist*, 42.8: 1368–1392.

Holm, Peter. 1995. The Dynamics of Institutionalization: Transformation Processes in Norwegian Fisheries. *Administrative Science Quarterly*, 40: 398–422.

Hurley, Michael. 1998. An Ecumenical Community: The Origins of the Columbanus Community of Reconciliation. In *Christian Unity: An Ecumenical Second Spring?* Dublin: Veritas, 317–340.

Ingram, P. 1998. Changing the Rules: Interests, Organizations, and Institutional Change in the US Hospitality Industry. In M. C. Brinton and V. Nee eds., *The New Institutionalism in Sociology*, Stanford, CA: Stanford University Press, 258–276.

Jamieson, Alan. 2006. Post-church Groups and Their Place as Emergent Forms of Church. *International Journal for the Study of the Christian Church*, 6.1 (Mar.): 65–78.

Jarzabkowski, Paula. 2004. Strategy as Practice: Recursiveness, Adaptation and Practices-in-Use. *Organization Studies*, 25.4: 529–560.

Jeffrey, Steve, Michael Ovey, and Andrew Sach. 2007. *Pierced for Our Transgressions*. Wheaton, IL: Crossway Books.

Jepperson, Ronald L. 1991. Institutions, Institutional Effects, and Institutionalism. In Powell and DiMaggio, 143–163.

Joas, Hans. 2013. *The Sacredness of the Person: A New Genealogy of Human Rights.* Washington DC: Georgetown University Press.

Johnson, Cathryn, Timothy J. Dowd, and Cecilia L. Ridgeway. 2006. Legitimacy as a Social Process. *Annual Review of Sociology*, 32: 53–78.

Jones, Anthony Hawthorne. 2011. *The Relational Ecclesiology of the Emerging Church Movement in Practical Theological Perspective.* PhD diss., Princeton Theological Seminary.

Jones, Tony. 2009. *The New Christians: Dispatches from the Emergent Frontier.* San Francisco: Jossey-Bass.

———. 2011. *The Church Is Flat: The Relational Ecclesiology of the Emerging Church Movement.* Minneapolis: JoPa Group.

Jorgensen, Danny L. 1989. *Participant Observation: A Methodology for Human Studies,* Applied Social Research Methods Series. Newbury Park, CA: Sage.

Kalberg, Stephen. 1990. The Rationalization of Action in Max Weber's Sociology of Religion. *Sociological Theory,* 8.1 (Spring): 58–84.

Khan, F., K. Munir, and H. Willmott. 2007. A Dark Side of Institutional Entrepreneurship: Soccer Balls, Child Labour and Postcolonial Impoverishment. *Organization Studies,* 28.7: 1055–1077.

Khomiakov, Aleksei Stepanovich, and Ivan Kireevsky. 1998. *On Spiritual Unity: A Slavophile Reader.* Trans. Boris Jakim and Robert Bird. Hudson, NY: Lindisfarne Books.

Kilde, Jeanne Halgren. 2002. *When Church Became Theatre: The Transformation of Evangelical Architecture and Worship in Nineteenth-Century America.* New York: Oxford University Press.

Kim, Hyojoung, and Peter S. Bearman. 1997. The Structure and Dynamics of Movement Participation. *American Sociological Review,* 62.1: 70–93.

Kim, Hyojoung, and Steven Pfaff. 2012. Structure and Dynamics of Religious Insurgency: Students and the Spread of the Reformation. *American Sociological Review,* 77.2: 188–215.

Kimball, Dan. 2003. *The Emerging Church: Vintage Christianity for New Generations.* Grand Rapids, MI: Zondervan.

———. 2004. *Emerging Worship: Creating Worship Gatherings for New Generations.* Grand Rapids, MI: Zondervan.

King, Brayden G., Elizabeth S. Clemens, and Melissa Fry. 2011. Identity Realization and Organizational Forms. *Organization Science* 22.3: 554–572.

King, Brayden. G., and S. A. Soule. 2007. Social Movements as Extra-institutional Entrepreneurs: The Effect of Protests on Stock Price Returns. *Administrative Science Quarterly,* 52: 413–442.

Kitchener, Martin. 2002. Mobilizing the Logic of Managerialism in Professional Fields: The Case of Academic Health Center Mergers. *Organization Studies,* 23.3: 391–420.

Knights, David. 1992. Changing Spaces: The Disruptive Impact of New Epistemological Location for the Study of Management. *Academy of Management Review,* 17: 514–536.

Knights, David, and Glenn Morgan. 1991. Strategic Discourse and Subjectivity: Towards a Critical Analysis of Corporate Strategy in Organizations. *Organization Studies,* 12: 251–273.

Koene, B. A. S. 2006. Situated Human Agency, Institutional Entrepreneurship and Institutional Change. *Journal of Organizational Change Management,* 19.3: 365–382.

Kraatz, M. S., and J. H. Moore. 2002. Executive Migration and Institutional Change. *Academy of Management Journal,* 45: 120–143.

Kraatz, M. S., and E. J. Zajac. 1996. Exploring the Limits of the New Institutionalism: The Causes and Consequences of Illegitimate Organizational Change. *American Sociological Review,* 61: 812–836.

Labanow, Cory E. 2009. *Evangelicalism and the Emerging Church: A Congregational Study of a Vineyard Church.* Surrey, UK/Burlington, VT: Ashgate.

Langenohl, Andreas. 2008. How to Change Other People's Institutions: Discursive Entrepreneurship and the Boundary Object of Competition/Competitiveness in the German Banking sector. *Economy and Society,* 37.1: 68–93.

Latour, Bruno. 1987. *Science in Action: How to Follow Scientists and Engineers Through Society.* Milton Keynes, UK: Open University Press.

Lawrence, Thomas B. 1999. Institutional Strategy. *Journal of Management,* 25: 161–187.

Lawrence, Thomas B., and Nelson Phillips. 2004. From Moby Dick to Free Willy: Macrocultural Discourse and Institutional Entrepreneurship in Emerging Institutional Fields. *Organization,* 11.5: 689–711.

Lawrence, Thomas B., and Roy Suddaby. 2006. Institutions and Institutional Work. In S. R. Glegg, C. Hardy, T. B. Lawrence, and W. R. Nord, eds., *Handbook of Organization Studies.* London: Sage, 215–54.

Lawrence, Thomas B., Roy Suddaby, and Bernard Leca. 2011. Institutional Work: Refocusing Institutional Studies of Organization. *Journal of Management Inquiry,* 20.1: 52–58.

Leblebici, H., G. R. Salancik, A. Copay, and T. King. 1991. Institutional Change and the Transformation of Interorganizational Fields: An Organizational History of the U.S. Radio Broadcasting Industry. *Administrative Science Quarterly,* 36: 333–363.

Leca, B., J. Battilana, and E. Boxebaum. 2008. Agency and Institutions: A Review of Institutional Entrepreneurship. Harvard Business School Working Paper 08-096. Cambridge, MA.

Leca, B., and P. Naccache, P. 2006. A Critical Realist Approach to Institutional Entrepreneurship. *Organization,* 13.5: 627–651.

Lee, Shayne, and Phillip Sinitiere. 2009. *Holy Mavericks: Evangelical Innovators and the Spiritual Marketplace.* New York: New York University Press.

Lenin, Vladimir Ilyich. 1940. *What Is to Be Done? Burning Questions of Our Movement.* New York: International.

Levy, David L., and Maureen Scully. 2007. The Institutional Entrepreneur as Modern Prince: The Strategic Face of Power in Contested Fields. *Organization Studies,* 28.7: 971–991.

Lings, George. 2006. Unravelling the DNA of Church: How Can We Know That What Is Emerging Is "Church"? *International Journal for the Study of the Christian Church,* 6.1: 104–116.

Lok, Jaco. 2010. Institutional Logics as Identity Projects. *Academy of Management Journal,* 53.6: 1305–1335.

Lounsbury, Michael. 2002. Institutional Transformation and Status Mobility: The Professionalization of the Field of Finance. *Academy of Management Journal,* 45: 255–266.

———. 2007. A Tale of Two Cities: Competing Logics and Practice Variation in the Professionalizing of Mutual Funds. *Academy of Management Journal,* 50: 289–307.

———. 2008. Institutional Rationality and Practice Variation: New Directions in the Institutional Analysis of Practice. *Accounting, Organizations and Society,* 33: 349–361.

Lounsbury, Michael, and Ellen T. Crumley. 2007. New Practice Creation: An Institutional Perspective on Innovation. *Organization Studies,* 28.7: 993–1012.

Lounsbury, Michael, and Mary Ann Glynn. 2001. Cultural Entrepreneurship: Stories, Legitimacy, and the Acquisition of Resources. *Strategic Management Journal,* 22.6–7: 545–564.

Luhr, Eileen. 2009. *Witnessing Suburbia: Conservatives and Christian Youth Culture.* Berkeley, CA: University of California Press.

Luhrmann, T.M. 2012. *When God Talks Back: Understanding the American Evangelical Relationship with God.* New York: Vintage Books.

Lukes, Steven. 1974. *Power: A Radical View.* London: Macmillan.

Lynch, Gordon. 2003. *Losing My Religion? Moving on from Evangelical Faith.* London: Darton, Longman and Todd.

———. 2012. *The Sacred in the Modern World: A Cultural Sociological Approach.* Oxford: Oxford University Press.

Lynch, Gordon, and Ruth Sheldon. 2013. The Sociology of the Sacred. A Conversation with Jeffrey Alexander. *Culture and Religion: An Interdisciplinary Journal,* 14.3: 1–15.

MacArthur, John. 2007. *The Truth War: Fighting for Certainty in an Age of Deception.* Nashville, TN: Thomas Nelson.

Macquarrie, John. 1972. Liberal and Radical Theologies: An Historical Comparison. *Modern Churchman*, 15.4: 214–223.

Maguire, Steve, Cynthia Hardy, and Thomas B. Lawrence. 2004. Institutional Entrepreneurship in Emerging Fields: HIV/AIDS Treatment Advocacy in Canada. *Academy of Management Journal*, 47.5: 657–679.

Maguire, Steve. 2007. Institutional Entrepreneurship. In S. Clegg, and J. R. Bailey, eds., *International Encyclopedia of Organization Studies*, London: Sage, 2: 674–678.

Maguire, Steve, and Cynthia Hardy. 2006. The Emergence of New Global Institutions: A Discursive Perspective. *Organization Studies*, 27: 7–29.

———. 2009. Discourse and Deinstitutionalization: The Decline of DDT. *Academy of Management Journal*, 52:1 148–178.

Maguire, Steve, N. Phillips, and Cynthia Hardy. 2001. When "Silence = Death," Keep Talking: Trust, Control and the Discursive Construction of Identity in the Canadian HIV/AIDS Treatment Domain. *Organizational Studies*, 22.2: 285–312.

March, J. G., and J. P. Olsen. 2005. Elaborating the New Institutionalism. WP 11, Centre for European Studies, University of Oslo, Oslo, Norway.

Marquis, Chris, and Michael Lounsbury. 2007. Vive la Résistance: Competing Logics in the Consolidation of Community Banking. *Academy of Management Journal*, 50: 799–820.

Martens, Martin L., Jennifer E. Jennings, and P. Devereaux Jennings. 2007. Do the Stories They Tell Get Them the Money They Need? The Role of Entrepreneurial Narratives in Resource Acquisition. *Academy of Management Journal*, 50: 1107–1132.

Marti, Gerardo. 2005. *A Mosaic of Believers: Diversity and Innovation in a Multiethnic Church*. Bloomington: Indiana University Press.

———. 2008. *Hollywood Faith: Holiness, Prosperity, and Ambition in a Los Angeles Church*. New Brunswick, NJ: Rutgers University Press.

———. 2010a. Ego-affirming Evangelicalism: How a Hollywood Church Appropriates Religion for Workers in the Creative Class. *Sociology of Religion: A Quarterly Review*, 71.1: 52–75.

———. 2010b. The Religious Racial Integration of African Americans into Diverse Churches. *Journal for the Scientific Study of Religion*, 49.2 (June): 201–217.

———. 2012a. The Adaptability of Pentecostalism: The Fit between Prosperity Theology and Globalized Individualization in a Los Angeles Church. *Pneuma: The Journal of the Society for Pentecostal Studies*, 34.1: 5–25.

———. 2012b. "I Determine My Harvest": Risky Careers and Spirit-Guided Prosperity in a Los Angeles Church. In A. Yong and K. Attanasi, eds., *Pentecostalism and Prosperity: The Socio-Economics of Global Charismatic Movement*. New York: Palgrave Macmillan, 131–150.

———. 2012c. *Worship across the Racial Divide: Religious Music and the Multiracial Congregation*. New York and London: Oxford University Press.

Marti, Gerardo, and Paul Olson. 2013. The Emerging Church Movement: A Quantitative Portrait. Paper presented at the annual meeting of the Society for the Scientific Study of Religion, Boston, MA.

Martin, John Levi. 2003. What Is Field Theory? *American Journal of Sociology*, 109.1: 1–49.

Martin, J., M. J. Hatch, and S. B. Sitkin. 1983. The Uniqueness Paradox in Organizational Stories. *Administrative Science Quarterly*, 28:438–453.

Marwell, Gerald, and Pamela E. Oliver. 1993. *The Critical Mass in Collective Action*. New York: Cambridge University Press.

McAdam, Doug, J. D., McCarthy, and M. N. Zald. 1988. Social Movements. In N. J. Smelser ed., *Handbook of Sociology*, Newbury Park, CA: Sage, 695–737.

McAdam, Doug, and Ronnelle Paulsen. 1993. Specifying the Relationship between Social Ties and Activism. *American Journal of Sociology*, 99: 640–667.

McAdam, Doug, and W. Richard Scott. 2005. Organizations and Movements. In *Social Movements and Organization Theory*. New York: Cambridge University Press, 4–41.

McCarthy, J. D,. and M. N. Zald. 1977. Resource Mobilization and Social Movements: A Partial Theory. *American Journal of Sociology*, 82: 1212–1241.

McCracken, Brett. 2010. *Hipster Christianity: When Church and Cool Collide*. Grand Rapids, MI: Baker Books.

McIntyre, Alice. 2008. *Participatory Action Research*. London, Sage.

McKendrick, David G., Jonathan Jaffee, Glenn R. Carroll, and Olga M. Khessina. 2003. In the Bud? Disk Array Producers as a (Possibly) Emergent Organizational Form. *Administrative Science Quarterly*, 48.1: 60–93.

McKnight, Scot. 2007. Five Streams of the Emerging Church. *Christianity Today*, 51. 2 (Feb.): 35–39.

———. 2011. Scripture in the Emerging Movement. In Scot McKnight, Peter Rollins, Kevin Corcoran, and Jason Clark, eds., *Church in the Present Tense: A Candid Look at What's Emerging*. Grand Rapids, MI: Brazos Press, 105–122.

McLaren, Brian D. 2001. *A New Kind of Christian: A Tale of Two Friends on a Spiritual Journey*. San Francisco: Jossey-Bass.

———. 2003. *The Story We Find Ourselves In*. San Francisco: Jossey-Bass.

———. 2004. *A Generous Orthodoxy: Why I am a missional, evangelical, post/protestant, liberal/ conservative, mystical/poetic, biblical, charismatic/contemplative, fundamentalist/Calvinist, Anabaptist/Anglican, Methodist, catholic, green, incarnational, depressed- yet hopeful, emergent, unfinished Christian*. Grand Rapids, MI: Zondervan.

———. 2007. *Everything Must Change: Jesus, Global Crises, and a Revolution of Hope*. Nashville, TN: Thomas Nelson.

———. 2008. *The Last Word and the Word After That: A Tale of Faith, Doubt and a New Kind of Christianity*. Hoboken, NJ: John Wiley and Sons.

———. 2010. *A New Kind of Christianity: Ten Questions That Are Transforming the Faith*. New York: HarperOne.

———. 2011. *Naked Spirituality: A Life with God in 12 Simple Words*. New York: HarperCollins. 3.

McLoughlin, William G. 1978. *Revivals, Awakenings, and Reform*. Chicago: University of Chicago Press.

McManus, Erwin Raphael. 2005. *The Barbarian Way: Unleash the Untamed Faith Within*. Nashville, TN: Thomas Nelson.

Merilänen, Susan, Janne Tienari, Robyn Thomas, and Annette Davies. 2004. Management Consultant Talk: A Cross-cultural Comparison of Normalizing Discourse and Resistance. *Organization*, 11: 539–564.

Meyer, John W. 1994. Rationalized Environments. In W. Richard Scott and John W. Meyer, eds., *Institutionalized Environments and Organizations*. Newbury Park, CA: Sage, 28–54.

Meyer, Renate E., and Hammerschmid, Gerhard. 2006. Changing Institutional Logics and Executive Identities: A Managerial Challenge to Public Administration in Austria. *American Behavioral Scientist*, 49.7: 1000–1014.

Meyer, John W., and Ronald L. Jepperson. 2000. The "Actors" of Modern Society: The Social Construction of Social Agency. *Sociological Theory*, 18.1: 100–120.

Meyer, John W., and Brian Rowan. 1977. Institutionalized Organizations: Formal Structure as Myth and Ceremony. *American Journal of Sociology*, 83: 340–63.

Michels, Robert. 1915. *Political Parties: A Sociological Study of the Oligarchical Tendencies of Modern Democracy*. Trans. Eden Paul and Cedar Paul. New York: Free Press.

Miller, Donald. 2003. *Blue Like Jazz: Nonreligious Thoughts on Christian Spirituality*. Nashville: Thomas Nelson.

Miller, Kent D. 2002. Competitive Strategies of Religious Organizations. *Strategic Management Journal*, 23.5: 435–456.

Minkin, Lewis. 1997. *Exits and Entrances: Political Research as a Creative Art*. Sheffield: Sheffield Hallam University Press.

Mische, Ann. 2007. *Partisan Publics: Communication and Contention across Brazilian Youth Activist Networks*. Princeton, NJ: Princeton University Press.

Mitchell, Claire, and Gladys Ganiel. 2006. Turning the Categories Inside-Out: Complex Identifications and Multiple Interactions in Religious Ethnography. *Sociology of Religion*. 67.1: 3–21.

———. 2011. *Evangelical Journeys: Choice and Change in a Northern Irish Religious Subculture*. Dublin: University College Dublin Press.

Mobsby, Ian. 2010. The Importance of New Monasticism as a Model for Building Ecclesial Communities out of Contextual Mission. In Graham Clay, Ian Mobsby, and Aaron Kennedy eds., *New Monasticism as a Fresh Expression of Church*. Norwich, UK: Canterbury Press, 12–18.

Mohr, John W., and Roger Friedland. 2008. Theorizing the Institution: Foundations, Duality and Data. *Theory and Society*, 37: 421–426.

Moody, Katharine Sarah. 2010. "I Hate Your Church; What I Want Is My Kingdom": Emerging Spiritualities in the UK Emerging Church Milieu. *Expository Times*, 121.10: 495–503.

———. 2012. Retrospective Speculative Philosophy: Looking for Traces of Zizek's Communist Collective in Emerging Christian Praxis. *Political Theology*, 13:2 (Apr.): 182–198.

———. 2014a. *Post-Secular Theology and the Church: Truth, Tradition, Transformation?* Eugene, OR: Cascade, Wipf and Stock.

———. 2014b. *Radical Theology and Emerging Christianity: Deconstruction, Materialism and Religious Practice*. Aldershot, UK: Ashgate.

Morgenthaler, Sally. 1999. *Worship Evangelism: Inviting Unbelievers Into the Presence of God*. Grand Rapids, MI: Zondervan.

Morrill, Calvin, and Jason Owen-Smith. 2002. The Emergence of Environmental Conflict Resolution: Subversive Stories and the Construction of Collective Action Frames and Organizational Fields. In M. Ventresca and A. Hoffman eds., *Organizations, Policy, and the Natural Environment: Institutional and Strategic Perspectives*, Stanford, CA: Stanford University Press, 90–118.

Moynagh, Michael, and Philip Harrold. 2012. *Church for Every Context: An Introduction to Theology and Practice*. London, UK: SCM.

Munir, K.A. 2005. The Social Construction of Events: A Study of Institutional Change in the Photographic Field. *Organizational Studies*, 26.1: 1665–1687.

Munir, K. A., and N. Phillips. 2005. The Birth of the "Kodak Moment": Institutional Entrepreneurship and the Adoption of New Technologies. *Organization Studies*, 26.11: 1665–1687.

Murthy, Dhiraj. 2008. Digital Ethnography: An Examination of the Use of New Technologies for Social Research. *Sociology*, 42.5: 837–855.

Mutch, A. 2007. Reflexivity and the Institutional Entrepreneur: A Historical Exploration. *Organization Studies*, 28.7: 1123–1140.

Navis, Chad, and Mary Ann Glynn. 2011. Legitimate Distinctiveness and the Entrepreneurial Identity: Influence on Investor Judgments of New Venture Plausibility. *Academy of Management Review*, 36.3: 479–499.

Nelstrop, Louise, and Martyn Percy. 2008. *Evaluating Fresh Expressions: Explorations in Emerging Church*. Norwich, UK: Canterbury Press.

North, Douglas C. 1990. *Institutions, Institutional Change and Economic Performance*. New York: Cambridge University Press.

Oakes, Leslie S., Barbara Townley, and David J. Cooper. 1998. Business Planning as Pedagogy: Language and Control in Changing Institutional Field. *Administrative Science Quarterly*, 43: 257–292.

Oakland, Roger. 2007. *Faith Undone: The Emerging Church—A New Reformation or An End-Time Deception*. Silverton, OR: Lighthouse Trails.

Oliver, C. 1992. The Antecedents of Deinstitutionalization. *Organization Studies*, 13: 563–588.

Orr, Philip. 2008. *New Loyalties: Christian Faith and the Protestant Working Class*. Belfast, Northern Ireland: Centre for Contemporary Christianity.

O'Connor, Flannery. 1988. *The Habit of Being: Letters of Flannery O'Connor*. New York: Farrar, Straus and Giroux.

Ó Tuama, Pádraig. 2010. In the Name of the Father . . . In Andrew Walker and Aaron Kennedy, eds., *Discovering the Spirit in the City*, London: Continuum, 78.

_____. 2012. The Task Is Ended. In *Readings from the Book of Exile—Poems by Pádraig Ó Tuama*. Norwich, UK: Canterbury Press.

Pache, Anne-Claire, and Filipe Santo. 2010. Worlds Collide: The Internal Dynamics of Organizational Responses to Conflicting Institutional Demands. *Academy of Management Review*, 35.3: 455–476.

Pacheco, Desirée F., Jeffrey York, Thomas J. Dean, and Saras D. Sarasvathy. 2010. The Coevolution of Institutional Entrepreneurship: A Tale of Two Theories. *Journal of Management*, 36: 974–1010.

Packard, Josh. 2011. Resisting Institutionalization: Religious Professionals in the Emerging Church. *Sociological Inquiry*, 81.1: 3–33.

_____. 2012. *The Emerging Church: Religion at the Margins*. Boulder, CO: Lynne Rienner.

Packard, Josh, and George Sanders. 2013. The Emerging Church as Corporatization's Line of Flight. *Journal of Contemporary Religion*, 28.3: 437–455.

Pagitt, Doug. 2005. *Preaching Re-Imagined: The Role of the Sermon in Communities of Faith*. Grand Rapids, MI: Zondervan.

_____. 2008. *A Christianity Worth Believing*. San Francisco: Jossey-Bass.

Pagitt, Doug, and Tony Jones. 2007. *An Emergent Manifesto of Hope*. Grand Rapids, MI: Baker Books.

Pally, Marcia. 2011. *The New Evangelicals: Expanding the Vision of the Common Good*. Grand Rapids, MI: Eerdmans.

Parker, Ian. 1992. *Discourse Dynamics: Critical Analysis for Social and Individual Psychology*. London: Routledge.

Perkins, John. 1993. *Beyond Charity: The Call to Christian Community Development*. Grand Rapids, MI: Baker.

Perkmann, Markus, and André Spicer. 2007. "Healing the Scars of History": Projects, Skills and Field Strategies in Institutional Entrepreneurship. *Organization Studies*, 28: 1101–1122.

Pettigrew, Andrew M. 1979. On Studying Organizational Cultures. *Administrative Science Quarterly*, 24: 57–81.

Pfeffer, Jeffrey. 1981. Management as Symbolic Action: The Creation and Maintenance of Organizational Paradigms. In L. L. Cummings and B. M. Staw eds., *Research in Organizational Behavior*. L. L. Greenwich, CT: JAI Press, 13: 1–52.

Phillips, Nelson, Thomas B. Lawrence, and Cynthia Hardy. 2004. Discourse and Institutions. *Academy of Management Review*, 29.4: 635–652.

Polkinghorne, Donald E. 1988. *Narrative Knowing and the Human Sciences*. Albany, NY: State University of New York Press.

Poloma, Margaret. 2003. *Main Street Mystics: The Toronto Blessing and Reviving Pentecostalism*. Walnut Creek, CA: Altamira Press.

Poppo, Laura, and Todd Zenger. 2002. Do Formal Contracts and Relational Governance Function as Substitutes or Complements? *Strategic Management Journal*, 23: 707–725.

Powell, Walter W. 1991. Expanding the Scope of Institutional Analysis. In Powell and DiMaggio, 183–203.

Powell, Walter W., and Paul J. DiMaggio, eds. 1991. *The New Institutionalism in Organization Analysis*. Chicago: University of Chicago Press.

Power, Maria. 2007. *From Ecumenism to Community Relations: Inter Church Relationships in Northern Ireland 1980–2005*. Dublin: Irish Academic Press, 118–164.

Purdy, Jill M., and Barbara Gray. 2009. Conflicting Logics, Mechanisms of Diffusion, and Multilevel Dynamics in Emerging Institutional Fields. *Academy of Management Journal*, 52.2: 355–380.

Putnam, Robert D., and David E. Campbell. 2010. *American Grace: How Religion Divides and Unites Us*. New York: Simon and Schuster.

Rao, Hayagreeva. 1998. Caveat Emptor: The Construction of Non-profit Watchdog Organizations. *American Journal of Sociology*, 103: 912–961.

Rao, Hayagreeva, and Simona Giorgi. 2006 .Code Breaking: How Entrepreneurs Exploit Cultural Logics to Generate Institutional Change. *Research in Organizational Behavior*, 27: 269–304.

Rao, Hayagreeva, P. Monin, and R. Durand. 2003. Institutional Change in Toque Ville: Nouvelle Cuisine as an Identity Movement in French Gastronomy. *American Journal of Sociology*, 108: 795–843.

Rao, Hayagreeva, Calvin Morrill, and Mayer N. Zald. 2000. Power Plays: How Social Movements and Collective Action Create New Organizational Forms. In B. M. Staw, R. I. Sutton, eds., *Research in Organizational Behavior*. New York: Elsevier/JAI, 237–281.

Reay, Trish, Karen Golden-Biddle, and Kathy Germann. 2006. Legitimizing a New Role: Small Wins and Micro-Processes of Change. *Academy of Management Journal*, 49.5: 977–998.

Reay, T., and C. R. Hinings. 2005. The Recomposition of an Organizational Field: Health Care in Alberta. *Organization Studies*, 26: 351–383.

Reay, T., and C. R. Hinings. 2009. Managing the Rivalry of Competing Institutional Logics. *Organization Studies*, 30.6: 629–652.

Reckwitz, Andreas. 2002. Toward a Theory of Social Practices: A Development in Culturalist Theorizing. *European Journal and the Social*. 5.2: 243–263.

Reed, Mike. 1998. Organizational Analysis as Discourse Analysis: A Critique. In D. Grant and C. Oswick, eds., *Discourse and Organization*. London: Sage, 193–213.

Reimer, Jeffery W. 1977. Varieties of Opportunistic Research. *Urban Life*, 5: 467–477.

Reinharz, Shulamit. 1992. *Feminist Methods in Social Research*. Oxford: Oxford University Press.

Rhodes, Carol, and Andrew D. Brown. 2005. Narrative, Organizations and Research. *International Journal of Management Reviews*, 7.3: 167–188.

Riker, William H. 1995. The Experience of Creating Institutions: The Framing of the United States Constitution. In J. Knight and I. Sened, eds., *Explaining Social Institutions*. Ann Arbor: University Michigan Press, 121–144.

Rindova, Violina, Daved Barry, and David J. Ketchen, Jr. 2009: Entrepreneuring as Emancipation: Introduction to Special Topic Forum. *Academy of Management Review*, 34.3: 477–491.

Robnet, Belina. 1997. *How Long? How Long? African-American Women in the Struggle for Civil Rights*. New York: Oxford University Press.

Rochon, Thomas R. 1998. *Culture Moves: Ideas, Activism, and Changing Values*. Princeton, NJ: Princeton University Press.

Roers, Everett M. 1995. *Diffusion of Innovations*. New York: Free Press.

Rollins, Peter. 2006. *How (Not) To Speak Of God*. Croydon, UK: Paraclete Press.

———. 2008. *The Fidelity of Betrayal*. Brewster, MA: Paraclete Press.

———. 2009. *The Orthodox Heretic and Other Impossible Tales*. Brewster, MA: Paraclete Press.

———. 2011. *Insurrection: To Believe Is Human; to Doubt, Divine*. New York: Simon and Schuster.

———. 2012. The Sin of Abstraction. In Chris Lewis ed., *Letters to a Future Church: Words of Encouragement and Prophetic Appeals*. Downers Grove, IL: IVP Books, 61–67.

———. 2013. *The Idolatry of God: Breaking Our Addiction to Certainty and Satisfaction*. New York: Simon and Schuster.

Ryrie, Charles C. 1995. *Dispensationalism*. Chicago, IL: Moody.

Sargeant, Kimon Howland. 2000. *Seeker Churches: Promoting Traditional Religion in a Nontraditional Way*. New Brunswick, NJ: Rutgers University Press.

Schmalzbauer, John. 1993. Evangelicals in the New Class: Class Versus Subcultural Predictors of Ideology. *Journal for the Scientific Study of Religion*, 32.4: 330–342.

Schmalzbauer, John. 2003. *People of Faith: Religious Conviction in American Journalism and Higher Education*. Ithaca, NY: Cornell University Press.

Schneiberg, Marc. 2007. What's on the Path? Path Dependence, Organizational Diversity and the Problem of Institutional Change in the US Economy, 1900–1950. *Socio-Economic Review*, 5: 47–80.

Schneiberg, Marc, and Michael Lounsburg. 2008. Social Movements and Institutional Analysis. In R. Greenwood, C. Oliver, R. Suddaby, and K. Sahlin eds., *The SAGE Handbook of Organizational Institutionalism*. Thousand Oaks, CA: Sage, 648–670.

Schwadel, Philip. 2013. Changes in Americans' Strength of Religious Affiliation, 1974–2010. *Sociology of Religion*, 74.1 (Spring): 107–128.

Scott, W. Richard. 1995. *Institutions and Organizations*. Thousand Oaks, CA: Sage.

_____. 2001. *Institutions and Organizations*. Rev. 2nd ed. Thousand Oaks, CA: Sage.

Scott, Richard W., and John W. Meyer. 1994. *Institutional Environments and Organizations*. Thousand Oaks, CA: Sage.

Scott, W. Richard, Martin Ruef, Peter Mendel, and Carol A. Caronna. 2000. *Institutional Change and Healthcare Organizations*. Chicago: University of Chicago Press.

Seo, Myeong-Gu, and W. E. Douglas Creed. 2002. Institutional Contradictions, Praxis, and Institutional Change: A Dialectical Perspective. *Academy of Management Review*, 27.2: 222–247.

Sewell, William F. 1992. A Theory of Structure: Duality, Agency, and Transformation. *American Journal of Sociology*, 98.1: 1–29.

Shepherd, D. A., E. J. Douglas, and M. Shanley. 2000. New Venture Survival: Ignorance, External Shocks, and Risk Reduction Strategies. *Journal of Business Venturing*, 15: 393–410.

Sherer, Peter D., and Kyungmook Lee. 2002. Institutional Change in Large Law Firms: A Resource Dependency and Institutional Perspective. *Academy of Management Journal*, 45: 102–119.

Simmel, Georg. 1990. *The Philosophy of Money*. 2nd ed. New York: Routledge.

Sluss, David M., and Black E. Ashforth. 2007. Relational Identity and Identification: Defining Ourselves Through Work Relationships. *Academy of Management Review*, 32: 9–32.

Smith, Christian. 1998. *American Evangelicalism: Embattled and Thriving*. Chicago: University of Chicago Press.

Snider, Phil. 2011. *The Hyphenateds: How Emergence Christianity Is Re-Traditioning Mainline Practices*. St. Louis, MO: Chalice Press.

Snow, David A., and Robert D. Benford. 1992. Master Frames and Cycles of Protest. In D. Morris and C. M. Mueller eds., *Frontiers in Social Movement Theory*. New Haven, CT: Yale University Press, 133–155.

Snow, David A., E. Burke Rochford, Jr., Steven K. Worden, and Robert D. Benford. 1986. Frame Alignment Processes, Micromobilization, and Movement Participation. *American Sociological Review*, 51.4: 464–481.

Snyder, Timothy. 2011. Innovating with Integrity: A Case (Self) Study. In Snider, 127–14.

Sotarauta Markku. 2005. Shared Leadership and Dynamic Capabilities in Regional Development. In I. Sagan and H. Halkier, eds., *Regionalism Contested: Institution, Society and Governance*. Aldershot, UK: Ashgate, 53–72.

_____. 2009. Power and Influence Tactics in the Promotion of Regional Development: An Empirical Analysis of the Work of Finnish Regional Development Officers. *Geoforum*, 40: 895–905.

Sotarauta, Markku, and Riina Pulkkinen. 2011. Institutional Entrepreneurship for Knowledge Regions: In Search of a Fresh Set of Questions for Regional Innovation Studies. *Environment and Planning C: Government and Policy*, 29.1: 96–112.

Stark, David. 1996. *Heterarchy: Asset Ambiguity, Organizational Innovation, and the Postsocialist Firm*. Ithaca, NY: Cornell University.

Stark, Rodney, and Roger Finke. 2000. *Acts of Faith: Explaining the Human Side of Religion*. Berkeley, CA: University of California Press.

Stimson R, R. R. Stough, and M. Salazar. 2009. *Leadership and Institutions in Regional Endogenous Development*. Cheltenham, UK: Edward Elgar.

Strang, David, and John W. Meyer. 1993. Institutional Conditions for Diffusion. *Theory and Society*, 22: 487–511.

———. 1994. Institutional Conditions for Diffusion. In R. W. Scott and J. W. Meyer eds., *Institutional Environments and Organizations: Structural Complexity and Individualism*, Thousand Oaks, CA: Sage, 100–111.

Strang, David, and Sarah A. Soule. 1998. Diffusion in Organizations and Social Movements: From Hybrid Corn to Poison Pills. *Annual Review of Sociology*, 24: 265–290.

Suchman, Mark C. 1993. On the Role of Law Firms in the Structuration of Silicon Valley. Paper presented at the annual meeting of the Law and Society Association, Chicago.

———. 1994. On Advice of Counsel: Law Firms and Venture Capital Funds as Information Intermediaries in the Structuration of Silicon Valley. PhD. diss., Stanford University, CA.

———. 1995. Managing Legitimacy: Strategic and Institutional Approaches. *Academy of Management Review*, 20.3: 571–610.

Suddaby, Roy, and Royston Greenwood. 2005. Rhetorical Strategies of Legitimacy. *Administrative Science Quarterly*, 50.1: 35–67.

Sullivan, Andrew. 2012. The Forgotten Jesus. *Newsweek*, Apr. 8, 26–31.

Sweet, Leonard. 2003. *The Church in Emerging Culture: Five Perspectives*. Grand Rapids, MI: Zondervan.

Taylor, James R., Francois Cooren, Nicoce Giroux, and Daniel Robichaud. 1996. The Communicational Basis of Organization: Between the Conversation and the Text. *Communication Theory*, 6.1: 1–39.

Thornton, Patricia H. 2004. *Markets from Culture*. Stanford, CA: Stanford University Press.

Thornton, Patricia, Candace Jones, and Kenneth Kury. 2005. Institutional Logics and Institutional Change: Transformation in Accounting, Architecture, and Publishing. In Candace Jones and Patricia H. Thornton, eds., *Research in the Sociology of Organizations*. London, UK: JAI, 125–170.

Thornton, Patricia H., and William Ocasio. 2008. Institutional Logics. In R. Greenwood, C. Oliver, R. Suddaby, K. Sahlin-Andersson, eds., *The SAGE Handbook of Organizational Institutionalism*. Thousand Oaks, CA: Sage, 99–129.

Thorton, Patricia H., and W. Ocasio. 1999. Institutional Logics and the Historical Contingency of Power in Organizations: Executive Succession in the Higher Education Publishing Industry, 1958–1990. *American Journal of Sociology*, 105: 801–843.

Thumma, Scott, and Dave Travis. 2007. *Beyond Megachurch Myths: What We Can Learn from America's Largest Churches*. San Francisco: Jossey-Bass.

Tickle, Phyllis. 2008. *The Great Emergence: How Christianity Is Changing and Why*. Grand Rapids, MI: Baker Books.

———. 2012. *Emergence Christianity: What It Is, Where It Is Going, Why It Matters*. Grand Rapids, MI: Baker Books.

Tomlinson, Dave. 1995. *The Post-Evangelical*. London: Triangle.

———. 2008. *Re-Enchanting Christianity: Faith in an Emerging Culture*. Norwich, UK: Canterbury Press.

Townley, Barbara. 1993. Foucault, Power/Knowledge and Its Relevance for Human Resource Management. *Academy of Management Review*, 18: 518–545.

Tracey, Paul, Nelson Phillips, and Owen Jarvis. 2011. Bridging Institutional Entrepreneurship and the Creation of New Organizational Forms: A Multilevel Model. *Organization Science*, 22.1: 60–80.

Troeltsch, Ernst. 1913. Religiöser Individualismus und die Kirche. In E. Troeltsch, *Gesammelte Schriften*, vol 2. Tubingen: Mohr, 109–133.

Tsoukas, Haridimos, and Robert Chia. 2002. On Organizational Becoming: Rethinking Organizational Change. *Organization Science*, 13: 567–582.

Turner, Bryan S. 2011. *Religion and Modern Society: Citizenship, Secularization, and the State.* New York: Cambridge University Press.

Valente, Thomas W. 1995. *Network Models of the Diffusion of Innovations.* Cresskill, NJ: Hampton Press.

Van Dijk, Stephan, Hans Berends, Mariann Jelinek, A. Georges L. Romme, and Mathieu Weggeman. 2011. Micro-Institutional Affordances and Strategies of Radical Innovation. *Organization Studies*, 32: 1485–1513.

Van Gestel, Nicolette, and Bas Hillebrand. 2011. Explaining Stability and Change: The Rise and Fall of Logics in Pluralistic Fields. *Organization Studies*, 32: 231–252.

Van Maanen, John. 1988. *Tales of the Field: On Writing Ethnography, Chicago Guides to Writing, Editing, and Publishing.* Chicago: University of Chicago Press.

Walker, Andrew, and Aaron Kennedy, eds. 2010. *Discovering the Spirit in the City.* London: Continuum.

Warner, R. Stephen. 1994. The Place of the Congregation in the American Religious Configuration. In James P. Wind and James W. Lewis eds., *American Congregations*, vol. 2, *New Perspectives in the Study of Congregations.* Chicago: University of Chicago Press, 54–99.

————. 1998. Introduction: Immigration and Religious Communities in the United States. In R. S. Warner and J. G. Wittner, eds., *Gatherings in Diaspora: Religious Communities and the New Immigration.* Philadelphia: Temple University Press, 3–34.

Watts, Duncan J. 1999. *Small Worlds: The Dynamics of Networks between Order and Randomness.* Princeton, NJ: Princeton University Press.

Webber, Robert E. 1999. *Ancient-Future Faith: Rethinking Evangelicalism for a Postmodern World.* Grand Rapids, MI: Baker Academic.

————, ed. 2007. *Listening to the Beliefs of Emerging Churches: Five Perspectives.* Grand Rapids, MI: Zondervan.

Weber, Max. 1978. *Economy and Society: An Outline of Interpretive Sociology.* Berkeley, CA: University of California Press.

Weick, Karl E. 1995. *Sensemaking in Organizations.* Thousand Oaks, CA: Sage.

Weik, Elke. 2011. Institutional Entrepreneurship and Agency. *Journal for the Theory of Social Behaviour*, 41.4: 466–481.

Wellman, James. 2012. *Rob Bell and a New Christianity.* Nashville, TN: Abingdon Press.

Wenger, Etienne. 1998. *Communities of Practice: Learning, Meaning, and Identity.* Cambridge: Cambridge University Press.

Whittington, Richard. 1992. Putting Giddens into Action: Social Systems and Managerial Agency. *Journal of Management Studies*, 29: 493–712.

————. 1996. Strategy as Practice. *Long Range Planning*, 2.5: 731–735.

Wicks, D. 2001. Institutionalized Mindsets of Invulnerability: Differentiated Institutional Fields and the Antecedents of Organizational Crisis. *Organization Studies*, 22, 659–692.

Wijen, Frank, and S. M. Ansari. 2007. Overcoming Inaction through Collective Institutional Entrepreneurship: Insights from Regime Theory. *Organization Studies*, 28.7: 1079–1100.

Wilford, Justin. 2012. *Sacred Subdivisions: The Postsuburban Transformation of American Evangelicalism.* New York: New York University Press.

Williams, Rowan. 2012. Fresh Expressions, the Cross and the Kingdom. In Graham Cray, Aaron Kennedy, and Ian Mobsby, eds., *Fresh Expressions of Church and the Kingdom of God*, Norwich, UK: Canterbury Press. 1–12.

Wollschleger, Jason. 2012. Off the Map? Locating the Emerging Church: A Comparative Case Study of Congregations in the Pacific Northwest. *Review of Religious Research*, 54: 69–91.

Wright, Stephen C. 2009. The Next Generation of Collective Action Research. *Journal of Social Issues*, 65: 859–879.

Wuthnow, Robert. 1989. *Communities of Discourse.* Cambridge, MA: Harvard University Press.

————. 2012. *The God Problem: Expressing Faith and Being Reasonable.* Berkeley, CA: University of California Press.

Yukich, Grace. 2010. Boundary Work in Inclusive Religious Groups: Constructing Identity at the New York Catholic Worker. *Sociology of Religion*, 71.2: 172–196.

Zilber, Tammar B. 2002. Institutionalization as an Interplay between Actions, Meanings, and Actors: The Case of a Rape Crisis Center in Israel. *Academy of Management Journal*, 45.1: 234–254.

———. 2006. The Work of the Symbolic in Institutional Processes: Translations of Rational Myths in Israeli Hi-tech. *Academy of Management Journal*, 45.1: 81–101.

———. 2007. Stories and the Discursive Dynamics of Institutional Entrepreneurship: The Case of Israeli High-tech after the Bubble. *Organization Studies*, 28.7: 1035–1054.

Zucker, Lynne G. 1983. Organizations as Institutions. In S. B. Bacharach, ed., *Research in the Sociology of Organization*. Greenwich, CT: JAI Press, 1–42.

———. 1988. *Institutional Patterns and Organizations: Culture and Environment*. Cambridge, MA: Ballinger.

# INDEX

"c." indicates chapter and "n." indicates material in endnotes.